RICHARD LEVITON has been interested in angels and mythology since an early age, and he is a frequent visitor to the British Isles. The author of eight other books, including *The Galaxy on Earth: A Traveler's Guide to the Planet's Visionary Geography* (2002), Leviton has been a professional journalist for 25 years, having published hundreds of articles in the fields of health, natural ecology, psychology, and spirituality. He has also edited a national magazine on alternative medicine, and, more recently — in his professional capacity as Senior Editor for Hampton Roads Publishing Company in Virginia, USA — he has developed a line of innovative alternative medicine self-care titles as well as authoritative and well-written metaphysical books.

WHAT'S BEYOND
THAT STAR

Other Books by the Author:

Seven Steps to Better Vision. Easy, Practical & Natural Techniques That Will Improve Your Eyesight (1992)

Weddings by Design. A Guide to Nontraditional Ceremonies (1993)

The Imagination of Pentecost: Rudolf Steiner and Contemporary Spirituality (1994)

Brain Builders! A Lifelong Guide to Sharper Thinking, Better Memory, and an Age-Proof Mind (1995)

Looking for Arthur. A Once & Future Travelogue (1997)

Physician. Medicine and the Unsuspected Battle for Human Freedom (2000)

The Healthy Living Space: 70 Practical Ways to Detoxify the Body and Home (2001)

The Galaxy on Earth. A Traveler's Guide to the Planet's Visionary Geography (2002)

WHAT'S BEYOND THAT STAR

A CHRONICLE OF GEOMYTHIC ADVENTURE

RICHARD LEVITON

CLAIRVIEW

Clairview Books
An imprint of Temple Lodge Publishing
Hillside House, The Square
Forest Row, East Sussex
RH18 5ES

www.clairviewbooks.com

Published by Clairview 2002

A catalogue record for this book is available from the British Library

ISBN 1 902636 32 5

Cover by Andrew Morgan Design
Typeset by DP Photosetting, Aylesbury, Bucks.
Printed and bound by Cromwell Press Limited, Trowbridge, Wilts.

For Judith Ann Lewis,
visionary, artist, sculptor, writer, partner.

Introduction

This book records the true story of one man's spiritual awakening and his subsequent adventures on the metaphysical quest for the Grail. The action takes place during a summer stay in Glastonbury, England, in the mid-1980s. Refreshingly for an account of psychic experience, the author utilizes an iconoclastic, humorous and slightly mischievous style. The result is something like Robert Monroe crossed with Jack Kerouac, or Carlos Castaneda meets J.D. Salinger; an entertaining spiritual journey like you've never read before. But the writing style does not detract from the fact that, essentially, he is recounting actual events, experiences and revelations which took place during a definite period of time; albeit, as with all spiritual experience, understanding deepens retrospectively.

The development of Leviton's spiritual vision was as unexpected as it was sudden. Although he had spiritual interests in his youth and later, nothing prepared him for the panorama of entities and unknown dimensions which became visible to his inner eye during that summer.

By any comparison, Richard Leviton had a fairly straightforward North American upbringing. Raised a Protestant — which in his experience meant 'you believe in nothing in particular' he later took an interest in Buddhism and other Eastern religions. For years he practiced Zen Buddhist meditation, although ultimately he found this unsatisfying. With its strict disciplines and its denouncing of any kind of visionary experience, he found it did not resolve deep-seated existential questions. In his twenties he took an interest in channeling, UFOs, and other paranormal phenomena. Later, he met the esoteric Jewish Cabala teachings, which had the opposite effect to Zen Buddhism, answering more questions than he ever thought to ask. Along the way he also studied and was enthused by Rudolf Steiner, Tolkien, and the tales of King Arthur.

During this time Leviton was something of a young capitalist entrepreneur, creating three businesses: a whole-grain bakery, a tofu factory, and a technical trade magazine on soyfoods production. At the age of 33, experiencing something of a mid-life crisis, he closed his current business and headed to England. Following earlier visits to sites connected with the Holy Grail and King Arthur, Leviton went to Glastonbury in Somerset – with which he had already become enchanted – arriving on Easter Sunday. This is where his 'rebirth' as a Grail Knight took place, and the events described in this book follow his inner and outer journeys during this period.

Leviton's initiation – the birth of his spiritual vision – came out of nowhere. As he describes: 'The spiritual alarm clock rang, the angels gave me my itinerary, a few nudges and clues and carrots, and I kept my rendezvous on time.' One day he was an ordinary person relying on the relatively dense perception of the five senses, the next he was seeing angels, gnomes, demons and dragons. His initiation was orchestrated by the family of angels whom he refers to as 'Blaise', and he was guided by his psychic friend Russell, to whom he refers in the book.

His spiritual awakening came just at the right time. Leviton recalls: 'I probably would have died of boredom or something like that if it hadn't happened. I was at a dead-end, standstill, cul de sac. I had nothing better to do. I thought: only an idiot would say no to the Ofanim telling him it's time for a fascinating initiation.'

Read with an open mind, enjoy, and remember — one day it could happen to you...

SG

1

I've never been the same since that night when the demons intruded into our cozy circle of angels and kicked it all to hell. On the other hand, let me tell you about my love affair with Blaise.

Do you know the word jackanapes? That was me back then — a metaphysical jackanapes. All I knew about angels was what I had read as a boy in *The Pilgrim's Progress*. I didn't know you could fit forty million of them on the head of a — pin? No, in a pinprick of brilliant light two inches above my belly button and a little bit inside. Nor did I know that they'd — Blaise, or should I say, the Blaises? — had the Marx Brothers as script writers and the Supreme Being for copy editor. Or that most of the world had never heard of them, but ought to.

I suppose it all started that morning in Glastonbury when I woke up with the phrase 'What's beyond that star?' in my mind. I didn't just wake up; no, it was more like being ushered back into the physical world and my body by the most attentive, softly luscious — it was like being wrapped up in a blanket of love.

I usually hate talking this way in public about things like love and lusciousness, but there is no other way to evoke the amazingly affectionate regard in which I was escorted back from dreamland into this world and my tiny second-floor room at Level's View Bed and Breakfast atop Wearyall Hill. Who escorted me? I have no idea, but I doubt it was people. I can't remember ever feeling that kind of unconditional love before. But if not people, then who? And what star?

All day long I felt there was something extra in my life, something additional around me, like an aura made of that same ineffable sweetness that had glided with me back into my waking state. Except every now and then I felt a chuckle, a sly giggle ripple through me, as if someone — actually, it felt like a group — was trying to keep some big laughs down so as not to ruin the surprise and betray their presence. It was as if first having given me a taste of the glorious sweet presence, they now wanted to send it all up in a swell of amusement at my expense.

Well, at the end of the day, what's any of it to do with King Arthur anyway? That's why I was in Glastonbury, this crazy, millennialist-mad village in Celtic Somerset, this bizarre living museum of myths about the Grail, Camelot, Avalon, Excalibur, Merlin, King Arthur and about fifty other unverifiable oddities of cultural memory. I shouldn't carp. I was here to add yet more confusion to this vast melange of speculation, scholarship, inflation, conflation, and expectation. After all, King Arthur was coming back, as soon as he woke up and dragged his sorry ass out of the hollow hills where he and his knights were sleeping until the time was right and Merlin gave them the wake-up call.

I was tired of history, tired of culture, tired of the United States, tired of reality. The world of myth sounded more interesting; at least it would be a summer's distraction, perhaps something publishable I could take back home when I got sick of England. I remember fantasizing one evening back in the U.S. I had just finished reading somebody's retelling of the basic Arthur story and I had pretensions of writing for *The New Yorker*. I was contemplating one of those elegant, urbane, slightly whimsical and exceedingly polished and well-researched fact pieces they excelled in and which since my adolescence had so thoroughly seduced me into believing represented the pinnacle of good writing.

'We recently paid a visit to Glastonbury of King Arthur fame to see what currency, if any, the venerable myth of the Round Table might still enjoy in these parts,' I fantasized telling William Shawn over lunch at the Algonquin. This would be my opening line for the article; Shawn of course, being an astute editor, would assign me the story immediately and even approve a generous travel budget and I'd be off to Celticland with *New Yorker* imprimatur in hand.

You can fantasize anything you want of course, and that's all this *New Yorker* daydream remained. My actual reality was that I had taken the summer off – realistically, I was between jobs, or out of one, whatever – and was holing up at Level's View to check the Arthur milieu out on my own penny. One aspect of the story that had recently grabbed my attention was the way certain actions were rooted to specific places in the landscape. Arthur fought here, the Grail was seen here, Camelot was situated there, Excalibur was tossed here. In fact, the Arthur story and the Grail myth were all over the British Isles, like confetti dropped from a height and scattered by the ocean breezes across the islands.

In some strange way, I sensed the myth had roots into the landscape, that it somehow lived in the landscape, depended on it, thrived in it. If it was all made up, then why the landscape specificity? If it was true, then why these places and not others? But then how could it be true? The scholars didn't give much credibility to that notion.

As for the psychics, most of them claimed they were King Arthur or Morgan le Fay redux, so you couldn't put much credence in them either. But the myth in the landscape – surely that is a mystery worth investigating, I thought to myself, as I was doing nothing much on an old, mostly broken down bench perched on Wearyall Hill. Below me sprawled Glastonbury, a busyness of reddish-orange roofs and funny-looking green hills, and a ruined cathedral.

But I felt that otherworldly regard around me again. It was basically a nice sensation, only marginally intimidating because I didn't know its source. I must have drifted off because I awoke suddenly as if somebody nudged me. Then I remembered where I had been, or dreamed I had been. I was at my childhood home, and I was perhaps six or seven. I floated out of my bed onto the roof of our home and walked into a six-pillared gazebo miraculously parked there. It was very bright. I almost had to shield my eyes as I approached it. I could have used sunglasses.

There were a few short steps leading into the white gazebo, and in its center was a brilliantly lit round table of some kind, made of light or crystal or lit by a dozen 300 watt bulbs. For some reason I wasn't the least bit alarmed or even surprised. This was as familiar to me as walking into the kitchen to inspect the refrigerator contents for something sweet and fattening to eat. I couldn't remember this part well at the time, but it seemed I smiled at some old friends inside this marve-lous mobile gazebo, and that as I did there was a wink, a rushing sound, an explosion of light, the peculiar sense that it had all collapsed into a single pinprick of intense light. We went somewhere, but I can't remember where. On the whole, it felt pretty good.

I spent the rest of the day walking around the town, up the High Street, up the Tor, over Chalice Hill, into Chalice Well, down to Pomparles Bridge, and up the backend of Wearyall Hill to Level's View again. Your basic walking tour of what one local savant calls the geomythic landscape, the land floriated with old, impossible stories, the myths that live on, incorrigibly, inarticulately, like dandelions in the land that all the rationalists want to expunge with weed killer. But there was one strange thing.

Every now and then, as I relaxed into my newest perch, parked comfortably on the ground, my butt absorbing the Earth energy and getting damp, but otherwise doing nothing, just watching, daydreaming about the myths, the landscape seemed to twinkle at me, like it was one giant eye with a sparkle of amusement in it. It was different than seeing stars, that unsettling aural experience when you bump your head or you stand up quickly. There was only one star, and it seemed sentient, inhabited, purposeful.

I know this sounds a bit daft, for what on Earth is a star doing in the landscape twinkling at me in the middle of the afternoon in dreamy Avalon, yet there it was: a star in the landscape was twinkling – no, *winking* – at me. I got a wink at the Tor, Chalice Hill, the Well, Pomparles, and the top of Wearyall. Not exactly *New Yorker* material. One thing I've learned in my few weeks in England is that everybody, even foreigners – especially the worst kind: Yanks – gets a license to be eccentric, free of charge. So I was being seriously eccentric.

I was having a pot of Earl Grey at Level's View around five o'clock after a leisurely day on the quest and thinking about that queer experience of stars winking at me when I remembered something else odd from my childhood. Actually, it was both intensely pleasant and deeply distressing, if you can feel excited and alarmed at the same time. Many times as a young boy I would lie awake in bed, under the covers, barricaded in with pillows and heavy blankets, and think about things.

Often I would read under the covers with a flashlight, long after I was officially instructed to go to sleep. Who could sleep when I didn't know how things turned out in *The Pilgrim's Progress*? I particularly liked the part when Pilgrim gets helped by an angel when he's ready to pack it in from despair. When I tired of John Bunyan's world, I would try to figure something out in mine. I would think about distances.

It's about fifty feet from my bed to Richie's house. It's a twenty-five minute walk from my house to school. It takes two hours by car to get to Uncle Isaac's house. Then I thought about how far away Boston was, because I had been there once already with my parents. But what about the Moon? That was far away, and the Sun was even farther. And the stars were farther away still. I could feel the tremendous distances like a chasm inside me, sense the immense space between everything, but things – stars – were now so far away from me I couldn't begin to calculate the distances, and my head spun.

It always happened this way. I got to the distances between the stars and me and a great gap would yawn open before me, an abyss I couldn't measure. The stars are impossibly far away, but what's on the other side of the stars? There must be something. How big is infinity? And what's on the other side of that? And what will happen to me in that infinity? Will I die?

My body would get big, huge, hollow, tingling and vibrating. It was like having a body made of a fully inflated balloon with nothing but air and space on the inside and a thin, expanding membrane on the outside. When I was really feeling daring with this sort of fun nightmare, I would look inside the balloon that was now my body and see billions of points of light, an uncountable number of tiny pinpricks of light. Stars. Galaxies. Inside me, and I was still expanding, ready to hold more. Despite this immensity of stars inside my balloon body, I knew there was still something else beyond them all, on the other side of the balloon. But what?

I was only six, too young to be a detached philosopher. My balloon always popped when I realized the ramifications of all this infinity: I would die one day. That's what it all meant. If there is infinity and the great mystery called God, then it meant I was real and alive and *that* meant I could and would die.

The next day I was sitting on a fairly lush hillside behind the Tor. The landscape was flushed with a shade of late afternoon summer soft green luminescence I'd never seen in the United States, or anywhere. The grass is fragrant and I almost envy the cows down the valley for their salad bar. The landscape before me is still, complacent, majestic, and full of stars, no doubt, if I were to indulge that deliciously odd experience from the other day.

I admit it: I was happy, possibly even delighted, about nothing in particular, just being here. I was even smiling and my smile as it deepened seemed to include the landscape as well, absorbing it in a motherly kind of way. I feel wrapped in a cotton duvet spun of wings – angel wings, I suppose, not that I know anything about that. But my body feels flooded with a creamy warmth as if somebody has emptied a pitcher of light into my head and its contents were flowing velvety and irresistibly like syrup through me.

My palms feel itchy, like something very small is scratching them. I pry open my eyes from this intoxicating envelopment and look at my cupped hands. There's a star in them and it's twinkling at me. No, it's not a twinkling star. It's a star going supernova. No, that's not it either. In fact, it's not in my hands anymore. The twinkling, supernovaing star has turned into something else, and they're standing right in front of me. Before me, in an effulgent arc of wings stand six angels, and each one is winking at me, like the joke's on me.

That's Blaise of course. They like their dramatic entrances. They like their little mysteries, their enigmas, their paradoxes. Why do I call them Blaise? Their official name in the membership roles of the angelic hierarchy is *Ofanim*, which is Hebrew for 'wheels,' but they like to call themselves Blazing Star. We started calling them Blaise early on because in Malory's *Le Morte d'Arthur*, Merlin has a mentor named Master Blaise who lived in the North of England and to whom he would pass on the gossip from Camelot. We figured let's keep it all mythological, so we dubbed these six winking angels Blaise and they didn't seem to mind. In fact, it seemed to grow on them.

Later we'd call that delicious soft duvet velvety feeling the Blaise Wrap; it was their way of letting us know they were back in town, back from God knows what else they do with their time besides talking to us. Later, not only would we get the Blaise Wrap, we'd be treated to the Blaise Drone.

Imagine you're sitting in your living room late one evening in a house out in the quiet countryside; it's so quiet even the cows are quiet, gone to bed. Your house is in something even smaller than a hamlet, a little conclave of six houses and a manure-splatted lane. But it has its own name – Wick – and it's about a mile from a town called Langport, large enough to have several churches and a cramped used book store.

Now suddenly it sounds like an eighteen wheel tractor trailer truck has pulled up outside your window and is idling. Except there's nothing in this farmlane that passes itself off as a road. In fact, when you go into another room, you can't hear the idling; come back into the living room and there it is again, unmistakably loud, vibrating your bones, but there's no truck.

Once we asked Blaise what this sound was: 'Oh, that's the sound of one of our wheels touching down,' they answered, expecting that would clear it all up.

The us in this case was myself and two others, Russell and Berenice Pendleton. I moved in with them when the proprietors of Level's View got sick of having me constantly underfoot, typing away upstairs, talking to myself, demanding miso soup for dinner, giving them no chance to close up the place and take a holiday. The Pendletons are their friends and now they're stuck with me and my little King Arthur investigation. They rent me a room upstairs. Russell does pottery, Berenice is a homeopath. They stay at home a lot and drink lots of weak tea, and thank God they don't mind having a busy-body American writer in their midst.

I mentioned the living room. That's where the Blaise Drone

happened. Maybe it's the house. It is very cozy, very old, moderately dysfunctional, and full of quirky charm. Frankly, to an American brought up in exurbia, it's a fantasy house, something out of C.S. Lewis' Narnia. It's one of those 300 year old stone manor houses with a dozen cramped rooms and low ceilings and crooked, uneven staircases where you crack your head coming down the landing because the second floor is so low because people used to be shorter and didn't need high ceilings and probably paid more attention anyway coming down the stairs.

There were two fire places: one was big enough for a slumber party for four; the other was where we had our evening fire in the grate as we enjoyed another cup of weak tea. Berenice's idea of a good cuppa was one inch of hot water, four inches of milk, and an anemic teabag thrown in for flavor. Russell's idea was just keeping filling the cup, thank you. He'd drink anything hot.

Occasionally, I weaned him off the Earl Grey and fed him a Guinness. On this particular evening, we had both knocked back a stout, one half each, and were feeling frisky, a little inebriated. Neither of us drank much alcohol so a little can be quite economical for cheap drunks like us. We were playing with Edmund's little toy cars. The Pendletons have two children, Edmund, six, and Celia, four.

I often got stuck babysitting them which was like being thrown into a swimming pool never having touched water before and not wanting to swim in the first place. But tonight the Pendletons were handling the babysitting and we were drag racing Edmund's toy cars around the lips of our beer mugs, seeing who could finish 20 laps first. Then Russell ditched his Mazerati in the foam. 'You shouldn't mix drinking with driving, you know,' I chided him.

I thought we had been a little drunk and quite silly, but suddenly all that was gone. We were rivettingly awake and focussed, as if somebody had turned up a dimmer switch to full intensity. A gigantic truck was idling outside the window. The oak logs in the grate were twinkling with stars. An amusement of wings settled over us. Reality seemed to melt, loosing all its hard edges. I almost felt like hugging somebody. There they were, the same six very tall angels I had encountered on the hillside behind the Tor. Except now Russell and Berenice were with me, and they saw them too.

I'm not saying the Ofanim condensed themselves into actual pinchable physical forms in that living room at Wick. They met us half way. Russell and Berenice were both a bit psychic, and I had my moments too, so given our raw talent, Blaise helped us see them by impressing themselves a little more firmly into our senses than they might normally do with more upmarket psychics.

Of course, over the years many times I wished Blaise would come down into matter and put their feet up with us. They said they had never been in human form, but one day they would have their chance. They even gave us the date: starting in 2020 they would start coming into our world as little Blaise babies, Blaiselets, little celestial wheels in infant's bodies. No doubt they'd be winking at an early age. It would be a once in Creation occurrence, and would actually signal the start of good things for the world. That was nice, but from where we sat in Wick that was a lot of years away still. I'll be worrying about my prostate by then. What have you boys got for us now?

We called them 'the boys,' partly out of amusement and partly because how else do you relate to high-ranking angels who are just inches from God without irony and jokes? I mean, why are they talking to us in the first place? What did we ever do to impress them? I only got a C- in Zen Buddhism after all. I flunked the *koans* and never moved up the corporate ladder in the Zen world. It was the same with the Boy Scouts. No climbing instinct I guess.

Sure I meditated, but my knees would get sore and I'd fidget and sneak a look at my wrist watch to see how much more of this nonsense I had to put up with. Russell got infected with Buddhism too and was sick for a long time with the Dharma, but he got over it too. Let's hear it for the lapsed.

It took us a long time to understand why Blaise bothered with us, but we finally got it. The Marx Brothers. The Three Stooges. Curley Howard, that outrageous mix of two year old and mad dog, must have studied with Blaise. Remember that wink? What's behind a wink but a tinkle of amusement, and what's behind that but a grand sense of the comedy of it all, the divine chuckle. Even the Ancient of Days has a funny bone.

This I what we got: even if you're a jackanapes and a complete failure at *koans*, if you get the joke, you're in. Blaise likes to laugh. The Old Man likes to laugh. Most of the angelic hierarchy, at least the top end of it, is full of cut-ups. I say most of it because, confidentially, the Elohim can be glum at times, and the Seraphim come across as a bit flighty.

But Blaise likes their lightness, their levity, their *levitony* – a species of giddiness inspired by angels. An antigravity particle twinkling away in every human. We once asked Blaise: how come you're talking to us and not the big shots in Shambhala or highly evolved masters and such? Because they take themselves too seriously and, believe it or not, they can't see us, Blaise said. Humor is the key that opens the door to where and what we are.

As I said, we called them the boys, although Berenice didn't appreciate this. She saw Blaise as females, we saw them as males. Of course they are neither, or both, or more than both. It doesn't matter. In fact, they told us they had been many forms, all the ones in the book, actually, even elephants. They once created a stir as a Hindu deity named Ganesh. Remember Ezekiel's fairly grandiose vision of the divine chariot that everybody thinks was a UFO? Blaise was there as the wheels of the Merkabah.

There were always six of them, identical, eight-foot tall angels with wings out to here, full of jokes and the answers to cosmic mysteries, responsible for all kinds of arcane tasks in the universe, on friendly terms with just about anything we could imagine – Martians, Pleiadians, all the gods and goddesses of every pantheon on Earth – and a great deal we couldn't imagine.

Another reason we called them the boys was that they didn't want us to put them up on a great marble pedestal and make celestial gurus out of them. Sure they were wise and educated beyond belief; sure they had a really impressive wingspan and could travel faster than light and visit us yesterday if they got a notion to now, and instantly take us to places like Mount Meru, the Crystal City, or Shambhala, at the drop of a hat. And sure we were a few not too clever humans who liked to drink weak tea and relax in comfortable chairs by the fire and occasionally lose all motor control over half a stout.

The point is: they needed us. It's a shocking proposition, but true. The angels need us to complete their work, and we need them to make being human palatable. They have all the answers and no bodies; we have bodies but no answers. Let's do lunch! I think Gurdjieff called this reciprocal maintenance, and it's a good term.

Later I thought of it in terms of a dimmer switch. You're in a dark room and want some light. You reach for the dimmer switch but find it won't move unless there's another hand there next to yours. Your hand and the angel's hand. Turn it on slowly, or else you'll make everyone blind. Move the dial slowly and bring light to the planet. Actually, you need a third hand on the switch to make it work right, but I'd learn about that later on.

So they were the boys to us, senior colleagues, if you will, and it seemed we had some things to do. But first we had to fall in love with them because you need a star to do the Grail Quest, and you need an angel to get your star. I didn't know this until much later. I didn't get how we had to sit back and enjoy the seduction for a few months until we had cultivated enough certainty that we could be trusted with a little field-work on their behalf. What's it like to fall in love with an angel, to be wooed by six attentive Ofanim with a forty million backup team if one of them gets stage fright?

Forty million? Remember the silly question that used to vex medieval theologians, the one about how many angels could dance on the head of a pin? That's one of those little irritating cosmic mysteries Blaise answered for us: 40.3 million. Here's the math: they have 144 major manifestations, and 6 to the power of 6 lesser manifestations. Each time they increase, they do so in multiples of 6. So that's 40.3 million and change. They can be in a lot of places at once, if they feel like it. Their resting, ultimate state is as a pinprick of brilliant light; then when they come down a scale, they're six angels; when they're feeling really expansive, they're 40 million. I once asked Blaise: how come six?

'How come there is only one of you?'

'One is hard enough to deal with.'

'One can do so little. Six can do so much more.'

I forgot to mention that not only does Blaise live in the universe, they live inside us, inside every human, frankly, whether they like it or not. I don't mean Blaise is some kind of angelic squatter, looking for bodies in which to perch. It's to do with the spiritual constitution of the human in general. People like Rudolf Steiner explained that all the angels, the stars, the whole celestial hierarchy helped create the human and still keep an active hand in the running of our affairs, and this includes digestion, breathing, seeing, thinking, and probably joke-telling.

Remember that wild vision of my body as a balloon full of stars? There's actually something to that and Steiner was probably right. Blaise has a legitimate, God-appointed place in every human: two inches above the belly button and two inches inside. It's not that somewhere amidst the cells and fatty tissues in your abdomen you will find a burning star. It's slightly more metaphorical than that, or perhaps I should say, rarefied. The star is definitely there, but it's in your energy body (or call it the etheric body, or aura, whatever) in the same place, just above the navel and a little inside. Look there and you will find a tiny blazing pinprick of angelic light twinkling back at you. Giving you attitude. Giving you a pick-up wink. Giving you Love from Above.

That's how we started to fall in love with Blaise. We couldn't get them out of our minds. Everywhere we went in the house, in Wick, in Glastonbury, there they were. We'd wash the dishes and there would be Blaise winking and waving from the suds. We'd cut up an onion for the miso soup and the six Blaises would wave to us from the cutting board. I'd vacuum the living room and hundreds of little Blaises would be grinning from the carpet fibers. I'd feel this scratchy, ticklish feeling at my navel, lift up my shirt, and there they'd be, sitting around the great wormhole of my physical body like it was the Harvard Club on a slow night.

One time I went to London to look something up in the British Museum (when they still had that fustian rotunda and the Victorian card catalog). Hundreds of Blaises with reading glasses down on their noses were studiously examining books on the second level of the rotunda. As I drove down Shaftesbury Avenue, every taxi had a Blaise passenger; some even sat on the roofs of the cars. On the motorway back home, we passed a small airplane taking off; a dozen Blaises clung to the tail like kite strings, and they didn't forget to wave. One time I was riding my bike home at dusk, having been out at a landscape site meditating and chasing cosmic mysteries. The six Blaises settled on my head as if it were their drawing room, sipping tea, reading the *Times*.

Another time, biking it home after dark, they set up a brass sextet on the top of my head and gave me some Mozart for the ride home. They set up some spotlights too so other cars wouldn't run me off the road since I had no lights on my bike and there were no street lights. I have no idea if the other cars saw Blaise's lights, but they didn't run me over, so something must have worked.

It's too bad pejoratives have been dumped on the idea of navel gazing. There's actually something to it: a conversing, winking, flying, shape-shifting, wisecracking, talking-to-God star. I spent as much of my time as I could keeping my eye on that star. I would have done it all day long if my mind didn't keep wandering, getting distracted, chasing bones the way those Zen dogs are known to do. The dog runs after the bone: that's the clever way the *roshis* would tell their students that their mind had no more brains than an easily distracted puppy who's off like a flash at the merest suggestion of a bone. Well, this dog runs after the star, after the coattails of eighty million wings. Woof, woof!

Everywhere I went, it was star, star, star. I kept seeing that blazing pinprick of light at my belly button, twinkling, waving, regarding – loving – me. It felt like an old friend, older than you could have had a friend, even if you figure in reincarnation. This was a friendship that was older than even the first life any of us ever had here.

The star was my closest, most confidential, most sagacious friend, an invisible helper I could have all to myself never forgetting – and somehow the paradox didn't vex me – that everyone else on this planet, in this solar system, this galaxy, universe, multiverse, the whole spacetime black bowling ball – I'll tell you about this later – could rightfully say the same thing. We are your Blazing Star, Blaise always said, but that 'your' encompassed a lot of beings.

I'd see Russell at lunch and ask him if he'd heard from Blaise. It didn't matter we had spent two hours talking with Blaise last night until two o'clock in the morning. It didn't matter that I'd just had a ten minute complimentary guided vision of one aspect of the angelic hierarchy, courtesy of Blaise. It didn't matter that I felt Love from Above streaming out of my belly star like heat waves across a summer land-scape. I wanted more: I wanted to hear more, know more, see more, be more. It's that craziness you get when you're twen-tysomething and seriously infatuated with a love interest. Even five minutes away from the erotic fire and you feel homesick for your lover.

So Russell and I would discuss what we'd heard from Blaise since breakfast. A wink, a twinkle, a little pressure on the aura, a slight nudge in understanding, the seed of an interesting concept, a fascinating connection. Anything. We couldn't keep Blaise out of the discussion. Why should we anyway? What more intriguing subject could there be?

It was like suddenly, miraculously, and unexpectedly, you find a secret entrance into the Great Man's office at the top of the high rise, and you can bypass all the middle level bureaucrats, the secretaries, gophers, ass-kissers, sycophants, dunners, confidence men, everyone in the organization who would prefer you didn't have direct access to the chief without going through them, without an appointment, credentials, a referral.

Forget the teachers and priests, the gurus with their busi-ness cards and websites. When we were with Blaise, it was as if we could see God through them, get a feeling for the Architect of it All through Blaise's sheer proximity. The sheer fact that

Blaise existed, was talking to us, showing us amazing things, was irrefutable proof that atheists were wrong.

Yes, sometimes we'd hear from Blaise between breakfast and lunch, and it would be like the Saturday morning kid's cartoons. Six Blaises in sunglasses standing − strutting? − cockily on a lilac beach under an intense sun. 'It's very bright where we are,' as if they needed an excuse for the shades. Five of the Blaises shaking their heads in dismay and disapproval as the sixth Blaise staggered about, his wings shredded and plucked. 'He flew too close to the Concorde today. Wings everywhere.' God, who writes their material?

Of course, they could ask the same question of us: who writes the thoughts in our heads? Sometimes they'd plant a little thoughtlet, the possibility of an interesting line of thought, and good Grail dog that I was, I'd fetch it and worry it all day, often driving Blaise a little crazy. It happened with tin. Joseph of Arimathea, the guy who bankrolled Jesus and brought him to the British Isles, even, if you believe the legends, to Glastonbury, supposedly owned or operated some tin mines in Cornwall. So they said Joseph was a tin merchant.

Metaphysical doyens, we figured there must be something esoteric to this story. What's tin spell in Hebrew? Greek? When you factor in the number equivalencies? Where would it fit on the Tree of Life? Does it correspond to a Tarot image? Russell and I obsessed about tin all the way into the evening when it was time for Blaise to visit again. 'Do you know what tin spells backwards?' they asked first off. 'It spells NIT.' As in nitwit, but they were too polite to say it.

But they wouldn't hold it against us. If they thought we were terminally obtuse, they'd never have bothered to make contact in the first place. Their way of leaving was often amusing too. A fat box that looked like a family-size detergent box, with the word 'ALL' printed in brazen colors. Under the brand name the box read, 'The answers to all your questions.' Another time Blaise said: 'And so. It's been a long day in the sun. We need ... oh, a bath. We're going over to the Dead Sea for a dip. See you later, Our Love. Wish you were here.'

The days passed like this. With every gesture, every step, every little activity, climbing the stairs to my room, carrying out the trash, raking the compost pile, brushing my teeth — these irrepressibly happy Blaises are with me, mirroring everything I do. Then in the evening the Blaise Wrap would start.

They would usually announce their arrival about an hour before they showed up. It got so I would just sit on the sofa and do nothing, waiting for the first sign of Blaise. It was like staying up all night and waiting for the sunrise. It was like dowsing. It was like waiting for your lover to come home from a trip, from her day at work, from the next room, from looking away for a second.

They would slowly approach our world, like an exquisitely slow strip tease, long before they congealed into form and speech. The room would start to feel attentive, as if populated with eyes and ears, as if we were being regarded. Normally, we go about our days observing the world, but how often does the world look back? As Blaise slowly approached, you'd feel watched, observed, noticed, but in a wonderful, almost narcissistic way. You could almost like yourself under the influence of this kind of wonderful mushy affection.

It's as if Blaise watches us from within reality, beholds us from within our own awareness. You end up observing yourself the way they are. You start having deeper thoughts, more organized thoughts; they start running in interesting grooves; you start understanding things. You feel you're getting some help. Things grow warm, happy along the edges; things melt into a sweetness that flows like blood through us. I suppose mystics call this bliss.

Like a dimmer switch that is slowly, steadily strengthening the illumination in the room, Blaise meditates us, reminds us who we are, who they are, what the Mystery feels like. The little pinprick of light at your navel grows larger, like a star rushing towards you, like a star milliseconds away from going supernova. Soon their presence is almost palpable. The room seems inexplicably brighter, fuller, as they keep turning up the dimmer switch of their presence.

We feel as if 'translated into Heaven,' as Malory often said of the more fortunate Grail Knights in their angelic encounters. You almost can't stand it it's so delicious. You want to feel this way forever. It's so full you feel you will burst, and then Blaise speaks, organizing this lush angelic presence, this Love from Above, into words.

'We come as a Blazing Star. We come as a pinpoint of light. Feel for this pinpoint of light inside yourselves. Feel for this tiny Blazing Star just above your belly buttons and a little inside. Breathe with your Love from Above to this Blazing Star as we breathe with you. . . .' We'd comply, and start to melt away into bliss city, then Blaise would say some more. 'Think of us, as you wish, as six columns of enveloping white light, making a circle around you.'

This one woke me up: the gazebo on the roof of my parent's

house. That was Blaise. I've since refined my perception of this a bit and now describe it as a rotunda. It turns out Russell and Berenice often experienced Blaise in this form; in a sense, this was Blaise's office, a six-pillared collapsible rotunda. Often we'd visualize this rotunda set in a lush green lawn: walk in the rotunda, wink at the six white pillars (Blaise pretending not to look like angels, hiding their wings behind the columns), sit down at the table as they zipped the rotunda up into a pinprick of light and went somewhere.

Blaise continued: 'Think of us as a blazing pinpoint of Light. Think of us as the *Nimitta*, the comet of consciousness, as a very fine point of light within a lilac flame.' This Nimitta reference was interesting. It's a Sanskrit word and means something like the ultimate point of focus, or a refined quintessence of consciousness. Experientially, the Nimitta is a diamond with forty million facets. Just think of it: picture a sparkling diamond, say, the size of a two-story house. It has forty million facets, each twinkling, each winking, each a doorway. You can walk through any one.

We never got a straight answer out of Blaise on this one. It seems the star is the condensed brilliance that comes out of the Nimitta, but it also seems that the Nimitta is what you find inside the star, the manifoldness before it concentrates itself into a point of light. It doesn't matter; it's real either way.

Part of the Blaise experience, we learned, is that you want your star to go supernova. It starts as a pinprick of light at your navel; focus, smile, grin, wave, and send Love from Above to it, and it swells, enlarges, expands, rushes at you until it envelops you in a blaze of light and disappears. Now you are inside the star. You've turned inside out. First the star was in you; now you're inside the star. You're a walking, talking, winking star. You're in Blaise, or at least the outer fringes.

Aside from this being rather a fun thing to do, it's essential for the Grail Quest and all the other geomythic things Blaise had us do. To get your star to go supernova, it's sometimes easier to see it as the Nimitta instead. Walk through any window. As soon as you're through, your star is supernova. This is good, and the start of a progression that actually leads you to the Round Table, Holy Grail, the Christ, the Buddha Body and other high-end ineffables.

The Nimitta is also handy if you want to remember your past lives. They're all in there, even the ones you don't want to remember, when instead of being an amazing Atlantean priestess-starlet or wizard manque, you were tortured, maimed, disemboweled, humiliated, and generally abused beyond belief. Yeah: death pictures. But it's not all horror show.

The real problem is that it can be a hall of mirrors, a seductive fun house with always another fascinating door to open. It's like the Tarot image of the Wheel of Fortune. You keep going round and round as you explore yet another past life, mostly out of curiosity. I once had a clear visual (metaphysically speaking, it was an analogy) of this records room inside the Nimitta: You stand in the center of a large circular room along whose perimeter are thousands of doors. Open a door and walk through into a past life memory. Stay as long as you like. But watch out, you might.

Some days I'd climb up the small hill behind the manor house and look out over the Wick countryside. There were the little drainage ditches called *rhynes* running through the somewhat boggy fields; there was the train track along which a couple times a day a train sped in a hurry; there was the River Parett, an out-of-work has-been of a stream with just enough life force to keep moving along; there the Holstein milkers from the dairy farm crossing the tiny footbridge over Dur-leaze-drove rhyne. The Somerset landscape is minutely domesticated, known, described, labeled, and mapped. Every two-foot wide rhyne and single-person footbridge gets vali-dated. I'd perch and wonder: what does Blaise do during the day? On the weekends? What is time like for them?

You have to start with the fact that they've been here a very long time. Not on Earth. In existence. When was Blaise born? 29,900,000,000 years ago, actually earlier than this universe and some of the angelic hierarchy were created, they told us. Twenty-nine billion years and never in a body. Twenty-nine billion years old and masters of time and space, coming and going, backwards and forwards, as they pleased. To be pre-cise, as God pleases. They've seen it all in this universe, and that 'all' encompasses a great deal more than I know I am presently able to comprehend.

A lot of their time with us had to do with planetary history, how things got here, who did what, and why. Reading between the lines, I also got a sense of how angels are restrained from doing certain things because they would interfere with our free will to be complete idiots. In other words, they set up the place, the whole geomythic temple that is Earth, showed us how it works, but then under orders from above, had to step back and let us use it intelligently or stupidly. Occasionally, they'd be allowed to mop up the mess.

One day they were explaining ley lines and their relationship to sacred sites, holy sites, power points, vortexes – they're called lots of things, but in this case Glastonbury Tor, Chalice Hill, and Beckery, a not well known but important site on the edge of town. Blaise said that the ley lines – for now, think of them as energy lines running between points – shouldn't be tampered with because it was complicating their work.

'Man is foolish to tamper with these lines unless under specific guidance through thought forms to deal with them in the material plane. His foolishness creates more work for us, gives the dark more of a chance. Tell people to leave what they don't understand alone until they understand more. Put this in big letters. Otherwise we will never finish our work.'

'And you're talking about a long time,' I offered.

'Right, a long, long time. Imagine a day spent waiting for a ten ton weight to drop on you. Can you do that? It would make time very long, wouldn't it? Imagine thousands of years like that.'

One time they had to curtail their evening visit with us to sort out a problem in the third star of Sirius. Some bad guys were trying to commandeer this star and, I guess, basically take over the galaxy. Another time, they called us from the road, en route to the Pleiades where they gave regular reports on what we were up to on Earth – not just me, Russell, Berenice, and the kids, but everybody, the whole race. By the way, I asked them how long it would take them to get to the Pleiades from where they were, which was more or less in our solar system, maybe even near Earth. About six hours, they said. How do you guys travel? Blaise said it's like we all look through a long telescope and try to imagine we're already at the other end of it, say, in the Pleiades. As soon as most of us can see ourselves there, we're there.

Another time they were going to Arcturus but they weren't planning on making much of a report there due to insufficient interest. Last winter they spent four months on a planet related to the star Polaris in the Little Dipper where apparently a lot of souls from Earth hang out for a while after death. Blaise vaguely hinted there was a beach there, with lilac sand, and that they might, on an off day, have spent a few moments kicking back in the sunlight.

One time they had to leave to help out at a meeting in Glastonbury where business interests were trying to do something to Chalice Well that would have been bad news for the planet's energy body, Blaise told us. One time they visited us and said they actually weren't even here; this was a video recording they made earlier, but which they scheduled to be activated and shown when we reached a certain point in time and understanding that would trigger the start button. Video recording or not, we still had a lively chat with them, they answered questions, evaded others, made some jokes, dished out assignments, and left, never having been here.

Recognizing I couldn't match my mind to their level of consciousness at this moment, I asked them what was surely to them a dumb question. What did you guys do today? 'We will give you an extraordinary piece of information,' they said, in that mock solemn tone that always has a twinkle or quip lurking just behind the syntax. 'We will speak to you of the life of an angel. We read from 'Today:' Awoke. Found we were already awake. Looked around and thought, This is it. It is this. Knew it was no thought, knew it was inspired. Knew we didn't know, knew we had work to do, knew it was joy. Knew we would return to Earth one day. Knew one day we would have bodies like yours. Knew we would try to help as many humans as possible. Hung around a few church spires here and there. We were mainly in Europe and North Africa today, though two of us made a significant presence in Central Mexico.'

Among their other daily duties there is zodiac cleaning. That is, tending the galaxy and its many constellations. 'We love the zodiac on behalf of those above. We are like dentists. When you brush your teeth, if you don't brush them all correctly, then some will rot and drop out. They will decay and need external help. Now, if you care for each tooth with love, with toothpaste and toothbrush, each tooth will be whiter than white. It will shine from within your mouth like a star. This is what we do with each part, every part of each place, even the dark crevices of humanity. We send some love into even those places. We try and get rid of the decay so that we may all become one again in the brightness of the big star we are.'

Blaise as God's peripatetic dentists, gallivanting all over the galaxies treating stellar gingivitis and patching up caries. I didn't know it at the time of course, but Blaise had a career in zodiacal dentistry in line for me as well.

One thing Blaise never tired of telling us and which we never tired of not understanding was that they remembered us from before the Fall. Presumably they meant the Garden of Eden or some pre-incarnational state. We'd sit there, being with Blaise, listening to them, swimming in their Love from Above, knowing the boys knew something major about us that we can't even remember. They also implied that somehow we had come from them, had once been with them, and gone off on some kind of hare-brained assignment, and hadn't written home much.

It reminded me of the situation of Odysseus's crewmates when they hit Circe's island. Being a magician and evidently ill-disposed to Greeks in ships, Circe turned most of Odysseus's men into pigs. Odysseus escaped this fate, but he suffered nonetheless at seeing his former shipmates snouting around in a porcine misincarnation. A few of the crew were still in the ship moored off the island; they were still humans, unenchanted into pigs by Circe.

I came to think of Blaise as the shipmates still whole and hale on the ship in their original state; the rest of us had already bit Circe's bullet and were groveling in the mud, oblivious to our former state of existence, or, if we did know we weren't originally pigs, not remembering how we got here or how to get back to being human — or in this analogy, one of Blaise.

One of the most startling pronouncements Blaise made in those days was about angel envy. They truly thought humans had something they lacked. Imagine: they have the joy, the bliss, the awesome knowledge, the proximity to God, a non-money based lifestyle, total recall, complete mobility, and they envy us? What do we have? The need to eat, bloat, get heartburn, scratch mosquito bites, not understand most things, get headaches, be quarrelsome, evade responsibility, pretend to be atheists. However, this kind of oppositional thinking doesn't wash with these boys.

'The Architect of All Absolute Existence made you in His image. We are not so fortunate. You have Buddha Nature. You have Christ Spirit. You and He are one. We only serve. We have to come back in your forms to rejoin with Him. No possibility for us until our time is right. To have human form is a rare and extraordinary event. We are envious of it. Each of you who occupy this form has an opportunity of uniting with the highest, with the Lord Absolute. We do not have this possibility in our present form. We are not complaining, you understand. Just trying to put things in perspective for you. We are more than happy. We are in a state beyond your experience.'

We think being in a body is a bit of a nuisance, and we'd rather be angels. Blaise thinks being an angel is pretty okay, but they've got unfinished business they can do only in a body. They envy us the chance, we envy them in general. Studying this basic conundrum, I realized I had left something out of my equation, but what that was, I didn't know.

Their basic strategy was to plant seeds of Love from Above while they were still the Ofanim. Then when they get their once in 15 billion years chance and incarnate, they would reap a little Love from Above as anonymous gifts from the seeds they had already planted just in case people forgot to be nice to them. These guys are good planners. The game plan was that when the next Golden Age arrived – circa 2020 AD – they would achieve bliss in the human body, transcend all limitations, and definitively be out of here in one life, back with the Old Man – technically, one with the Old Guy – where they belong.

However, and this is where we came in, for that Golden Age to commence on Earth, for Blaise to bliss out in those human bodies, certain obstacles had to be removed, certain things set in place, a little bit of Grail questing had to be done on behalf of the big plan. That's why Blaise was visiting us every night. Somebody had to get trained in being a Grail Knight and they thought I was a likely candidate. Or else everybody else they asked already turned them down. Either way, the job started the next day.

2

The first thing I learned on the Quest is that you need a gnome.

Funny little guys. Gnomes haven't gotten much attention for the last couple of centuries, since around the time of the Industrial Revolution. They didn't care for the noise of the new machinery, and they retreated further into the wilds of Ireland, Scotland, Scandinavia, and the deep old North. Of course the men with machines never gave the gnomes another thought, and forgot all the odd tales of their grandparents. The tales may be odd, but they're true.

Before I came to England to look for traces of King Arthur, I didn't think I knew anything about gnomes. Never seen one, talked to one, or even thought about one, or so I thought. But I had this recurring dream as a child. It was about two secret rooms in my parent's house. The first was in the attic. You climb the stairs, go around to the back, then open a door that you hadn't realized was there. It was a private chamber — mine, of course — full of amazing books. Much later I understood this was a veiled dream memory for going into the Blaise gazebo on the top of the roof, the books being all the great things Blaise told me.

The second secret room was in the basement. You go down the stairs, pad across the cold linoleum floor to the boiler room, open the door, and go left. Normally there is a woodpile there, but in the dream there is a door, known only to me. On the other side is another marvelous library. As a boy I was crazy for books, so this was a most excellent carrot to get me into these arcane rooms. This one – again, it took decades before I got it – was actually a gnome den.

No, there wasn't a gang of gnomes squatting in my parent's basement dependent on my tact to keep them shielded from unsympathetic human eyes. Somehow I had left the world of my parents and their notions of reality and what's possible in it, and went off with the gnomes into their world. Naturally I told nobody about these outings; why should I have anyway? I thought they were dreams.

So what's a gnome? They're players; they're needed; they have a God-appointed job. They have a tendency to be goof-offs; they can be mischievous, playful, even deceitful, but they are wonderfully loyal and unarguably helpful for the Grail Knight out in the field staggering around without a clue. Blaise on occasion has tactfully pointed out that the gnomes some-times need a little discipline to keep their eyes on the target. Rip van Winkle and his unexpected twenty year's sleep up in the gnomefied Catskill Mountains is a good example of what happens when you don't give these boys a little discipline and focus.

In the Grail stories, the Knights had gnomes but the chroniclers called them dwarves; so did Tolkien. Yes, they're short, something like three feet tall from our point of view. When you're with them, though, it seems you're the same height as they. There are female gnomes, but it's mostly the male gnomes who have to do with humans, especially Grail Knights. Celtic lore describes them as short in stature, rotund, jolly, bearded, capped, waist-coated, high-booted, wearing late eighteenth century garb. Frankly, you could just as well dress them up in L.L. Bean gear, or even Armani, if you like.

For the most part, the visuals are optional. You make contact with their energy, your brain forms some kind of reasonable image, and you leave it at that. Once I saw a gnome's face close-up, especially the eyes. They were utterly foreign, nonhuman, different. I was probably registering them a little more clearly than usual that time. The fact of the matter is this: I really like gnomes, they're a lot of fun, and I need them for my work, and so will you if you get a notion to go on the Grail Quest.

There was a place about a twenty minute's walk from the house at Wick along a muddy track and across two open fields. The locals called it the Fairy Dell, or maybe it was just Russell and Berenice who called it that. It was a good pick-up place for fairies, gnomes, elves, sylphs, even the great god Pan, all of whom I encountered on this queer little round hill edging up to a patch of blackberry bushes and a small copse.

You walk across the field, avoiding the tussocks and cow splats so you don't twist your ankle and stain your sneakers until you cross the tiniest trickle of a stream. Stepping across this inconsequential streamlet, it feels like you've just entered a different world, like you parted the curtains of a sybaritic grotto in the Venusberg and you are now in foreign but intoxicating territory, a little devic paradise.

Don't think I could see gnomes right off the bat. No, it took some time to acclimatize myself to their vibration, to let their energy congeal into a negotiated image of their form. First you feel them, and here I had Russell's help. He had been seeing gnomes, fairies, angels, and lots of supersensible beings for years. We'd perch on the brow of the Fairy Dell, be as still as possible like we were waiting for rabbits to come sit in our laps, and sense the gnomes as they gathered around us. Russell would tell me what was happening. A couple of gnomes are sitting in front of you; one's smoking a pipe, the other is squinching up his face, trying to figure you out. A couple dozen more are sitting in a half circle about fifteen feet away from you. This one says its name is Battingley.

Once I matched the energy sensation to the concept, an image of a gnome formed in my brain and Battingley was there before me, puffy-cheeked, a bit wrinkled, and merry. He wanted to show me something. Granted, it took me a couple of weeks to see it, coming to the Fairy Dell every day, sharpening my vision and confidence so I could see Battingley and some of his world without much effort and with a great deal of amusement and interest. He and his buddies seemed to enjoy my company as well, so we got on fine. I gathered they hadn't had many visitors in recent years. One time Blaise commented with just a touch of regal detachment: 'We are aware the gnomes like you.'

The thing Battingley wanted to show me doesn't seem to have a name in myth or folklore, so I call it a gnome egg. It basically looks like one, and it does hatch something. Imagine a hollow golf ball about fifty feet high and wide, set somewhat into the ground, and made of misty white light. It's like a golf ball in that its white surface is pockmarked with numerous shallow depressions. Inside the gnome egg are innumerable chambers or cells and in these dozens, maybe hundreds, of gnomes are busy with activities.

The gnome egg is a kind of district headquarters for the gnomes of a region. They always come back to the egg, touch base, get assignments, and set forth again into the great outdoors. The gnome egg, as I would soon learn, is also a kind of skylight for what could be described as a vast underground citadel.

Battingley offers me his hand and we enter the gnome egg. No longer is it an elliptical white mist set halfway into the Fairy Dell; on the inside, the gnome egg is a multicolored spherical palace of huge dimensions. Actually that's what I see after I get there, but the way there is a little breathtaking as well. I went down a long gently sloping tunnel passageway with Battingley, walking, running, floating, flying – it's hard to be precise about the kind of movement. It seemed like we traveled in this tunnel for several hundreds yards, maybe even a few miles. Then we got to the palace.

One thing you need to know about the Grail Quest is that you need to be prepared for the unapologetically mythical. You'll see things you only heard about from myths but never thought were true, always thought couldn't possibly be true. Like gnome kings. The walls in this long rectangular marble-encased hall had recessed niches in which small statues of gnome royalty were enshrined, like sculptural portraits of midget kings.

But as I started to look at one, it came alive; more precisely, it was as if I had suddenly entered a movie version of the statue, was watching its life and accomplishments as a bystander. I can get as much detail about this particular former gnome king as I like, or I can have the short version. The more I watch, the more intently I engage myself, the more detail I get; as my attention flags, so does the video's depth of coverage. It's very interactive.

Either way, this is a kind of hall of records for gnome royalty: press the button (basically, just focus your attention on it) and you get the whole epic movie. You could easily get swept up in the drama of a single former gnome king and never make it to the end of the hall to the current one.

Here's where things got really mythological. If you've ever read about gnomes you know they have a fondness for jewels and a tendency to be associated with dragons. I offer you Alberich, the avaricious gold merchant in Wagner's *Das Rhinegold*. Gnomish to the end, he was enchanted, besotted, ruined by that infernal lump of gold he stole from the Rhine-maidens at the bottom of the river. To be fair to gnomes, this is an exaggeration; Alberich was a special case. There is some truth to the tales of their attraction to precious metals and jewels, but it's more of the order of a job description, a responsibility, a duty. They're supposed to be interested in them. You have to see things from their perspective.

While we were waiting to see the gnome king, Battingley filled me in on the history and duties of the gnomes. I'll give you the short version to save time. You'll be wondering: what — gnomes talk? They do, but like their appearance, what I hear is an approximation, a compromise, a best guess. They communicate something, and the brain translates it into reasonable, probable, understandable words, images, even pictures. It'll do; all you need is a clue, the gist of it.

After a while, it's no big deal, talking to gnomes, no different than talking to your wife, the grocer, or an old friend in another country. If you have an ornate syntax, then so will your gnomes; if your inner voice sounds like Hemingway at his most laconic, your gnome speech will be clipped and monosyllabic. It doesn't matter as long as you don't propose to publish it as received gnomic gospel. They wouldn't like that. They're much more loose and fluid, like the magnetic field waves they walk.

The first thing I realized about gnome reality is that the Earth looks different to them than to us. In some respects their Earth is more the real Earth. Their primary reality is a planet of magnetic field lines. They see them just like we see hills and mountains. 'The world to us looks like the ribbed surface of a seashell,' Battingley told me, the ribbing being the magnetic flux lines. This world has connections with another, subtler one laying like the next skin in an enormous onion.

They call the connection points between worlds the 'splice.' One world is that of the magnetic field contour lines; the other is a parallel world of energy nodes and lines of light; the splice is the ladder between one world and the next. Later I would understand that one of the gnomes' duties is to help novice Grail Knights such as myself at the time make their way through this splice.

To gnomes, the magnetic field lines are palpable grooves and ridges in the landscape, and they spend a lot of their time walking these grooves, tuning them up. The sound analogy is apt. To a large degree, the gnomes perceive these grooves as sound ridges raised up in the soft earth, and they maintain them — and I don't mean it jokingly, though it sounds like a put on — by humming a tune. In a sense, any tune will do, as long as it's a gnome tune. It's their essence itself, their essential sound, that gets imparted to these magnetic sound ridges and keeps them clean.

'Our singing, which is our basic life vibration, purifies, strengthens, and amplifies the sound qualities of the waves,' Battingley explains. Largely it's humans who dirty the lines. Our thoughts, emotions, discordant feelings and expressions, our negativities, wars, and generally bad behavior stain and distort the lines, so the gnomes have to clean them up. They're like tuning forks, reminding the sound ridges what their vibration is supposed to be like. 'We don't do anything special. It's our nature to correct the sounds by the way we are.'

Battingley's memory is deep, and encompasses days in the history of Earth that even mythology doesn't remember. He says that once, in the beginning of things, the entire planet was a single web and that they danced through it everywhere. It wasn't broken or disrupted anywhere. 'Now it's a terrible mess, jangled and discontinuous,' and they can walk the waves only in certain places. There are some locations — he calls them 'black knots,' we call them cities — where it's very hard, highly unpleasant, and almost impossible for gnomes to do their ridge walking. 'We cannot heal them. The waves there are broken, and we have abandoned the black knots. They kill our ears.'

Then he tells me something fantastic. About an ancient contract humans have with the gnomes. They haven't forgotten it; obviously we have. In this antique time even before myth, when humans were still mostly celestial beings making reconnaissance visits to a virginal Earth, when the entire planet was the Garden of Eden, prephysical, but heading there, you extruded gnomes and angels from your bodies of light, said Battingley. The whole world was inside you. You were the whole world.

The Earth was a field of flowers — giant, exquisite floral lotuses of light and consciousness — and you inhabited these flowers like suns. You projected the gnomes and other elemental families, the sylphs, salamanders, fairies, and undines, from out of yourself. It's like you went three ways: from out of your head flew the angels; from your feet walked the elementals, and what was left standing was you, the human.

But this was both a creation and a fall, for where there had been one, now there were three: the angelic, the human, and the elemental. The angels made a pact with us: we'll help you remember God. And so did the gnomes and their colleagues: we'll help you maintain your world. Angels above, gnomes below, humans in the middle. The angels will raise you up and you will raise us up. This is the ancient contract. These are the hands on the dimmer switch, the gnomes being the third hand without which you cannot turn on the lights.

'Angels and gnomes are equal parts of your human being,' said Battingley. 'Your angelic side remembers Heaven. Your gnome side remembers Earth. You are in between — in a muddle. You've forgotten both, the above and the below. But we remember how your face looked when your being split into three, when you started looking outside yourself for your world. You have forgotten the mirror that showed you how you contain the entire world. You have forgotten the web. We are an aspect of your memory, walking at large in the world you created. We remember it for you. That is our part of the contract.'

It was time to meet the gnome king. He was a dignified,

regal type of guy, kingly, exuding importance, but, at the end of the day, still a gnome. I think I know how angels regard some of our follies and pretensions. I think it's with a kind of tactful, respectful amusement. So I model my deportment after Blaise and how he treats us, bow to the king, and ask him how's it going. He sits on a throne at the end of the rectangular hall, flanked with two rows of fluted pillars on each side, and all of it topped by an elegant mottled Islamic blue domed roof. He's surrounded by piles of jewels and crystals. The king hands me a palm-sized green crystal, possibly an emerald. Battingley gestures for me to cup it carefully in my hand and to follow him.

On the way to wherever Battingley is leading me, he explains that in this world what I see as jewels is really the mineral frequency spectrum on and in the Earth, the gradations of the earth element, which, after all, is the gnome's province. Think of the totality of the jewels as a kind of garden the gnomes tend, says Battingley. But it's also a control panel, a push-button display board for the gem hoard around the planet, a way of keeping track of the mineral element on Earth and making changes in it when needed. 'And there's a third side to it,' Battingley added, gesturing to my right.' The jewels are all part of the dragon's eye.'

I suppose I should have taken it all in my stride. After all, here I was, consorting and conversing with gnomes, bowing to gnome kings, and in arm's length of the world's greatest jewel horde, and I wasn't unbalanced at all. I wasn't even nonplussed. It all seemed pretty believable. But the dragon threw me a bit. He was a *big* guy, no question about that, and I didn't even see all of him. I surmised his full girth from the part I did see, which was mostly the head. But the eyes – it was the eyes that did it. It was as if the entire fantastic jewel horde of the gnome king was embedded in the dragon's eye, was the eye.

Battingley indicated I was to hold the green emerald in my hands as close to the dragon's head as I could. 'Don't worry, he won't bite,' Battingley assured me. As soon as the emerald came in contact with the dragon, it flared into bright green flames and I felt the stone vibrating in my hands; when the flames died down, the stone was gone and I was holding an arrow-shaped two-foot long emerald sword instead. 'That's your gnome sword, Grail Knight,' said Battingley, clearly amused. 'Never go on the quest without it.'

I followed him back to the central gnome king hall. This time I noticed a multifaceted ruby set in a circle at the center of the hall. The circle is more like a spreading ripple, like what happens when you drop a pebble into a still pond. 'The ruby is the seed the king of the gnomes planted to make this gnome egg,' Battingley tells me. 'Each gnome egg has a jewel seed, but they are all different colors, just like the king's jewel horde by his throne. That connects him to all of them around the Earth.'

Battingley told me that when you put all the gnome egg seed crystals together, that's the eye of the dragon. That's why the dragon's eye seemed like it was made of embedded crystals. It is. There are about ten thousand gnome eggs around the planet and each one has a jewel seed equivalent to this ruby. The eggs are also often close to dragons, within twenty miles or so. The gnome egg grows out of the jewel seed – it can be any kind of jewel – and together they comprise the dragon's eye. Each gnome egg gives the gnomes an eye into the dragon's world and makes it possible for them to work with the dragons.

I had a momentary vision of the dragon's eye. In it I could see hundreds of gnome eggs around the Earth, and thousands of gnomes scurrying around inside them, and a jewel seed at the center of each egg. I understood that each gnome egg is a porthole for dragons to look into our world and see what we're up to. This seemed like an elegant, symmetrical set-up, then I caught myself short.

What am I talking about? Dragons with eyes made of thousands of gnome jewels? What did they put in my miso soup this morning? I realized the gap between what I was experiencing and what I thought was possible was shockingly wide. Then I calmed down and resumed the adventure. You get these epistemological goose-bumps now and then on the quest, but after a while, they don't bother you so much and you just get on with your vision and quit worrying about whether it's possible.

I was about to thank the gnome king for the sword and the visit, but I had already left. I was back at the Fairy Dell with the Grail *derrière* settled on the damp ground. Battingley was gone but I still had my gnome sword, whatever that is.

So my life was filled with gnomes after that. It seemed everywhere I looked, I saw gnomes. I saw Battingley almost every day. It wasn't always about getting more information; sometimes we just hung out. I think it was partly to get me accustomed to the gnome vibration, so I would feel comfortable with them, be able to discern their frequency from among, as I would discover, a great many others.

I went to the gnome egg every day and meditated, my

gnome sword at my side. I still didn't know what to do with it. Sometimes it didn't seem like meditation; more like a casual attunement with the devic world. I'd sit there, surrounded by two dozen gnomes, none off us saying anything, just watching, and sometimes, not even doing that. I didn't knowingly enter the gnome egg again although I sat next to it and occasionally patted it. One day Battingley said, 'We can see the stars in the daytime,' and that image kept me going for hours. Sometimes when I returned home after an afternoon at gnome head-quarters, Russell would remark how my face looked gnomish, like I was half in their world now and starting to molt a bit of my humanness.

Over the years, there would be occasions when I would call on Battingley, and, actually, a succession of gnome colleagues, for assistance in a landscape job. Battingley, old sport, I need about four dozen gnomes to help anchor some incoming energy at such and such a place. Can you accommodate me? They'd be there instantly, ready to anchor. Other times I would call on Battingley to give me a precis of the energy configuration and history of a place before I did anything else. And sometimes they were eager for my company, possibly for anybody's company if that anybody could see them and believe they were real.

Once I went to a small town in central Norway on a Blaise assignment. The gnomes practically ran to the taxi the minute I rolled into town. They were hanging off the signs and buildings in town like the monkeys drape themselves over ancient statuary in India. They were everywhere, ready for business. Their spokesman, a gnome who called himself Rareal, could hardly contain himself. The minute I found a comfortable, quiet perch he gave me a complete – and highly useful – report on the geomantic condition of the town and environs.

After a while, the Blaise world and the Battingley world started to come together. Blaise would ask me to go visit a site, some hillside, copse, the edge of a stream, or a corner of Glastonbury Tor. They'd say it was important to sit in just the right spot, but they wouldn't tell me where that spot was. 'Ask the gnomes for guidance,' Blaise would say. So I did.

One time Blaise wanted me to meditate for two hours on a wooded hillside outside Glastonbury. He wanted me there – the place was called Ivy Thorn Hill – at 1.30 a.m. for the equinox. I'd never been to the hill, didn't even know where it was exactly. I borrowed Russell's car, a beat-up old Citroen that had this queer way of sitting down on its haunches when you turned off the motor. This was for me traveling in luxury; the rest of the time I got around on my fifteen-year old ten-speed Dawes bicycle.

I found the hill, parked, then stood frozen in pitch darkness. There were no streetlights; there wasn't even starlight. Just another slatey grey overcast night sky. I don't think Blaise wanted me to meditate in the little lane where I had parked, but I had no idea where they did want me to park myself for a couple of hours. So I called on Battingley.

He appeared before me instantly, looking for the most part the way we had agreed he would look. He was waiting for instructions. I told him Blaise wanted me to sit someplace special on this hill – could he show me where it was. He offered me his hand and I took it. I hope you can appreciate how odd this is. I mean it's odd if you're fresh to the world of the Grail Quest, gnomes, dragons, and midnight assignations prescribed by angels that look like wheels. How could I take Battingley's hand when he didn't have a hand I could feel? Certainly he has a hand, but it's not made of flesh and bone like mine or yours; how would I know I was actually holding it? Then there's the matter of following him. Was I making it up? Would he really lead me somewhere useful, correct, intended?

These seemed like insoluble, vital questions, but it was almost time to get started so I shrugged my shoulders and abandoned these complexities of reason. I took Battingley's hand, focussed all my attention on it, and followed him through a blackberry thicket into the woods and part way down a slope. I sat down and had a pretty interesting vision of traveling to another planet and meeting King Arthur, so I guess Battingley got me to the right place.

I also got an inkling of what to do with that gnome sword. Battingley made a gesture of inserting it into the ground, like sticking a butter knife into a cake. I shoved my emerald blade into the ground next to me and felt a jolt of connection with the planet. Later Blaise would tell me: 'The gnome sword enables you to ground elemental energy in the Earth and the human world.'

In fact, I asked Blaise one night about gnomes. How did they see them? What are they, for that matter? 'Would you prefer to call them morphogenetic impulses from your superconscious mind as inspired by Blazing Star? They are called many things. Why not just call them gnomes? Whatever is in you is out there. They are on Earth to harmonize all elemental forces, to assist with the elemental balance, to assist in the cooperation with the human and plant kingdoms.'

Blaise also said the gnomes are involved in the conscious evolution of the planet, just as we are, or should be. 'They are here to enact certain preset, preordained missions that can be activated only in cooperation with the human kingdom. The elementals are intermediaries between the Earth and humans just as angels are intermediaries between humans and the Creator. As the angels wish to communicate with the elementals, it is only possible through humans.'

So Blaise knows about the contract too. At Ivy Thorn Hill I had learned that one thing the gnomes assist we humans in is getting our butts ensconced at the right spot on unfamiliar hillsides for the purposes of participating in arcane angelic rituals otherwise known as Blaise assignments. The reason Battingley could so easily, so expertly, guide me to the place Blaise intended for me is because they know the micro-structure of the geomythic terrain. They know all the bumps, ridges, nodes, lines, and high points of the subtle landscape, all the places a Grail Knight needs to get to on the quest. They know the web, the terrestrial mirror of the celestial human as it was in the beginning. This, I would appreciate later, is crucial to the Grail Quest and why Blaise is here.

Years later, Blaise would confide to me the purpose behind all my dealings with the gnome egg in these salad days of the quest. 'The interface between the Earth and the angelic kingdom is very strong at this location,' Blaise said, referring to the Fairy Dell. 'It was an important place for the birthing of the first Grail Knight in this time. We facilitated the cracking of the gnome egg. It was also warmed by the resident gnomes when you arrived. Then you meshed into the spacetime sequence already programmed for you. The gnome egg was the egg preprogrammed for your work and also for the beginning of a new cycle.'

So sure, I had a roadmap that got me to the physical hill called Ivy Thorn, but the gnomes have their own maps of the energy terrain of Ivy Thorn, and that got me to the angelically designated spot. Why is one place designated and another not? Because the designated spot will induce a heightening of consciousness; it will give me a little more lift into the subtle realm where all the action is. The designated spot has a little more starlight inherent to its makeup, and it is this starlight – this emanation of Blaise – that makes all the difference in the Grail Quest. In a sense, the Grail Quest is all about collecting these droplets of celestial light throughout the planetary landscape and drinking them like a precious elixir capable of restoring immortality and complete recall.

Gnomes can be handy if you happen to get lost on a mist-enshrouded hill in the middle of Wales at dusk and you have no idea which end is up or where the hell you parked your car. I was on assignment at Cader Idris in Wales. My gnome host was Bejerinen who was kindly escorting me around the mountain, showing me the various spots at which to meditate in accordance with Blaise's plan for my experience of the sacred site. The day went smoothly, and Bejerinen proved to be an able tour guide, and he didn't laugh too much when I fell into a stream immediately after I had patted myself on the back for my admirable, unflappable sense of balance. The dicey moment with the mist happened the next day.

We – I was traveling with a friend, mainly because she had a car, and I didn't, and she didn't mind driving me — had spent the day on Eagle Mountain, a mostly treeless hill in the Preseli district of South Wales. It had been a pretty good day on the Quest: we had witnessed the Archangel Michael and tons of his colleagues do stunning things in the geomantic landscape. We were journalists covering the remarkable event for a newspaper yet to be founded that would even contemplate publishing a report of such goings on.

It was almost dusk, and Eagle Mountain was looking ever more moorish, bleak, and indomitable as the light diminished. An alarm sounded inside me: Uh oh, read about this. Excellent way to get seriously lost. There wasn't an official trail. In daylight, you walked up and down any way you felt like; at night, this hiker's free-for-all could be a recipe for a broken ankle and exposure. I called on Bejerinen for assistance. Say pal, could you please guide us down in an efficient, safe, and humanly friendly way?

I make all these qualifications for a reason. Gnomes are mostly well-intentioned, but our world looks different to them in their world, if you follow me. I see rocks, branches, bushes, gulleys, but they see a straight line of light, or, as I said earlier, curving sound ridges. The straightest, quickest way across a landscape for a gnome may be perilous for a human; it may certainly be inconvenient and strenuous. This is something to remember if you're ever leading a group to a numinous spot on a hillside you've never been to before and you're following a gnome who knows the way. He may not necessarily take you there in the most comfortable way. You may find yourself going straight up a cliff or practically climbing trees. So it's advisable to qualify your requests.

Bejerinen was qualified, and guided us down Eagle Mountain safely and without unpleasant incident. As an extra service to we Grail Knights in mild distress, at my suggestion, he held a bulb of orange light in his right hand so I could be doubly sure I was following him in the growing dark. Which is yet another paradox of course because where they are, it's not light or dark especially, so if he's not walking in the dark (even though I am), what difference does it make that it's dark where I'm walking?

This is another of those vexing rationalistic conundrums you get into when you let your mind have a look at current conditions. We picked our way carefully but surely down the long steep hillside, overall visibility being about fifty feet and mist blowing past us like fast-moving luminous shreds of rag.

While I'm on the subject of following gnomes at close quarters, I'd like to point out that sometimes you have to be careful. There are a few rotten apples in the gnome barrel, just as there are among the angels: fallen angels, fallen gnomes. It's a bit like the bad Hobbits in Tolkien's world; most Hobbits are wonderful, impeccable lads, but a couple, Frodo and his pals found out, had gone south. Occasionally this happens with gnomes.

Once, very early in my training, I was contemplating having a meditate around dusk. I had a special place in the woods where I liked to go. Blaise had suggested that I not visit the place after dusk during the two weeks in which the Moon was waning because I was not prepared to handle the influences that were stirring in the world at that time each month. That's the demon stuff I mentioned at the start of this chronicle, but I'll tell you about that later.

I went to the head of the Fairy Dell farm track. Battingley was there, and so were about six other gnomes. Battingley held up his hand, palm facing me, indicating I should stop and go no further. A couple of his colleagues countered this signal by waving me on, telling me there was no problem, nothing to worry about, that they'd walk with me to my meditation spot near the gnome egg. I was confused: stop, go, go on, go back – who should I listen to? The other gnomes started to look like Battingley, and that confused me even more. I figured insofar as gnomes are the good guys and all of this is commissioned by Blaise, and they're the extra-good good guys, what's there to worry about?

I won't go into it now, but I got in trouble. Not with Blaise, not with the gnomes, but with *them* – you know, the bad guys. I had been confused then beguiled by a few gnomes of ill intent and I had exposed my immortal soul – really just my completely inexperienced waking world self – to unwhole-some influences at a time when I had no clue what they were or how to handle them. Remember, my own guy had been faithfully waving me off, but I managed to disregard or dis-count his prudence and blundered on ahead, bullishly, breaking all the china in my own china shop and getting billed for the mess.

After this, I devised a secret handshake for Battingley. It was something only he and I would know so that I could tell him apart from the impostors. It wasn't actually a handshake, though. I had him display a twinkling emerald crystal made into a certain shape in his right hand. When I saw the jewel, I knew I had the right gnome and could proceed as before, with aplomb, insouciance, and restored naivete.

The gnomes know their way around this geomantic star-infused terrain. In fact, that's their job, to know every inch, every subtle gradation of sound and light and numinosity, to know them so well they can guide greenhorn Grail Knights around the place so they can have visions and start to wake up to this awesome reality. That's why you need a gnome on the Grail Quest; without one, you'd have almost no idea where to go, and you'd surely have less fun.

Come to think of it, it's a gesture of selfless service on their part because neither gnomes nor angels can go on the Grail quest. The gnomes can't because they're just gnomes and are part of what's quested; the angels because they don't need to and because they're also part of what's quested. But both facilitate our going on the quest. And when we the questers fill the Grail bowl with starlight on Earth, the gesture feeds the gnomes and satisfies the angels.

Of course, sometimes the gnomes can be a bit confusing about their directions. I don't know if it's because their attention was wandering that day or they felt like having some fun at the Grail Knight's expense. One time Blaise sent me to a place called Copley Wood. It was a good sixty minute trek on the Grail bike, about seventeen miles each way. I actually had to go there about six times over the months. There was a big plowed field where the farmer seemed to grow stones and boulders, a small forest, a mostly dried-up stream, and a wooded hill.

For some reason it was awfully easy to get lost in that small acreage, and I did so many times. I suppose you can't get lost in such a small place; call it disoriented. In fact, there are few places I've been to where I experienced so many variations in disorientation.

I can't say I'm an elegant, fleet-footed tracker when it comes to walking through the woods and over brambles. I made a fair mess of things and a lot of noise. I'd crunch branches, snap twigs, curse at cobwebs, slosh through the mud, trip, shout, lurch over gulleys, bat away insects, besmear my face with all kinds of woodland stains. The gnomes were watching me of course as I staggered around in a fit of misdirection; they probably thought I was in need of remedial walking. I thought I knew where I was going on this occasion; it was a reasonable assumption since this was my third trip to Copley Wood, but it was as if I'd never been here before. Nothing looked familiar; none of the trails I thought I knew led to where they used to. I was getting irritated.

Normally it's two hours from home to the top of Copley Wood. That's an hour on bike, an hour on foot. But today three hours had already elapsed and I was now peevishly walking in large futile circles. I had passed that well an hour ago and here I was at it again. I wasn't even near the top of the hill. Standing at the edge of the woods, I recognized a familiar field and thought I would walk along the edge of the copse keeping the field in sight.

Good plan, but it had no connection with reality. Somehow as soon as I set off, the field disappeared and I was disoriented again. Finally, I flopped on the ground, flung out some energetic curses at the universe, and said the hell with it. I closed my eyes and thought I'd have a nap. Maybe reality would sort itself out during the time out.

When I opened my eyes about ten minutes later, a half

dozen gnomes were peering down at me in concern, their heads only inches from my nose. 'What's with you guys? I thought you were my friends. Why are you letting me get so bloody lost in here?' The gnomes scratched their heads and respectfully retreated from the barking Grail Knight. I guess it wasn't their fault; I hadn't officially asked for their guidance through the woods. I eventually found my way and had the inner Grail adventure Blaise had intended, and the next time I went to Copley, I got the gnomes on my case before I even dismounted from my bike. Show me the way, boys – I'm in your hands!

Actually I was about to have one of them on my hands. I had spent the day at Copley Wood, meditating by an old stream quaintly called Magotty Pagotty, then I had climbed the hill, staggered through the woods again, and found another spot to meditate on Worley Hill, the official name for the top of Copley Wood. I'll tell you about Worley later, and Magotty Pagotty for that matter, for they are linked and have to do with something called a cosmic egg.

When I got back down to my seat at the edge of Magotty Pagotty, there was an egg there the size of a cantaloupe. Inside the egg was a squirming baby gnome. He's fully dressed, looking very gnomish, just a miniature version, and he winks at me like a puppy sticking its nose out of a kid's wicker basket at Christmas.

A Grail Knight is asked to do a lot of strange things during the quest. And we're asked to deal with a lot of baffling con-undrums. I had come on bike. That takes two hands. I didn't have a knapsack; this little guy was too little to walk. I couldn't leave him here: that would be irresponsible, and, bizarre as it struck me at the time, the gnomelet was evidently a gift to me, evidently inaugurating my new career as a white slaver.

I figured it was best to simply play along. Okay: there really is a baby gnome and I have to deal with it. Why not take the little fellow home and figure it out later? I put the gnome on my head and started for home. As I rolled up to Wick at dusk, Russell was in the yard, raking. He chuckled and pointed to my head, and said 'What's that on your head, Grail Knight?'

I kept the gnomelet in my bedroom on the top bookshelf, next to my books of Celtic folklore and fairy mythology. I thought maybe this would feel like familiar, if ancestrally so, surroundings as he found his bearings in my world or until I figured how to get him back to his. I sent out an all points distress call to Battingley. It was one thing to babysit the Pendelton's kids; they were at least susceptible to well-structured bribes in return for good behavior, but what do gnomes eat? Do little ones sleep? Get lonely? Miss their own kind?

I needn't have worried. Higher forces were at work. A few days later after lunch I feel drawn to step out into the garden, which is what the English call a mowed lawn bordered by flowers and what we would simply call the backyard. The place is filled with gnomes, packed, swarming with them. I guessed there were 150 gnomes sitting cross-legged in a couple of half circles waiting for me to show up. Immediately they got up, Battingley took the gnomelet from me — I had sensed the infant needed some fresh air — and we made a grand procession through the mud and ruts of the farm track to the Fairy Dell.

It had all the trappings of a religious procession, almost something you'd see in old Tibet. At the head of this gnome parade, several hefty gnomes carried the gnomelet in a litter with a golden cupola. Once at the Fairy Dell, the twelve dozen gnomes fanned out in a broad half circle like a Celtic torc, leaving me positioned where the clasp would go. On behalf of the group, Battingley said this rabble of gnomes was my personal Round Table of gnome attendants and assistants for the quest.

Then he said something that's even today a little hard for me to believe, but he said it and I heard it, so here it is: 'This golden gnome' — he was pointing to the gnomelet — 'is our new king and will be the first lieutenant of your Round Table.' Two dozen gnomes raised the cupola with the kingly gnome inside like a wineglass in a banquet toast. The curtains of the cupola were pulled open and inside was the golden gnome with crown, robes, and an amiable grin. 'Dalai Gnoma! Dalai Gnoma!' the gnomes chanted, applauding their new potentate.

I promised to return in a few days to give their new king — the whole gnome gang, in fact — a sip from my Grail bowl. But first I had to get one.

3

The next thing you need on the Quest is the Grail.

Everybody's got it wrong about the Holy Grail. You don't have to go searching for it. On the Quest, you start with it. The angels give you the Grail. What you have to do is figure out what it is and how to use it. It may also interest you to find out where it came from.

One of the first things you realize on the Quest is that all the myths about it — in fact, all the old myths about anything, period — are true, but they're distorted, twisted, fragmented, upside down, front to back turned inside out, misleading. You can't take them literally, but you shouldn't dismiss them either.

When the tales of King Arthur's knights speak of cranky dwarves accompanying the knights on their Grail errands, they're talking about gnomes. When they say the Grail chalice contains the blood of Christ, that's partly true, but you have to understand it outside of any official religious position or tradition. And when they whisper the marvels of the Grail Castle and how tricky it is getting inside it, don't start looking for some fantastic mountain-perched stone-built fortress with a Grail hidden in the upstairs oubliette. It's not there.

But there is most definitely a Grail Castle. I know because I've been in it, several times. But as I said, first you need to get the Grail. One night early in our apprenticeship with Blaise, they gave us the Grail — or shall I say, an early model edition of it. And being empiricists, they preferred to send me out in the field first and explain things later.

'We present you with an image,' Blaise said one night. 'A lilac flame burns over a golden Grail bowl that has no stem but two handles, one on each side. In the center of the lilac flame is a still point of brilliant pure light, a tiny blazing star. The bowl gives off a blue light and a blue light surrounds the bowl. It sits on the ground in a grassy meadow. On the outside of the bowl running around just under its rim are the symbols of the zodiac. They face outwards and each is enclosed in a hexagram except for Capricorn which is in a pentagram which points upward. Behind the bowl are two swords. One points up, from Earth to Heaven; one faces down, from Heaven to Earth, and is set in a scabbard with jewels. Bring this image into the center of your being.'

This was like trying on a three piece suit, fixing the bow-tie, and slipping on the wing-tips all at once while combing my hair and shaving and listening to someone explain one of the oldest cosmic mysteries. I placed the Grail bowl at my pelvis; the lilac flame rose up to about my chest; the little pinprick of light twinkled inside it. The sword going down had the handle at my shoulder blades; the blade went down through the top of my head and its point reached the base of my spine. This sword was set inside a jeweled scabbard. The other sword started at my pelvis, its cross-bar handle at my hips but the very end of it touching the ground. The top point of its blade came out just above my head. This sword had no scabbard. Both swords were enhaloed with lilac flames.

The next day I took my Grail equipment out for a spin at the Fairy Dell. It was a little odd walking around with all this stuff inside me. Of course, we rarely take the time to visualize our internal organs (or even to know where they all are inside, and why), and the details of our skeleton are for most of us a rumor still uninvestigated. But now I had all this Grail paraphernalia, this Quest regalia, and with every step I took, I tried to keep it in focus, and I tried not to slosh the contents. The Grail seemed to be filled this morning.

At the Fairy Dell, I sat down on the edge of the woods. Battingley is with me of course, but he seems to have invited all his friends. There is a gang of gnomes, a clutch of fairies, a couple of females of indeterminate age looking a bit like Disney's Snow White – 'Those are sylphs, silly,' said Blaise – and a large male with little horns on his head like cowlicks. His skin is dappled in green leaves, his face is wrinkled and mischievous, but the flute gives him away. Tell Thamus, that misinformed Greek sailor, that the great god Pan is not dead!

The gnomes make a circle around me, sitting cross-legged, smoking pipes, watching it all like amused guardians. Fairies drift down languorously like autumn leaves. The whole place seems suffused in a lovely emerald green shaft of light. I offer one and all the contents of my Grail bowl, and everybody has a good drink. Meanwhile I gorge myself on the ripe wild blackberries nearby, then I take a little nap in the bright sunshine.

When I awake I have an odd sensation that I had been swimming in the Grail, that doing a lazy backstroke across the blue light in the bowl I had swum right into the chalice and had become it. That was indeed a queer sensation: the bowl of course is circular and if it were to see the world, it would not see it from merely a single fixed place, such as we do because we have eyes. It would see everything all at once as if it had eyes in all three hundred and sixty degrees of its own circular being.

My sensation of this is that I am continuously transiting the Grail bowl so that my attention is uniformly distributed throughout it. I am no longer a rectilinear human with eyes at the top; I am a hollow golden sphere with eyes nowhere and everywhere. It's like I am a golden sun rapidly revolving around inside itself. I am both the sun that is briskly moving in a circle and the Grail bowl that seems to be made of the sun, as if the sun were some kind of molten metal poured into a Grail mould to set.

As I zip around in perpetual circles in this golden circuit, I sense somehow I am transiting stars and constellations, and am moving through but am more than the twelve zodiacal signs Blaise said were embossed on the outside of the Grail bowl. I sense that somehow I know everything there is to know about them; I am more mobile than they are. They are fixed; I am zipping. They are points, but I am the whole thing. They are stars, but I am the container for all stars. I am the container that knows what the stars know, and lots more. I'm not trying to get grandiose on you, but the Grail has something to do with big time knowledge, things really worth knowing, cosmic things, cosmic memory.

In the evening Blaise says I did good at the Fairy Dell. Bringing lunch to the devic world was a good idea. 'Your gift to the fairies will be replenished twice over. The gift you made will relate to the devic realms. Made without our suggestion, it will bring much support for you in the future as the word has been passed amongst them.'

There was no need to tell Blaise about my cool experience in the Grail merry-go-round. Whatever I experience they're already there, watching it, in it, and probably facilitating it in the first place. It was becoming evident to me the Grail is more than a devic lunch wagon driven by courteous Grail Knights. 'The nearest a human gets to the process of comprehending the Grail is allied to what you call memory. The *process* of remembering is very important. The Grail Quest is achieving the memory of that which existed at the point when consciousness decided, phylogenetically, to take human form. It is the process of remembering the condition *prior* to when consciousness came to be locked in a spacetime continuum within the human organism.'

Now I understood why Blaise was always saying, 'We remember you as you were before the Fall.' Before the Fall is the 'prior' condition, before whatever we were originally – all of humanity, the original Adam and its incalculable progeny – entered into human form for the *first* time. It's remembering what you were before you were *ever* a human, or ever even thought about becoming one, and perhaps before you ever even heard of the whole idea that you could become a human, and perhaps before God even came up with the idea of a human. We're talking about a memory that goes *way* back in time, possibly even before time. But the memory process has a subtlety to it, a kind of hidden clause.

'The principle of the Grail is the process whereby the unitive function, represented by the bowl, contains something, the process of individuation, which is the overflowing of the bowl,' Blaise explains. 'The Grail legend is the synthesis of

these two processes in consciousness, the unitive and individuative processes.'

This is the tricky part about the Grail, about being human.
You have to play out your own melodrama – you as a character appearing throughout history, making mistakes, cor-
recting them, having insights, forgetting them, remembering
your self, abandoning it, eventually getting it all together as an
individual voluntarily returning to your source, your head in
your hands. That's the individuative part. The unitive part is
that all of us – the whole phylogenetic mass of humanity over
time – is in this together, is really the same soul experiencing
the same drama over and over – you know, oneness. We're all
that same head born in the Grail Knight's hands.

'The process is demonstrated in the Arthurian legends
whereby only a small percentage of the knights could give up
their ego base and survive the process,' Blaise says. 'Only a
small number had a large enough spiritual background with
the facility to survive the personal death to reach the unitive
level. The Grail bowl is the receptive vessel for the unification
process, which is a continual process involving the essence of
human consciousness. Anyway, don't worry about it Grail
Knight. You can remember.'

So I took my receptive vessel for the unification process into
Glastonbury to see what shreds of memory I could collect.
Blaise had me start at Wearyall Hill and proceed down the hill,
up the main street of town, and around the back to the Tor,
over Chalice Hill, and down into Chalice Well gardens. I was a
one-man Grail parade. I guess it takes more than one to
remember for I had a gang on board for the Grail procession.
I'll describe the entourage for you:

Battingley brought about a dozen of his gnome friends; there were bouquets of fairies and one matronly sylph; at least six Blaises; the shade of my dead brother; the shade of Wellesley Tudor Pole, a Glastonbury savant, once a successful tea merchant (he secured Chalice Well for the public many decades ago) and Blaise colleague; and the spirit of Joseph of Arimathea, the guy who brought the Grail to Glastonbury two thousand years ago and buried it in Chalice Hill. Among his other postmortem duties, he is overseer of the Grail lineage, and I guess he wanted to see what a genuine American jackanapes Grail Knight manqué looked like and to be on hand if and when the Grail butt needed a swift kick or the Grail head a bit of an infusion of common sense.

I'll have to stop here for a moment and clear up the confusion no doubt generated by that last remark about Joseph. The myths say Joseph brought the Grail bowl containing a few drops of Jesus the Christ's blood as it flowed out of his body on Golgotha strapped up on that horrible cross. The myths also say Joseph stashed the Grail somewhere in Glastonbury, probably in Chalice Hill. You're probably wondering: if he buried the Grail in Chalice Hill, why all this get-up of swords and bowl, this complicated inner image? Why not just tear the hill apart and get the Grail and be done with it?

The irony is that the actual physical Grail is only a symbol of the real Grail; it is a worldly copy of something that is inherently much more subtle. Even if I had *that* Grail, I would still be as thick as bricks; it wouldn't benefit me a bit if I hadn't done the inner work of remembering. Even if I had *that* Grail, I wouldn't have the Grail at all. I wouldn't have even begun the Quest, and I would be seriously distracted.

Just for the record, I did see *that* Grail one afternoon while I was meditating at the Abbey (I'll tell you about it in a minute), but I wasn't impressed, nor should you be, because that's not the Grail we're concerned with. It's just a cheap knock-off of the real thing. If you spend your time looking for that one, you may as well stay at home and see what's on HBO and forget the whole thing.

Let's get it over with before I go any further. I'll tell you how I saw the Holy Grail, the one brought by Joseph of Arimathea, and buried in Glastonbury somewhere two thousand years ago, and then I'll tell you why it didn't make any difference. If you were to settle for that, it would be like thinking Noah's Ark was only a unique and singular physical object; you would completely miss the point. It's the same with the Grail, as I found out.

I was meditating at the unfinished Edgar Chapel, at the far end of the Glastonbury Abbey ruins, the part that's closest to Chalice Hill. Five lines of light intersect at that point and they somehow make a doorway into another place. I penetrate this nexus of lines and enter a circular frieze, like a giant color photograph, or a scene of live action frozen in time. It quickly melts into living color and action. I see a group of medieval monks in a fifteen-foot deep trench examining the entrance to a stone-lined tunnel that leads into Chalice Hill. I study the tableau more carefully and see a wall of cubic black stones that surround the entrance the monks are examining.

I pass through this entrance into an empty stone chamber presumably inside Chalice Hill. It's like a monk's cell, bare, clean, ready for meditation. There is a single window: it is a three-sectioned bay window. The room is gloriously illumined by light pouring in through this small window. The light is so intense, so effulgent, I can no longer see the window. I've never seen light like this in the physical world. Somehow I am able to see the source of this resplendent light. It is the Holy Grail.

I pass through this three-bayed window into an ocean of light. I can't say I remember much after that. That's the annoying thing about mystical experience. You always fall asleep at the crucial part and afterwards can't remember a thing. I find myself back in the solitary monk's cell. Now it has twelve bay windows and over each is a sign of the zodiac. There is a circular zodiac embedded in the floor, done in little ceramic tiles. I sit under the same window again and pass through it once more into that ocean of light. I swim through the light waves and reach the Grail, which is radiant, golden, and prodigiously, inexhaustibly overflowing.

In the midst of these events, I think to myself: So, this is where Joseph stashed it when he came to Glastonbury. I was glad to learn it is permanently protected against egress by any other than invited Grail Knights. Archeologists could probably tear the hill apart and never find the Grail even though it's there in the hill manifesting somewhere in that numinous nether dimension between matter and spirit. It was nice to know it was there, but it didn't quite make my day. I was after a different Grail.

At the Fairy Dell, I had gotten the impression the Grail in some respects was like a lunch wagon. At Chalice Well I discovered the lunch wagon has more than one customer. Sharing the angelic bounty with the devics is a good idea and wins you points with Pan, but you soon learn some elderly gent called the Fisher King is your prime customer on the Grail lunch route. When you meet the Fisher King, you have entered the Beverly Hills of mythic personages. This one is very upmarket. You can't get much more mythological than him.

Here's the main point about the Wounded Fisher King: the Grail Quest is done on his behalf. He's the guy who can't remember anything and is miserable on account of that. In fact, he's miserable to be around. So miserable he's turned his once lush kingdom into a wasteland.

The Grail sagas confuse the issue by saying he has a terrible wound in his thigh or groin and, invalided, has to spend his time on a couch as once a day the Holy Grail is brought before him. Nobody can heal him and he can't have the Grail. The whole thing is a metaphor. There's nothing wrong with the old man's thigh or groin. 'The Fisher King pertains to that aspect of consciousness that lies at the deepest level,' says Blaise. 'He rules over the deep past and the deep memories of the soul. His wounds are that which do not remember the soul's purpose and nature, its level of development, and the individual's ability to penetrate that veil.'

The wound is his blocked memory. His life energy in the groin can't connect with his crown, his highest spiritual principle. He's split, exiled, forlorn. He can't remember his origin, his *prior* condition. He's miserable, and he's made everyone around him, even the land, miserable too. He lives in the Grail Castle in daily sight of the Grail, but it's useless to him. He doesn't know how to use it to heal himself and remember. That's the job of the Grail Knight: get into the castle, give the old boy a drink from the Grail bowl, heal his wound, and help him remember. Then he becomes what he used to be: the *Rich* Fisher King.

Apparently Wellesley Tudor Pole worked with Blaise years ago to set up the Chalice Well garden to be a training ground for Grail Knights. I don't know how they did it, but as I climb the stone steps that lead out of Arthur's Courtyard (a lovely grotto with a tiny waterfall and overhanging trees in about the middle of the garden), I come upon an oak door. I knock on it four times, then enter a king's royal court and walk slowly along a carpeted path to the king who is expecting me.

I carry the Grail with delicacy and concentration, as if it's precious china, and I try to keep the swords and flames and stars all in the right place. People line the hall and observe my progress, and I have the feeling there hasn't been a Grail Knight through here in some time. Physically, I am walking very slowly up the garden path to the actual well of the Chalice Well; Blaise has arranged it so that nobody else is here today to witness my eccentric shuffle towards the king of cosmic memory.

The king is short and stout, his head is a bit squarish, his beard red, his hair long and straight, and he sports a golden crown. Aside from the crown, he reminds me of my high school biology teacher. But his expression gives it all away. He seems discontented, restless, peevish, unhappy, unhealthy, forlorn, hurt — he's a mess. We look each other in the eyes, then I retrace my steps, leave the Grail Castle, and return to Arthur's Courtyard for a time out.

Blaise nudges me to make the trek to the Fisher King again. This time it seems like I am high in the mountains, on some windswept peak — Eschenbach's *Munsalvaesche* perhaps, the medieval Castle of the Grail believed to have been situated at Montsegur, a craggy peak in the French Pyrenees. I knock on the oak door again, enter, and proceed as before, aware of the hundreds of eyes intent on my progress down the hall to the king.

I feel like a serving woman — a cross-dressing Grail Maiden, if you will — bringing the old fellow a drink. I notice there's a crown on my head too, and just before I reach the king, another king empties a basin of milk — it's probably light — into my Grail bowl. The Fisher King is seated just to the side of the well and he gestures for me to sit next to him. Together we survey the court, the flowers, the muralled walls, the courtiers. For some reason, everybody seems a little happier now that I'm here. I guess he doesn't get many visitors these days.

A few days later I visited the Fisher King again, but this time I paid a call to his actual residence, not his commuter's apartment. I went to the Grail Castle. The Palace Adventurous, the Castle of Wonders, Castle Carbonek, and *Caer Sidi*, the Revolving, Spinning Castle, as some have called it. I sat on Chalice Hill and focussed on my Grail image, making sure the swords, lilac flame, star, blue sphere, and Grail bowl were all in the right place. Then I concentrated on the Blazing Star, the one above my belly button and the one inside the lilac flame, for they are the same.

Somehow I find myself before a door again; it's not locked, so I push it open and enter what appears to be an enormous castle. There is a large foyer filled with framed portraits, possibly of previous Grail Knight visitors. Beyond the foyer is a large rotunda, and in the center of the open space on a chest-high platform is an emerald, bright green, three feet high, double terminated with six equal facets.

I put a Blaise tip to practical use here. I breathe as Love from Above to this seemingly impenetrable peculiar green stone, and suddenly I am in it, or it disappears, and I am in a royal hall, a regal throne room like the one at Chalice Well but grander, more opulent, as if this were the original, and the Chalice Well version the fair but scaled down copy. At the far end of the hall stands the Fisher King, looking grim but regal, holding a scepter. I carry the Grail to him, as I had done at Chalice Well. But he seems to float up to the ceiling of the Grail Castle; he inserts his scepter which resembles a lance into the source of the brilliant light that floods the hall. This makes the whole place get a lot brighter. Then he inserts his scepter into the Grail bowl, and sits down again. Then I see the whole thing again except from a different angle.

This time I insert my sword (the one in the scabbard and with the hilt at my head) in the Grail bowl, and I float up to the ceiling to change the light bulb, or so it seems. Now the Grail is much larger, no longer a bowl resting on my pelvis. It's the size of a large public fountain mounted on a pedestal; it is probably twenty feet in diameter and full of light. I fill my Grail bowl with this and approach the Fisher King — who is himself again and not me — empty its contents on his head, drenching him in light.

Then I tried to be clever. I've read the Grail stories and know that Parsifal always blows it on his first visit to the Grail Castle because he stands around stupefied and never asks the old king what the problem is. I thought I'd get on top of this problem from the outset, so I asked him: 'Whom does the

Grail serve?' The Fisher King answered, 'It serves you.' He was *supposed* to say it serves him. 'Who is you?' I ask. 'You and I are one.' So much for being clever. What happened to the rug I thought I was standing on?

That's when I realized I was being conned. That the whole Grail Quest and the Wounded Fisher King was a big con on me. Not just me, you, everybody. I kept thinking the Grail Castle was a place outside me, that the Fisher King was some fallen celestial being requiring my assistance. Wrong.

I am the Fisher King, and so are you and your brother, mother and father, your aunts and uncles, your neighbors, postman, baker, doctor, and mine too. Each of us is the king who can't remember his divine origin; each of us is the cranky, despondent, invalided monarch who thinks he can't be healed and likes to whine about it. We're all stranded here bereft of our memory of why. It's not a permanent, irreversible amnesia, though; that's the good news about the Grail Quest. Total recall is possible; in fact, it's the whole point of the game.

And the Grail Castle? Castle Carbonek: just think about it for a minute. Castle *Carbon*ek. It's the human body, my body, your body, based on carbon.

I think Blaise was patiently waiting for me to make this (to me) momentous discovery, because the minute I got it, they had this to say: 'At the time of the Arthurian myths, the predominant form structure and container for human consciousness was the carbon cycle, as in carbonic acid. The Castle Carbonek was the individual knight's exploration of his own inner temple.'

This was elegant. The whole quest to remember your origins gets cast outwards into a myth about a king and a castle and valiant knights who try to fix the problem. That's why the Fisher King looked like himself then like me, and why I saw things from his vantage point then from mine. I thought I was beginning to understand the set up, until Blaise threw me another curveball. I had been wondering: if the Grail Castle is just a spatial metaphor for the human body, why does it look like a castle instead of, say, a giant body?

It turns out there are more than one hundred Grail Castles around the planet. Each is the same in that once you enter it you could just as well be in any of the others. It's like a hundred doors opening into the same room. All the castles are copies of an original. Even so, 'The Grail Castle does not exist anywhere on Earth in the sense you know it,' Blaise explained.

'It is the etheric double of something in a different time and space mirrored here for a purpose. The castle at Chalice Hill and the ones elsewhere are all etheric doubles of this place. They were brought here and placed as 'buildings,' as etheric temples, for the evolution of the planet and its soul beings. Their purpose is yet to be fulfilled. A very small number of humans in the past had access to the particular level of consciousness necessary to perceive these castles in the etheric realm. Access was made from the etheric castles on Earth to the actuality of the castle in another dimension, but this has not occurred since Atlantean days. Access will become more available and this will be firmly established in a short time.'

I was glad to hear they'd be opening up the Grail Castle to the general public soon although I was disconcerted to have my provisional understanding of things kicked to pieces again. So it is more than a metaphor for deep memory. It is a real and mythological place, if you'll pardon the irony, which is not mine by the way. God's the one who made everything so complex. If there are dozens of these castles around the planet, that means everyone has a fair shot at visiting the Grail Castle and doesn't have to travel too many miles to the nearest replica.

It also means that somebody — Blaise and their pals, and their Boss — took the time to design the planet, or at least one aspect of it, in such a way as to make possible our remembering our cosmic origins while we walk around the place in bodies. They designed the planet to make higher consciousness possible. What a courteous gesture. In other words, somebody thought it worthwhile for humans to remember where they came from; somebody designed the Grail Castle as a workshop for that process of recollection; somebody organized to have more than a hundred copies of it distributed around the Earth; and somebody made up a clever story about it and passed it on to a few humans and eventually to the whole race of us who now dismiss it as a groundless fairy tale.

Everybody knows who the Somebody is, and this matter of attribution points out one of those strange ironies of the Quest. It's like an Agatha Christie detective novel turned inside out. Of course the butler did it, but what exactly did he do? We know *who* did it — God did it, and Blaise, and all their angelic cohorts — but *what* they did and *why* is what the mystery is about. Which reminds me of one of those almost self-congratulatory remarks Blaise once made when I asked him how come there was a Grail Quest in the first place.

'It is to stop humans from becoming depressingly boring, to indicate to humans joyful boredom. We hope the Quest will become something of a fad. Much can be transformed by this means.' Make the Mystery into a game show. Not a bad idea – inevitable, logical, really – if you're facing 15 billion years of evolution and you have to supervise a fairly obtuse species called human beings.

If you live in southern England and are in need of a Grail Castle as part of your process of reclaiming your cosmic memory, come to one above Chalice Hill. If you live in southern France, consider Montsegur; if you live in Iran, try Mount Demavend, If you live in Northern California, believe it or not, Alcatraz is your place; later I would discover a Grail castle replica moored in the ethers above the prison island in San Francisco Bay. Think of it globally. The Montsegur Grail Castle is the same place as the Alcatraz, Chalice Hill, and Mount Demavend Castles. Potentially humans from numerous diverse points on the planet could be entering the Grail Castle at the same time: would we see one another?

We would, and we do. It's called the Round Table. Knights who make it into the Grail Castle assemble at the Round Table as equals. It's round because there is no head and no foot, no hierarchy, only positions needing to be filled.

So how do you get to the Round Table? Go through the emerald. Remember the double-terminated six-sided emerald I saw at Chalice Hill? That was not a quirk of my particular imagination and visualization processes. It helps that the great mythographer of the Grail Quest, Wolfram von Eschenbach, declared that the angels brought the Grail to Earth in the form of a green stone. Nobody could ever understand what Wolfram was on about because they couldn't get past this question: how the hell can a green stone be a chalice? The answer is simple: it can't, and it's not supposed to. The Grail is *inside* the stone.

This business of the emerald is very complicated, and I don't plan to go into it much here. However, it is central to the whole story – Grail Quest, Castle, cosmic memory, the true nature of the human, the planet, the game. If you want to get inside the Grail castle and sit at the Round Table, walk through the emerald; any of the side facets will do; each is a doorway. The truly egalitarian thing about the set-up is that, technically, you needn't even find a Grail Castle replica moored over some mountain or prison island to get in. It helps, but you can shortcut the system. Here's how: the emerald is inside you.

The emerald is a secret part of your heart chakra, that energy vortex in the center of your chest. Not your physical heart, but its energy parents. Everyone has one, whether you like it or not, believe it or not, use it or not. It's a two inch vertical emerald situated just to the right of your sternum with its top starting at about the level of the third rib down on the right. Admittedly, it's a bit awkward – and silly to watch, too – to try to climb into a two inch green stone in your chest while occupying an adult human body. It's much easier to project it outside you and walk in the front door like it's a bank and you belong there.

I learned to project my emerald to be a two-story glass building. Walk through any of the six sides and pull up a seat at the Round Table. Here's a Grail Knight tip: first, breathe as Love from Above to the Blazing Star above your belly button. Intoxicate yourself with its angelic fumes to such an extent that the star goes supernova and you're inside it as the star. You'll find this to be a pale blue seemingly infinite curved space. Focus on the bottom part, and think of it like a slightly concave pale blue dish, a bit like a saucer for a tea cup. Set your emerald in this blue dish then walk right through.

I did this regularly in the early days of the Quest. It was like sneaking into a secret clubhouse, so secret I hadn't even known about it a few weeks ago. For a while it's like trying to see in the dark. What table? I don't see any round table. It's there, certainly, but you will probably have to pretend you see it at first. Once you've got the table in view, you can start looking for other visitors. Again, it may all be a blur for some time; it was for me. I started with the chair I was sitting on, bringing its shape and details clearly into focus. Then I worked on the roundness of the table, and I made it about fifty feet in diameter. Next I saw the other chairs. Eventually I started seeing some people.

Be careful here. Don't expect to see your friends, neighbors, parents, teachers, or anybody else recognizable. It's far more likely you'll see strangers. This is all paradoxical because, technically, you are all colleagues of the Holy Grail, and on a soul level, are probably closer, more consanguineous, than your waking world friends who may not disavow you for telling them about the Grail Castle but probably will not encourage you to expatiate on its wonders either.

There's a wonderful story from the Grail legends about a time when all the knights were assembled and the Holy Grail was brought down in the center of the great table, filling everyone with intense awe and unrelieved wonder. This is the state-of-the-art Grail Castle experience, the ideal of the whole set-up. For a while you may have to settle for more solitary epiphanies until everyone else shows up and you wipe the artifacts of sleep from your eyes.

I was sitting at the table one day. The table was getting well established in my 'sight' and I was studying its marvelous roundness and wondering what was that little seed of golden light in its very center. The more I focussed on the golden dot, the bigger it grew. Soon it was a refulgent golden orb; then it seemed I was flying into the Sun. It was so bright, everywhere was molten gold.

I disappeared – that is, my sense of occupying an upright male human body – and was swallowed up by this gold. Everywhere was gold. Even that's not correct because it presumes a specific point of cognition by which I realized everywhere was gold. I no longer had such a discrete point. Goldness was, shall we say.

Then the goldness slowly congealed itself into a form. I deduced it was the golden Grail bowl because I found myself zipping around the three hundred and sixty degrees of the circle again. I was the Grail and my attention was globally distributed through the bowl. My sense of myself was as a chalice, a bowl. I'm not saying I forgot who I was; I knew I was still this American Grail Knight who hung out with angels and gnomes and was interested in figuring out most of the cosmic mysteries. But my body of reference was no longer human, with all my awareness piled up inside a skull and with arms and legs and internal organs and circulating blood and all the rest. My body was this bowl thing and I was feeling very receptive.

Then I realized the Grail itself is not the memory of our cosmic origins. It is merely the means by which we can attain that memory. As Blaise said, it is the receptive vessel for that deep soul memory. A drop of brilliant scarlet blood fell into the bowl, into me, and distributed itself through the Grail. The instant the scarlet touched the golden chalice – my skin, so to speak – it flooded my awareness with this same quality of scarlet. Everything was scarlet now, just as before everything had been goldness.

There was no golden bowl, no more zipping around the circle. I melted into this scarlet, and when everything, even the voice in my head that still narrated these events and claimed an individuality for itself – when even this point of self reference dissolved into the scarlet and I heard the words 'Not I, but the Christ in me,' the scarlet itself vanished and there was a field of brilliant white. After some time, the whiteness seemed to assume a form, a kind of geometric shape, and once again I seemed to be inside an organized space.

It was like being inside a clear quartz crystal. It seemed to consist of a four sided-pyramid on top of another one, but they were pointing in opposite directions; in other words, the bases of both were touching, as it were, back to back, and the pointed parts were facing in opposite directions. Later I would understand this is an octahedron, esoterically known as the Buddha Body, Merlin's glass house, the eight-spoked wheel, and other interesting names. The last thing I was aware of was that the glass house started to rotate slowly as if somebody were spinning it like a top. It was a kind of pleasant sensation, even purposeful, the way a wheel at the end of an axle must feel when the vehicle starts to move.

A couple of weeks later I wanted to visit the original of the Grail Castle. I wanted to see Sarras for myself. 'The city of Sarras, the spiritual place' is a phrase Thomas Malory often used in Le Morte d'Arthur when he referred to the Grail. He implied that the Grail came from there or was kept there, but he never explained what Sarras was. I guess that would make things too easy.

I focus on the Chalice Hill Grail Castle and find myself high above it but at a forty-five degree angle to it. From above, the Grail Castle looks like a miniature spiral galaxy, a flat silvery disk with a golden mound in the center, like a plump egg yolk. In this visionary expedition, I stand on Chalice Hill and look up to see a brilliant golden sun set in a golden circle. I walk into this sun. A Shepherd of the Sun appears; he's dressed in white and bears a staff. He gestures to a series of standing golden rectangles about six feet high.

I walk through one and pass over a causeway across a deep chasm. At the end of this causeway is a small beehive chamber perhaps twenty feet across and a bit higher. Its walls are golden pentagons and upon them is a written script, and not in any letter-based script I recognize. The script is really living fire, and the living fire is actually angelic beings expressed as a living script of fire. The fire angels seem to sweat liquid fire into a golden phosphorescent puddle that quivers like mercury. 'This is Soma,' they say, the liquid fire of immortality. I dab some on the top of my head and it leaps into golden flames.

I should mention that one of the things consistently said about the Grail Castle is that there people live as long as the gods, enjoying bliss, perfect memory, and pretty much whatever they want to eat and drink whenever they want it. Total recall is considered the same as immortality in this scheme.

For variety, I thought I would switch my focus to the Montsegur Grail Castle to see if anything looked different from that vantage point. I see a medieval stone palace guarded by a dragon. In a sense, the castle is the dragon, and you enter the place through the dragon's mouth. Not to worry; they don't bite. The interior of the castle is the golden coils of the dragon which means the castle is circular, perhaps spirallic, in shape. The Fisher King's throne area is an eggshell pale blue. I don't directly see the Grail but I see its effulgence. The hall is filled, overflowing, super-saturated with intense golden light.

Beyond this is a misty space in which humans mill about. The mist clears and I see an apricot-colored outdoor amphi-theater, Grecian style. The people in the amphitheater all have laurels on their heads. The amphitheater fades away, or per-haps my attention shifts a bit, and I am drawn to a small stone-lined pool surrounded by lovely white birches set high in the mountains. I immerse myself fully in this pool in a kind of baptism.

I realize that the pool could very well be situated in the center of the amphitheater and the birches could be the people with laurels on their heads. Sequential visionary images have a way of being equivalent. The little baptismal pool is the inverse of the famous River Lethe in which souls about to incarnate immerse themselves so as to divest themselves of their soul memories of Heaven which would otherwise get in the way of being happily deluded and in the dark as alive men and women. This pool helps you remember, and I want to remember so much I dive into it and disappear.

It's a dimensional portal of course. Things are never just one thing or what they seem, especially in this otherworld. I arrive outside a huge white-stoned wall on a small hill overlooking a vast plain at sunset. I know that on the other side of this huge wall is a large city full of people and that I probably wouldn't mind too much if I met a few of them. I ask Blaise for a lift up over the wall and into the city, and they oblige. I am lifted up and deposited in the city. It's Sarras, I know it.

It is intensely emerald in here. Momentarily I see a crown comprised of thirteen different jewels atop a vast celestial being. At the center of this city is a towering version of the emerald, which is one of the thirteen jewels on the crown. So perhaps this emerald domain is but one of thirteen ascribed to this cosmic being. The emerald emits a feeling of morning freshness, of dawn, of the purity of the first morning star, of the first instant of unstained self-aware consciousness, of that primal morning when the gods awoke and knew existence was real.

Now I see a little more of this awesome being. It is something like a human, but much more like an angel, but even to say that is inaccurate. Numerous smaller angels make a circlet of winged pulsating light about this majestic and towering presence, and myriad more angels envelop this bringer of living light, this light bearer, in sparkling bands like folds in a robe. Not only the head, but the entire body is blazing with encrusted jewels, pulsating points and geometries of light.

Looking at this majestic celestial being, you can't help but think it is singularly organized for awareness, for self-conscious cognition. That somehow, miraculously, compassionately, beatifically, we came from this, this is the mould made for us, the Promethean fire-infused original. Consciousness gloriously prior to the phylogenetic 'Fall' into the human form.

'Sarras is an ancient word,' Blaise tells me. 'The Grail was earthed, in a sense, through this name in ritual. Amongst a particular group of beings, there was mutual agreement as to a particular place in which to ground their individual experiences of the Grail. That was Sarras.' I realized that not only does the Grail help an incarnated human remember where he came from, but from *here*, the viewpoint of a soul outside of incarnation, or prior to it, it's a way of collecting and distilling experiences in consciousness during an incarnation.

Think about it. The question we should be asking of life every day is what is matter? How did consciousness get into this form of flesh and bone, and — God! — why ever for? What's it been like, you ask yourself in this soul dimension, in Sarras, to have been a point of consciousness residing inside a carbon-based, oxygen-dependent body for fifty, seventy, ninety years? What was it like to bloat, to hiccup, to breathe in and out thousands of times, to feel so limited, so confined, so reduced, so dismembered, so damned amnesiac?

Some mornings (more than I'd like to admit) I wake up thinking I'm in a nightmare: what am I doing in this body? What are all these squishy organs inside my skin? Will I get out of here in one piece? I suppose it's a useful question to ask why is there consciousness at all? To me the answer is, why not? Questions like this are based on a false assumption. They assume we know what matter is, that it's our friend, our colleague, our home, and that consciousness is the strange visitor. I don't think we know much about matter at all; I think consciousness is our more familiar home, our base. The Grail proved that to me, but make up your own mind after you quest around a bit. Come to Sarras and see what you think.

I pass through this towering emerald at the center of the vast city and enter a giant meeting room dominated by a huge round table. All of this is familiar, only on a much larger scale than anything I've seen before. Various beings sit at the Round Table, most of them a bit odd. One in particular catches my attention. He has a long, pointed head, or maybe it's a head-dress; he looks like a member of the ancient Egyptian royalty, one of those godlike humans with unnaturally large heads, two crown chakras for the price of one cranium.

'He's from Sirius,' whispers Blaise. I understand that if I wanted to I could pass through this Round Table to another, more exalted meeting place in Sirius. But where's this? I ask Blaise. 'The Pleiades.'

I don't see the other people around the table, but I know they're present. I know that these are the key players, the ones who originally set up the Earth to be a workshop for the expansion and evolution of consciousness in a material base and who look after it even today to see how we're doing. These players have access to every human in existence through the emerald. It's like we all have a little green beeper in the chest. It's nothing to worry about. It's a good thing. Maybe I should say they have responsibility for the spiritual welfare of every human soul for their intentions are benign. Paradoxically, they are *our* intentions, were we to remember them. You start to see things like this in Sarras.

This council table in the original emerald city within the original Grail Castle is connected to every human through their own emerald. This instantaneous connection is the emerald modem operating across space and time, and before either. Each of us can dial up using the emerald modem and be in this place outside of spacetime and before incarnation. All of us are always, potentially, living here in Sarras, sitting at this table, as we were before the Fall. The emerald modem is always on even if we think we're computer illiterate.

'The emerald,' says Blaise, 'was dropped into Man's bio-physical organism at that point when form was brought into matter by the Lord of Light, at the time of 'the Fall.' There is intensively but one emerald. When a man or woman begins to awaken the aspect of themselves that is of the Lord of Light, the emerald glows within them. The light that the emerald contains is beyond any description. Were you to be exposed to the source of love and light within the emerald, you would lose your sense of spacetime continuity. Therefore you must progress gently towards this. Gaining familiarity with the emerald is also part of the preparation for the Christed initiation in the Buddha Body. You have already tasted a little of that experience through your visits to the Grail Castle.'

Naturally I asked Blaise what this Christed initiation in the Buddha Body is all about. 'We are instruments of the Archangel Michael in this activity. He brings the Christ spirit forward from the final event at the Hill of Golgotha. He prepares this initiation for the event of your future. It is the central theme of your work with us as a Grail Knight. It is about the event at Golgotha when matter became spirit.' Which is to say, when the Christ *remembered*.

4

You won't get too far on the Quest without a dome.

I realized this one afternoon while lying on Lollover Hill under its lovely dome. Lollover is a grassy rounded hill with a broad view of the other hills surrounding Glastonbury and the flat moorlands stretching green and low all the way to the Severn estuary up near Bristol. Frankly, this is a hill as if divinely prepared for lollygaging, for lolling over, upon which you can be a shameless lollygagger.

This is the kind of lushly comfortable hill, such a couch for indulgent lounging about in the open air, that you feel you could kiss it, snuggle up to it, which basically I'm doing. I'm on my back, palms cradling the back of my head, my knees facing the sky, legs crossed insouciantly, my left besneakered foot tapping the warm summer air indolently. There's nothing I have to do today, the Grail Quest is taking a breather, and I'm wondering when the domes are coming back.

Granted, they left such a powerful imprint when they were here, that it's as if they never left. Overhead I can see Zadkiel, archangelic leader of the Chasmalim, a family of bright angels, and I see them arrayed in dozens of clusters across the landscape for miles. They are emitting sounds. The whole thing, if seen from above, is like a vast sunflower in full bloom. Even though the domes, those traveling vaults of Heaven, are gone from the Earth for the moment, the numerous angelic choirs of the stars are still audible, still making an impression on the land, still *hearable*.

Way back in 1953 Arthur C. Clarke, that savant of science fiction, peered into our past and future and with prescience wrote in *Childhood's End* of the Overlord's silver gleaming ships descending upon the Earth in one apocalyptic moment, 'pouring out of the unknown depths of space,' to hover visibly over the planet's major cities. All the world watched as the great ships 'descended in their overwhelming majesty' and changed the history of the Earth, Clarke said.

That's pretty close to the truth, Blaise told me once. They prefer the term Cosmic Chaplains to Overlords, and the 'ships' — they call them 'domes' — will be more likely to settle each like a glorious canopy over various mountains rather than cities. In fact, when they come again, they'll settle exactly on the places they settled the last three times. Yes, they've been here three times already. Some of the dome sites became cities, but most were over volcanoes which became mountains when they calmed down, and still later, sacred mountains.

But I'm getting ahead of my story. I have to tell you about the Mump and how we first discovered the domes. . . .

I can see the Mump anytime I want from the edge of the back garden at Wick, right where it abuts the cow pasture that eventually takes you to the Fairy Dell. The Mump — it's proper name is Burrowbridge Mump and it's four miles from where I stand, directly overland — is a miniature Glastonbury Tor, smaller, oddly shaped, suspiciously manmade-looking, and topped with a ruined stone church. It's not as high as the Tor and doesn't get as many visitors, but according to Blaise, it's almost as important. It's a solitary bump in a flat landscape, a queerly contoured mound amidst the soggy *rhynes*, and it offers a fine view in all directions, including yet another vista on the shapeshifting Tor, which looks like a different hill from every new angle in which you happen to view it.

The Mump usually looks the same from wherever you view it, but this day it had something extra – above it. It was as if a giant translucent, pulsating rounded lampshade or multi-colored cake canister was set above and over the Mump and its sides, encasing it in light. This light canopy was perhaps four times larger than the hill itself and seemed to have a brilliant light bulb at its top center. Numerous spokes of light ray out from the lampshade giving me the impression of an immense radiant wheel; some of these radiating lines are spirallic, producing the image of a great deal of kinetic energy, like a whirling disc. Straight lines of intense light ray out across the landscape as if drawn with a pen and ruler; one goes to the Tor; some of them cross the curving lines.

If this were a tent and it had a tent pole, the light would be at the top of the tent pole. In fact, this visual analogy is not far off the mark. There was a kind of tent pole, but it was more like a spiraling, twisting, continually uprising current, like the old barbershop displays or a double helix of light. This twining light column seems alive; it is certainly active, as in 'on' if this were indeed a light switch, and there is continuous commu-nication between the center of the Mump and the inside top of the canopy over it. No, not canopy – *dome*, as in a cathedral's domed ceiling. That's probably where the church builders got the idea for a domed ceiling – from the domes in the land-scape.

For a moment, I'm there, inside the Mump, under its dome.

It's like being in a marvelous church – no, scratch that; it's like being in the original of all domed interiors, the archetypal rotunda, so to speak. A spiral of white light weaves upwards like a corkscrew in a transparent shaft towards a rotunda or domed ceiling. That ceiling is so brilliant I can't look at it for more than an instant. It's even brighter than looking directly into the Sun. Blaise says, 'You are inside a dome, a star in the landscape.'

I decide to run up Wick Hill, just behind the house and about forty feet higher, for a better view. The light canopy over the Mump now looks like two hands cupped in prayer forming a large oval shape between them; purple rays stream down from above and over the wrists onto the landscape. Once again, I sense myself inside the dome. The ceiling glitters with light, and is as elegant, symmetrical, and majestic as the high rotunda at St. Paul's Cathedral which I had recently visited in London. The curved walls and ceiling are pockmarked with portholes out of which beams of light are projected into the landscape. At the same time, uncannily, I feel as if I'm in the depths of outer space, out among the myriads of stars.

I didn't know it at the time but Russell and Berenice were actually on the Mump as I was having this little vision of the hill's secret energy anatomy. They had taken the kids there for a picnic and a romp. A little after I came down from Wick Hill and was filling up the kettle for some Grail tea, I heard the Citroen drive in noisily over the gravel. When I told them about my outing to the Mump, Russell said he had been aware of that and had in fact seen a few things on his own. 'The Mump was packed with angels. I counted at last sixteen, plus eight very large ones, plus an angel for each of us, including you.'

When I described the lampshade over the Mump, Berenice sniffed, indicating she was one or two steps ahead of me on that one. 'That's a dome, isn't it? I remember Blaise telling me about them. Maybe it was in a dream, I don't know. It looks like an upside-down flower-thingy with its green stalk rising right up into the sky and beyond. Its flower petals lay over the land. It looks rather like the head of a big flower, but it's all made of light. Or maybe I should say it's like a latticework of light, a bit like a lace doily suspended over the hill with lots and lots of blue lines raying out for lots and lots of places.'

Berenice's remarks seemed to trigger Russell's memory. 'Crikey, I almost forgot about this bit. There were lots more angels, come to think of it. Hundreds of angels of various colors and sizes, all dancing around us in a ring, like the fringes at the bottom of a lampshade. The spectacle filled the whole of the Mump. Blaise said they had brought some of their friends. I saw the dome overhead too. Light flowed down the sides of it in rivulets that changed color, from pale pastel lilacs to a rainbow spectrum. The dome covered all of the Mump, a bit like an upside down mixing bowl only transparent. How about you, love? Did you see anything else?'

Berenice enjoyed a long sip of her favorite weak tea flooded in milk, then answered. 'There was a golden staircase. I climbed it, and at the top, I saw an amorphous light being, almost undefined, although its arms extended to me in a welcome. It gave off such a happy, lovely feeling.'

'You know, it was like Blaise gave us a quick tour of an otherwise very secret place,' Russell added. 'It was as if, being who they are, they got us past all the red tape and security and passport control and all that, right into the heart of things. Straight to the top as usual.'

Russell's comment triggered a memory. I realized more had happened to me at the time than I had been aware of. Surprise, surprise! Just when I thought I knew what I had been doing. 'Wait. There was more, before I even got inside the dome. There was a line of people. It was so long it faded into the distance on the left along a dark, winding road. These people were lining up to get inside the dome. Then I saw a shepherd in a dark robe; he stood there with his staff like a tonsured friar before the entrance to a barrow — you know, a manmade cave on the ground with two upright stone slabs and a third laid across them like a lintel to frame the opening. He had a cross on a chain around his neck, and in the center of the cross was a golden figure — a blissful goddess figure of some type. A bit like Marilyn Monroe, actually. Then Blaise whispered that I ought to focus more clearly on the image. This time I saw an eagle inside a golden circle.

'On the inside of this cave door were a lot of gorillas. No, more like Chewbacca from *Star Wars* — eight foot tall, comfortably erect, lean, lanky ape beings. They even seemed intelligent, that they could communicate with me. One of them offered me a twig with button-like white flowers which he plucked from a large bush nearby. I carried this twig with white flowers as I went further into the cave. The twig is a kind of security card or visitor's pass. You know, like the golden bough. I came to a second door. This one was guarded by a man in a bronze spacesuit. He looked like a cross between an astronaut and a soldier, and he had a globular helmet and a long rod that was somehow a gun. For some reason he paid no attention to me and let me pass.

'I opened the door and passed through. There I saw a human involved in some kind of creative work; he was absorbed in deep thoughts, like an engineer conceiving a big project. Then I noticed something weird. A lot of these Chewbacca-gorillas were hanging by the arms from hooks, as if they were fur coats in storage or winter coats hung up in a mudroom after their occupants have come inside.

'Then I realized they weren't bodies on meat hooks; they were costumes, uniforms, skins — *bodies* they could put on like coats when they needed to. One of these figures without his gorilla suit stood benignly before me with a face that would pass as human. He smiled then gave me a leaf and a wand and gestured for me to look up. That's when I saw the corkscrew of light in the dome.'

Russell grinned and nodded. 'Grail Knight, those weren't gorillas. They are *Yetis*, you know, Sasquatch, the Abominable Snowman. I saw them too. They have something to do with guarding the entrances to these domes. They seem to escort those invited to visit the domes — whatever they are — into the interior.'

Naturally the matter of domes would be the first topic of discussion for us when Blaise made their daily tutorial visit with us this evening. In actual fact, it would not be a simple answer, and would encompass months of imparting information and arranging experiences. To explain what a dome is you have to explain the cosmos. To an extent, our extended Blaise tutorial did just this. But it is a big subject, and I'll just give the highlights here.

The domes were celestial devices that came here three times in the early days of the Earth. It was only during the third dome presence that there were any humans around, and only a few were capable of understanding what the domes were. It would be incorrect to call them ships, saucers, UFOs, or anything like that, yet they had some material substance and were able to effect matter. They came from a place, settled on Earth, then left, and they did this two more times. They traveled faster than the speed of light, which means they exist spatially in between what we normally call matter and spirit. I don't think you could walk up to a dome and tap its hull and hear anything; more likely, you'd get a deep sunburn and your ears would ring for weeks.

Even to say they came and went and will return is too unsubtle. Whatever. The important thing is they had a purpose here. 'The domes made the etheric structure of the Earth what it is by imposing a conscious matrix upon the planet,' said Blaise. 'This made the Earth a place for possible human evolution. After the domes departed, they left impressions on the Earth's surface. They left an oscillating pattern which will continue until the Earth ceases to exist or until they are reaffirmed by another visit. The domes will return one day.'

Nor did the domes come with emotionless little grey aliens in the cockpit, or praying mantis-like insect alien scientists, or any other kind of popular image of visiting ETs we might have. The ones driving the domes were called Cosmic Chaplains, and these were way beyond what we even think of as gods. There were no hands on the steering wheels because there were no hands or steering wheels. 'They are workers for the Architect of Cosmic Destiny. They are not describable in terms of angels. You might better refer to them as pure energy. Masters of Cosmic Destiny, architects and engineers of infinite capability, brought the domes to Earth in line with past proposals and future events.

'These Masters of Destiny described the portals of consciousness to Man and introduced the Grail Quest to humans as a representation of the divine source. Each dome has a portal. The Masters of Destiny, or Cosmic Chaplains, look out from the portals to see how Man fares in his conscious aspirations towards the Quest. The Masters watch to see which of humankind heed the directions and set forth on the Quest. Berenice, by the way, had a glimpse of one aspect of a Cosmic Chaplain.'

It turns out there were hundreds of domes, close to two thousand, arrayed all over the planet in a more or less symmetrical pattern. It was a bit like pasting a bit of the galaxy on the Earth, spreading out a couple thousand stars around the skin of the planet. Their impression remains today, and from our relatively thick-skinned sensibilities, it's as if they are still here. Ever hear of sacred sites, power points, holy places, energy vortexes? You're talking about a dome, or a dome cap, which is a subsidiary, smaller dome arrayed like flower petals around the center like the blooms in a sunflower head. Wherever you find a holy site today, long ago a dome had something to do with it. You're just picking up on the energy residue of their original awesome presence.

The entire planet was sacralized forever in the blink of an eye when the domes arrived and settled on the soft clay of a virginal planet. Lollover Hill, where I indolently lie today, was once soft clay newly domed. The Earth was highly suggestible in those days, open to imprints from the cosmos. Not only did the domes settle on the mountains; in most cases, they summoned the mountains up from out of the Earth, commanding the earth element to bask in the celestial sunshine as mounds and peaks. The mountains arose with such vigor and excitement that for a time they were volcanoes, then settled down into a long middle age as stone-sided mountains. People still remember them, if vaguely, as the homes of the gods.

From Blaise's point of view, that residue of energy and memory is a mere *soupcon* of the original majesty. Imagine you're in a dark closet, so dark you can't see a thing. Somebody turns on a 500 watt light bulb then turns it off. You're going to continue seeing that bulb for some time even when, technically, it's turned off. In fact, you're not going to forget that light bulb for a long time. Well, that's the theory. It turns out as a species we mostly did forget about the dome lights and only remember that there are some odd places around the planet where if you go there it sort of feels like maybe a bright light is present and you feel just a tad exalted being there.

But what's a dome? The answer to this kept me astonished and delighted for weeks. Each dome is a star on the Earth. Take the brightest eighteen hundred stars in the galaxy, or the ones most relevant to human life and its evolution on this kind of planet. Assign each star to a dome and then place the domes around the planet in some kind of esoteric pattern that is not, strictly speaking, like the star map of the heavens overhead, but still corresponds in some arcane way to what the stars are truly about. In other words, here is a mystery wrapped in a puzzle inside an arcanum. 'Experientially, each dome represents the life of a star as experienced on Earth,' Blaise explained. And it gets even better.

The domes are all connected by means of straight lines of light. We know these as ley lines. The individual domes emit curving, spirallic lines of light; these curving lines are also known as ley lines. At the ends of these lines are the smaller dome caps, often almost fifty of them per dome. So you have major stars (domes) and starlets (dome caps), which is to say, stars of lesser magnitude forming a kind of informal constellation around the bright one.

Multiply this pattern by about eighteen hundred times and distribute it around the Earth and you have an aspect of what Blaise calls the galaxy on Earth. It is Heaven incarnated as a planet, a terrestrial star map laid out upon the landscape. You have domes and dome caps everywhere in a vast energy matrix to support higher human consciousness and evolution, brought here as a gesture of Love from Above, and as a challenge to us to figure out the pattern.

You could connect all the dots and redraw the constellations right on Earth. In fact, if you don't it's very hard to understand the star grid at all. There might even be an important star in your backyard, especially if you live in a star-freckled place like Glastonbury. You could go on a star hunt to find these starfalls on the local landscape, collecting domes like Easter eggs in your Grail basket. You might even get a glimpse of the Easter rabbit. All the domes are linked — energetically 'wired' — to a central place, a very big original dome somewhere on the planet. This is the dome that spawned all the other domes. Blaise said they'd tell us about it later; in fact, they'd show us in person one day.

The really irresistible question is why and so what? What good does it do us if the galaxy is imprinted on Earth and everywhere we go we're walking among the stars? Most of us never even look up at the stars, and very few of us other than astronomers even think about them anymore. Mention 'stars' in America and people think of Hollywood. Or *Star Wars*. Or *Star Trek*. Or *Stargate*. But actually experiencing, say, Aldebaran in Taurus? Not likely.

Did you ever hear the expression, 'As above, so below?' This one gets some currency these days. It's an old Hermetic axiom to remind us that as humans we're built the way the cosmos is. That assures us we can get some orientation in the universe, that we can feel at home in the galaxy after the Fall — you remember, from before we needed the Grail. But it's missing a phrase.

That tidy phrase should say: 'As above, so below, and in the *middle* too.' It's the middle that provides the answer to the why and so what. The Earth too is built the way we and the cosmos are. The Earth is the middle part of the Hermetic equation. This assures us we can get orientation on a planet made of matter, and, believe it or not, feel at home here. Make yourself at home, humans, because we brought you the whole cosmos in miniature, Blaise and their buddies said to us long ago. The Earth is a compressed computer chip with mega-gigabytes of cosmic memory all for you. Start remembering: it's all here.

The Earth, human, and cosmos — same structure, same contents, same purpose. Same everything, really, just different shapes. Figure out one, you get the other two for free because it's the same pattern. They gave us the galaxy on Earth to give us a leg up on figuring out the pattern. In case it's not obvious,

I'll just mention that discerning the pattern is a big part of the quest. See the pattern and the Grail suddenly makes a lot of sense. Hang out with the Grail for awhile and you'll start getting wind of the pattern.

So not to worry: your galactic home is here, intact, just as you left it, precisely as you remember it — if you were to remember it — twinkling in and around matter. The middle part of Earth, our home away from home, is this immense energy matrix of stars and constellations — and a *great* deal more as I would learn over the years with Blaise — what for convenience we might call the Earth grid. It's where the Grail Quest takes place. It's where the Blaise training happens. It's the biggest mystery show in town.

This energy matrix is relevant to us because it's a mirror image of who we are as cosmic beings now inhabiting human bodies walking around in sneakers and lying insouciantly — lollygaging — on grassy green hills on a summer afternoon. The whole planet is one vast human body filled with stars. It's a big round version of ourselves, and we are upright, somewhat rectangular cheeky versions of the galaxy. To be a human is to put on a *yarmulke* scintillating with nearly two thousand pinpricks of light on the inside. Actually make that about eighty four thousand points of light, when you add all the dome caps.

Forget the *yarmulke*: those stars are *inside* our skull, on the inside of the cranium, projected downwards into us like a reverse planetarium. A cranium made of eighty-four thousand stars so tightly packed together it's a blur of cosmic light, so thick it's become bone, and each star has something to say to you, has its own little message, its own story, its own god.

Take Orion. This happened a few years after the day on Lollover Hill. I was at Mount Palomar in Southern California. I understood that the dome over this mountain corresponded to the middle star — *Alnilam*, or as it was earlier known, *Al Nitham*, 'String of Pearls' — in Orion's belt in that constellation. The name Orion supposedly derives from *Uru-anna* and means 'Light of Heaven,' and on that particular day, I needed some light from upstairs.

One of the myths about Orion was that as a giant he was besotted with Atlas' seven daughters. Atlas was a giant and the Pleiades (the Seven Sisters) were his daughters. Thinking them nymphets for the grabbing, Orion chased them with amorous intent. They were turned into stars to prevent their ravishment by priapic Orion, and even today, star-watchers and mythographers say Orion seems still to be hunting the Pleiades girls. Today in metaphysical circles Orion has an ambivalent reputation; some say he — the stars comprising the constellation — is aligned with the dark forces in the galaxy, others say he's with the good guys. I once asked Blaise which it was: is Orion a good guy or a bad guy in the cosmic scheme? 'Make up your own mind. We'll introduce you to him one day,' they said.

They made good on that promise when I found myself on this mountain and realized its affiliation. Blaise was doing something to the dome with some colleagues of theirs they called the Ray Masters (which I'll tell you about later), and as I sat meditating in a secluded spot on the mountain, I followed the dome back to the star. I don't mean I launched myself into outer space and had a quick reconnaissance at Orion, many hundreds of light years away. Yet experientially it was something like that. The paradox of the Earth grid is you don't have to go very far to really go far. The whole place is a vast wormhole matrix.

Bear in mind that the stars of Orion, even though they seem next door neighbors in a familiar connect-the-dots image, are in fact vast distances apart. Betelgeuse, the giant hunter's right shoulder, is 590 light years from here, but Alnilam is 1,630, and it's 163 light years just from *Al Mintaka*, one of the two other 'nearby' stars in the belt, the Three Kings, as the group is called. From a celestial viewpoint, Orion, only one of many dozens – ultimately, probably of thousands – of constellations in this galaxy, itself occupies an almost unimaginable amount of cosmic space. Light takes almost 170 years just to get from one star to the next in the belt alone. That's a long way to live from your nearest neighbor, yet all these stars are merely points in a gigantic stellar body we call Orion, and that of course is only one of many dozens of constellations.

One advantage to living on an Earth upon which the galaxy has been imprinted is that the distances you have to travel to get anywhere are remarkably reduced. I didn't have to travel 1,630 light years to get to Alnilam. I had only to place my attention on the blazing star above my belly button and let it – Blaise – transport me through the dome overhead to the energy of that star.

Let me pass on a tip: the blazing star above your navel is the key to the whole grid. It's too complicated to explain at the moment, but the whole Earth grid (and I suspect the stellar grid as well) is extruded like some intricate cobweb from this tiny pinprick of Blaise light. In a sense, being here on Mount Palomar under the Alnilam dome and being at Alnilam in

Orion isn't much different from a human point of view. Here's why, and this is the point of the story.

I had some Pleiadian karma that needed fixing. I won't go into this too much – it's family history that belongs in another book – but a lot of the events on Earth have to do with earlier events that happened in the Pleiades. As Blaise would explain over the years, the planetary grid is the collective work of a great number of what we would call extraterrestrials or spiritual beings.

Beings from the Pleiades were major players in this, and there were good Pleiadians and bad Pleiadians. Some of the struggles currently underway on Earth, both collectively and individually, can be traced back to situations existent a long time ago in the Pleiades and in their relations with other star systems and to all the factors that led to the design and creation and inhabitation of the Earth. Who knows? Maybe Orion was a good cosmic cop and the Pleiades were the bad girls. It wasn't ravishment but the lockup that was on the Hunter's mind.

Anyway, I had some karma from that time and it was getting to be a nuisance. Call it an impediment. I had traced my ancestry back to the Pleiades, although Blaise said that was only a recent residence, and other star systems could be named. It doesn't matter here. On this particular day at Mount Palomar I happened to be with someone who I soon learned was very much involved in this Pleiadian karma. I was beginning to dislike this person a lot, but didn't know why.

As I followed the dome back to the star in Orion, I sensed the great Hunter's presence, and I knew at once he was a good guy. Obviously my mind had to reduce and simplify –

domesticate, cognitively – something almost inconceivable for a human to some kind of proportion and familiarity, so let me say, with this caveat in mind, that it seemed that a figure touched my neck and released a black pyramid that had been blocking it and creating the impediment.

The pyramid disappeared and my throat felt liberated, as if I could speak forever and continually say new things. I could denounce people. I could praise them. I could speak any damn thing I wanted to. I understood that this colleague with me at Mount Palomar had been the one responsible for placing the black pyramid in my throat. It was a black magic thing from Egypt a long time ago, and I'll leave it at that.

Aside from the fact that I felt wonderfully freed and unfettered, I learned something keen about mythic memory. Here's the key fact: in astrology's human body map, the Pleiades are found in the throat. They are part of the constellation Taurus, the bull, and in that constellation they are found in the bull's neck.

So, Orion was not a skirt-chaser, not a testosteronically crazed male hunter god out to ravish the Seven Sisters, but a *protector* of the Pleiades and a colleague in good standing of Blaise. His job is in part to prevent the Pleiades from getting ravished by other celestial influences of an inimical persuasion, and to lend a helping hand to limping Pleiadian Grail Knights when requested. As usual, the myths got it backward; or maybe that's the reason myths last so long: they hide secrets out in the open but you have to read them with a mirror, in reverse.

Before I left Mount Palomar that day, I had a moment's vision of the entire constellation of Orion arrayed across the planet. If you were to map this out in a linear, topographical way, and find where all the Orion domes are, it might not look quite like the constellation overhead. Even so, I had a second's glimpse of the major stars in this celestial being.

Imagine a transparent planet with nothing in it or on its surface such as mountains and lakes: just a glass ball with a dozen or so points of twinkling light inside it. A three dimensional model of the stars of Orion takes up the whole of the ball's interior space giving you a figure of light inside a rolling see-through beachball – a virtual Orion upon the Earth. Do you see how you have to connect the dots to get the full picture?

There is still another angle to these domes, says Blaise, and this is really the payoff. Of course at the time it was just another enigma. 'The domes were brought to Earth to create a paradise for humankind. Each dome carried a light form, or seed crystal, of what was to be, both locally and globally, through the grid. Of these paradise seed crystals, some have been activated, but otherwise humanity has either not been aware of this divine potential or has not bothered to make use of them to create the intended Earth paradise.'

Meanwhile, a bit short of paradise and not having a clue what Blaise meant about seed crystals inside the domes, I was called back to the Mump. I was sitting on the north slope of the hill beside an old stump. Behind me, though buried, were the portals to a stone chamber inside the hill. In other words, I believed I was seeing the physical entrance, now buried, to an artificial cave inside the Mump.

This wasn't surprising; the same has been said of Glaston-bury Tor, that it was a deliberately constructed hill encasing an interior chamber of considerable size and basically other-worldly intent. As Blaise is fond of saying, things are not what they seem. It's getting to the point these days where often I can't even tell what they seem.

Not only was I aware of the gateway to the buried chamber, but huge translucent angels twice the size of the Mump were now encircling the hill. Their backs were facing in towards me. Elohim, whispered Blaise with a chuckle. (The Elohim, among others in the angelic hierarchy, work for Blaise.) My body comfortably ensconced on the hillside, I pass through the wooden door that seals the physical cave and am inside the stone chamber of the Mump. Except this is itself the portal to another dimension, a far larger chamber as it turns out. I pass through this dimensional overlap and enter a huge open space, resembling an amphitheater. Its walls seem to be six-sided cells, like a network of honeycombs.

Now the Elohim face into the amphitheater, standing at its far edges. They are very large, majestic angels; they seem like the sort that get things done, real executives, the kind you want in an efficient corporation. They pick me up and pass me around the circle, Elohim to Elohim, as if I were a precious object — I don't know about that for sure, but I certainly didn't want to be dropped: these guys are tall! — then put me down at last in a concavity that looks like a round table full of stars occupying the center of the amphitheater.

I drift into this starry table and float out amidst the myriad stars of the galaxy. In fact, I am a star myself, a little pinprick of light, a blazing star in the galaxy. This didn't surprise me too much: hasn't Blaise been telling us for months that each of us is a star? It may not have surprised me, but it sure astonished me.

Two Elohim, one male, one female, both wearing golden crowns, accompany me, one on either side of me, although I don't get how a star can have sides. An uncountable number of stars scintillate through the Elohim's diaphanous angelic forms as we proceed. I feel like I'm continuously falling forward, tumbling, rotating, yet also moving through space at a terrific clip. Eventually we reach a planet, except I can't shake the sensation that somehow I am the planet.

Leaving this enigma unsolved, I find myself more or less on solid ground, a grassy sward at the edge of a conifer forest. The Elohim carry me in a hammock across the field, through the forest, and into a gigantic building. I count seven stories, but it is much bigger than that. It seems to extend across the landscape for miles. Ribbons of light – gold, violet, blue – ripple like electric ley lines along the building's exterior, like a kind of sparkling aura.

The Elohim carry me – I'm still but a star – upstairs into a room that resembles a modern surgical theater. They put me into a six-sided emerald that stands on a dazzlingly white table. I am a minute speck of light inside a womb of emerald. Yes, it's the same emerald that's involved with the Grail. On a shelf near the table an infant is encased in a golden crystal – a different evolutionary stream perhaps, for I'm getting the sense that the Elohim are doing some basic genetic engineering here. That infant in the golden crystal is destined for some other place, probably not Earth, not now.

As for myself, things are happening. I am now a human fetus or a tiny fully-formed infant, still inside the emerald, though. The Elohim are finished here, and take me in a wicker basket to an impossibly tall mountain range overlooking a vast plain upon which sparkles a magnificent dome. That's Shambhala, Blaise whispers. We float down thousands of feet into the valley and enter the dome.

Once there, the Elohim immerse me — my body is still the emerald — in a luscious fountain of light. I feel wet with light, flushed with consciousness. I realize the Elohim are building my spiritual bodies prior to my physical incarnation. They put me inside first a silver then a golden tube of light, then into a kind of washing machine that tumbles me around in more light, then into a series of fourteen organ pipes, each a different color — the primary rainbow colors and variations on each. ('Ray Masters,' Blaise whispers. 'We'll tell you about them later.') Each pipe irradiates me, one after another. I feel like a walking rainbow — or I would if I had legs, but I'm still an emerald with six sides and no appendages.

I take stock of my situation and realize I am in four places at once. I am outside on the Mump, my rear end getting chilled from the damp ground; I am inside the Mump in the physical stone chamber; I am with the Elohim on their hospital table; and I am in Shambhala getting the bath of a lifetime. After thinking about this for a while and getting nowhere with the puzzle — for one thing: which is my primary place of being present? — I figured it didn't matter. I had bigger things to fret about, like the Sword of Damocles hanging worrisomely over me and the Mump. God knows who's holding the blade.

This keen sword is so bright it is blinding, and it is pointing directly at me as I lie on the Elohim's table. In fact, it points right at my chest. Suddenly an invisible hand thrusts the sword through the top of the Mump and my body. It cleaves my chest as easily as cutting soft clay. This reveals the emerald within my chest. Then the sword cleaves that and reveals a golden infant with a heart of rosy red petals. Nobody seems to be hurt for all the sword work.

Somehow getting cleaved by the sword sparks the golden child to life and he seems none the worse for having been born by a variation on the Caesarian section. The child emerges radiant from the lifeless carcass of the Grail Knight. Then like a pristine flower, it perches as an anther on a long style high above the petals of the Mump as if awaiting pollination by celestial bees. Despite all this cleaving, I, as the Grail Knight in sneakers whose legs are now asleep from having been crossed for so long as I sit on the Mump, am in one piece, disproving, I might add, the biological truism that men cannot give birth.

Later in the day Blaise filled me in on some further aspects of the Mump. 'It is a library, among other things. Do you remember the six-sided cells, the honeycomb of the dome at the Mump? A lot of the genetic engineering that took place in Lemuria and later in the second Atlantean period took place in the cells of the Mump. You saw a little piece of this, an aspect of your celestial birth and human phylogenetic birth, how the star and emerald were put into a living human being.'

So the dome over the Mump is a big memory producing theater. If I could clock in memories like this at all the planet's domes, that would be one spectacular reminiscence of my wild and crazy (and previously forgotten) cosmic life. Just before Blaise left for the evening, I asked them what star the Mump dome corresponds to.

'Aludra, close to the tail.' Aludra is from *Al Adhra* and means 'one of the Virgins.' It's the star in Canis Major, or the Greater Dog, at approximately the base of its spine. The well-known

Sirius, our galaxy's brightest star, is at the dog's neck or heart. As a star, Aludra is a luminous supergiant about 2,700 light years away and is as luminous as fifty-five thousand of our suns.

So this is where one of the stars from the constellation of the Dog touches down on Earth, appropriately, given the nature of my experience with the Elohim and their genetic engineering, at the procreative center of the canine's body. Those who talk about cosmic history and the prior involvement of star systems with Earth always bring up Sirius (and the Sirians) as major players. This discovery gives the thesis of Sirian involvement in Earth a bit of grounding.

Among other things, this information clarified a remark Russell had made earlier. It had made no sense at the time. He was recounting his experience of the Mump, when he and Berenice were physically there and I was there in imagination. He had said: 'There was a line of light from the Mump straight *up* to Sirius in Canis Major.' To the heart of the dog, as it were. I had no idea at the time how much this dog would feature in the next phase of the Grail Quest.

My attention back on Lollover Hill, I was wondering about that line of people queuing up before the dome. I've experienced two domes and their stars at a time on the planet when the domes are only residually here. What was it like when they were *really* here? Blaise drops the phrase 'wise domes' into my thoughts. Of course: people came to the domes for wisdom. After all, the gods were resident and the domes were their offices.

The difference between when the domes were here and now when they are residually present is 'e.' From wise domes to wisdom, from living presence to received tradition. The difference of course is the Elohim: the 'e' in wise domes and the 'e' that's missing in wisdom. In the transition from the first to the second, from that surrendering of a mere 'e,' is yet another Fall we've endured.

But then there's not much profit in lingering in that state of mind, dwelling on Falls and losses. The point of the revelation of the Earth grid is to realize it's all reversible. What we've forgotten can be remembered. What we've lost can be regained. If we once fell, we can now climb again. Blaise is fond of saying to us, 'We remember you as you were before the Fall.' The exciting thing is we can remember Blaise as they were before our Fall too. Walking among the stars on the Earth is a good way to start that project moving, and the way to really stay awake is keep reminding yourself that everything you see, all the wonders of Heaven are all inside you — are you. Even the angelic horsemen.

The perception of the horseman gradually dawned on me. The dimmer switch had to come on slowly I suppose so as not to blow out the windows with the light. I was thinking about dome caps, of a recent visit I had made to a couple dozen dome caps all associated with the same dome, which was a star in the constellation Aquarius, located north of here, up in Lincolnshire. Nearly each dome cap had a church occupying the site, and each site yielded an initial visual impression suggestive of its energy nature.

At one, I saw a large white astral dove stationary above the church surrounded by a corkscrew of white energy; at another, concentric gold rings in layers rising from the churchyard; at still others: a Madonna cupping her hands over the church, blowing it a kiss; an astral figure holding an open golden book upside down, so we could read it; half a dozen blue vertical pipes fifty feet tall with a human face at the end of each; a vortex uncoiling, wider at the bottom than top, with the face of a god on the bottom; another Madonna, welcoming, celebratory, opening the folds of her garments to reveal an eye or a pearl; the head of a saint, or perhaps Jesus, overlooking the church, sending down rays.

These were impressions gleaned from lived-in dome caps. They come with their own pure cosmic energy and intention; we live under them long enough and imprint our own desires and pictures on them. The result is a compromise, or per-haps a clear image somewhat distorted by our filters, in this case, religious ones. So what does the dome cap's original energy look like? I keep tapping the warm air on Lollover with my sneaker, waiting for an answer. How the hell should I know, I think. But I should know. My brain is hard-wired with this information. Everybody's is. All you have to do is remember.

So I tried to erase my images from the dome caps and sense the dome cap energy with less mediation of conventional images. I saw the Chashmalim again. They line the dome cap, a multitude of flaming winged humans, burning, but not burning up, made of fire, packed close together, thousands of them, like a lovely field of wheat, each stalk a flame, tall grass swaying in the mild breeze, leaves of grass aflame.

Chashmalim, one of the ten angelic families: the heavenly River Dinur, whose name means 'fiery river,' was said to have been made out of the flaming sweat of the Chasmalim. Hashmal, their leader, surrounds the throne of God as the fire-

speaking angel, and Ezekiel as part of his stupendous vision of
the heavenly hierarchy, said their sound was like the roaring
of the sea, like the noise of a huge army, like the voice of God
Himself, and that even when they stopped flying and folded
up their wings, there was still a sound emanating from the
tops of their heads.

I don't hear anything coming out of the Chasmalim, but
there are thousands of them parceled out among the 48 dome
caps around Lollover. They are attendants, accompanists,
outriders — for what? Ah, now I see it. Above me and seemingly filling all the sky is a burgundy-lilac horse and rider,
stars for eyes, pulling a magnificent golden chariot also made
of stars. The rider is also standing erect in the front of the
chariot holding the reins. It's not just one horse, but forty-eight
horses, all the same color, all with riders like him, only
smaller, like young princes, smaller stars, accompanying their
mighty king, a star god.

Now the sky in all directions is filled, packed with this
majestic tableaux of star god, chariot, outriders, and his glory.
The Chasmalim are the star god's strands of fiery glory, the
fire matrix that holds the entire apparition together: the god of
the star, his forty-eight outriders, the horses, the golden
chariot, the magnificent flame beings the glue that binds it
together.

The Chasmalim weave the energy field of the star and its
forty-eight associate stars into a fishnet web of fire beings,
dome and dome caps, major star and affiliate stars, star god
and retinue, riding towards me forever, right into Lollover
Hill, yet never coming any closer than where they are right
now, which admittedly is galloping right into my face, my ears

now as if pressed flat against the hill in defensive reaction to this vision.

I know all this, ultimately, is an attempt by my human mind to make sense of an incredible sight, but it has some classical support. The *Mahabharata*, India's epic of the gods and humans in a primordial moment in Earth's history, said that the gods and heavenly sages would appear before the ascetic *rishis* in their ethereal forms, 'standing in chariots and on mountain peaks.'

Some of the celestial big shots like Indra and Kuvera, who were guardians of the four quarters of the universe, became visible in their celestial chariots above human congregations. During the great battle recounted in the *Mahabharata*, Arjuna, the spiritual warrior, saw thousands of 'wondrous chariots carrying shining beings of great beauty' amassed in the sky over the battlefield. Krishna, Arjuna's psychopomp in the midst of this celestial visitation, explains that he has just seen the various gods in their respective spheres, has seen their shining abodes from the Earth as stars in the firmament, but now they're here, above him, as gods in chariots. The *Mahabharata* got it all, except for the domes.

I'm pretty much flattened out on Lollover, the spunk has gone out of my sneakers. I might go so far as to admit my tongue is almost hanging out of my mouth. Think of it, after all: to appreciate the impact of all the stars on the planet you have to multiply this almost indigestible apparition of celestial glory by eighteen hundred times.

There is one glorious stampede of riders, outriders, and burning Chasmalim per dome, each one the manifestation field of one star god and its cosmic particularities, biography, and assignment in consciousness – that is, to comprise some aspect of you and me, to have an influence on our awareness, to hold the space for one fraction of our totality in the mind of God.

Each of these domes, as grand and space-filling as the one over Lollover seems, is also a pinprick of light somewhere inside my cranium. The whole planetarium show is underway in there too. *And* contemplate the fact that domes are only a part of the human in our spiritual totality.

I emphasize *a part*, for domes, showstoppers that they are, are only one of *many* aspects of our true celestial nature – the nature we've completely forgotten we had and which, frankly, is fairly intimidating but occasionally amusing to start remembering – that have been brought to Earth for the purpose, I would guess, of essentially blowing our minds to pieces – in a salutary way of course.

5

I've already told you about the stampede at Lollover. I should mention that a dog is involved, and if you don't befriend this dog, forget the Quest.

I had taken a few days off from the Quest. I figured Blaise, the Lollover gang, the domes, and all the rest of this celestial congeries on Earth could get along on their own for a few days without me. Russell and Berenice didn't have much on their schedules either, so mostly we drank tea in the back garden, stared at the clouds, waved to the cows, and passed the lemon as the afternoons slipped by. Sometimes it seemed Blaise was lounging about around us in their own form of wing-tipped lawn chairs. Occasionally we amused ourselves by trying to figure out who Blaise really was, trying to crack their heavenly inscrutability. We were almost so relaxed we didn't care. That's when the dog barked.

I was lying pretty much supine on the lawn chair, on the verge of being too lazy to reach even for my tea cup. Then I remembered something I had seen from the top of Burrow-bridge Mump — God knows when. I must have forgotten all about it, or maybe it never percolated its way into my Earl Grey-soaked brain. It was the image of a huge black Labrador laid out across the landscape; this dog must have been at least five miles long, and pinpricks of light twinkled in its body like sequins. The Mump was its nose; nearby Oath Hill seemed to be its throat; Aller across the fields was its heart;

Wick was its navel; the All Saints Parish Church on the hill in Langport seemed to be its rear end; and still further out, another chapel was a bright star in its tail — the cynosure, I think they call it.

My sudden memory must have stirred Russell back into sentience for he remarked, ' I think the boys would like you to visit Oath Hill, if you can get yourself up out of that chair.'

I dutifully trudged down the lane, past the Fairy Dell, and along a few farm lanes until I climbed Oath Hill and tried to blend in with the lunching cows. You never know how welcome you are, if at all, in farmer's fields, especially when you're up to no good with Blaise and with rest of the galaxy that happens to be imprinted on fields and hills that landowners think is just earth, stones, foliage, and cow splats and something they own. The cows are busy with their bovine activities, eating, grunting, shuffling, pissing, splatting, lowing. I find a dry spot in the grass and plump myself down, ready for the cosmic mysteries.

I meditate on the Blazing Star just above my belly button for a while to get in the mood and to get ready. When you're with Blaise, anything can happen. What happened was a large German shepherd slowly walked up to me. It stopped a few feet from me, paused, sniffed me, then came closer and offered its paw to me. I shook it. We regarded each other solemnly. I know this dog.

'This is serious,' Blaise whispers to me. Serious? It's not like you guys to be serious, I respond mentally. You guys are always goofing off, looking for the laugh in everything. 'This is correct. We just found the laugh. We meant Sirius.' Sirius? I knew I was missing something here. Maybe I shouldn't have made fun of the cows. 'The Dog-Star, Grail Knight. This is Sirius. Now do you see?'

I remembered the five-mile long dog full of stars. That was a black Labrador, but this one is a greyish German shepherd, and it's a lot smaller. But that makes two dogs. Trying to give me the benefit of the doubt that, despite appearances, I was still quicker on the pick-up than my bovine colleagues, Blaise said tactfully, 'This is an image of the Dog-Star, the way your mind chooses to represent it to you. Before you can enter the temple of the stars, you must befriend the Dog.'

The fog started to blow out of the crevices of my brain and I began to get the picture. Of course: temple of the stars means the Glastonbury zodiac. Lots of people around here take this for granted, even though they can't explain it or account for it, that there is a circular stretch of Somerset landscape about ten miles in diameter whose terrain somehow resembles the traditional shapes of the twelve constellations of the zodiac plus the dog, also known as Canis Major. Some metaphysical wags called it the Region of the Summer Stars.

Books have been written and maps have been published suggesting the landscape affiliations for stars and constellations in this terrestrial zodiac, and places like Wick, Aller, Langport, and the Mump have been designated as parts of the Dog. The concept had fascinated me ever since I came to Glastonbury, but I never knew what to do with it or how to get beyond the question of so what? Maybe it had some reality. After all, Russell and Berenice had once told me their house was situated at the belly of the dog, according to this landscape figure. Now here before me was a visionary representation of this same Canis Major, or what local legend has always referred to as the Girt Dog of Langport.

Blaise gave me a few more clues. 'The Dog is the guardian. You couldn't even enter the zodiac without the blessings of the Dog. Without the warmth in the belly of the Dog, the zodiac is inaccessible.'

Later back at Wick I looked up Sirius in a few reference books. It started to make more sense. In Hindu myth, Sirius is the Lord of the Dwelling, the guardian of the thousand-gated House of Varuna. This is all code for saying this constellation is the watchdog on behalf of the galaxy and its billions of stars, a few of which we have imprinted in the Somerset landscape. You could say the Dog keeps the big starwheel grounded, intact, inviolate, free to go about its evolutionary business. But as I would learn, the Dog has another function: it is the zodiacal tour guide for Grail Knights.

It was time to get out the Grail bike. I had some dogs to visit. In those early days of the Quest, I didn't have a car, so I relied on my Dawes ten speed to get around the place. At a pinch, I could borrow Berenice's Citröen, but I didn't mind the pedaling. It was good for me, even entertaining sometimes.

My first stop was the dog's tail, out two miles beyond Langport in the village of Pitney. I sat outside the Church of St. John the Baptist, balanced, geomythically speaking, on the outstretched tail of the dog. It's amusing to note that a few miles further across the fields is a hamlet called Wagg. Somebody, long ago, in that great burst of etymological inspiration that led to place naming, knew about the Girt Dog.

This is where you start, if you're a neophyte Grail Knight new to the Region of the Summer Stars and its guardian dog:

at the cynosure. You take your bearings at Pitney, get your preliminary marching instructions for navigating the Dog temple, get the basic star map. I have a momentary flash of the entire geomythic dog with all its Canis Major stars twinkling, from here to the Mump and even beyond. Long ago, before Grail Knights had bikes, they would presumably hike down the valley from here, stride up Pict's Hill, and walk over to the small hill at Langport, near the business end of the Dog.

Pitney was a picnic compared to the church in Langport. Blaise had hinted there was a particular place inside the church where they would like me to sit, but it took a lot of pew-hopping for me to finally settle on what seemed to be their choice seat. I entertained myself during the several hours of confusion and delusion with observing various bizarre and distracting astral apparitions. Once four twelve-foot angels swooped down the aisle from the front door like Navy jets storming off an aircraft carrier. A woman came to freshen the flowers at the altar; she was probably real. When I remembered, I breathed as Love from Above to my star, figuring this would help. Finally the feature presentation started rolling.

I saw a man in Biblical garb standing before a grey stone basin about twenty feet across; he was accompanied by a dozen other men in long robes. This basin was set inside a small wooden chapel. A blazing ball of light descended into the basin, which absorbed it and passed the energy down into the Earth. I think the light emanated from the central figure. Then it flowed instantly through the entire extent of the Dog's geomythic body as if it were moving through pre-established channels, like a dried out riverbed ever-expectant of that big spring rain that will fill it with its life blood again and restore it to its glory. Even the Dog's nose at Burrowbridge Mump seemed to shine from this infusion.

But there was more. Where the stone basin had stood now I saw a two-petalled lilac heart in its place. A lilac flame surges up from this heart, ascends through the church's ceiling, and up into the sky. I feel wonderfully refreshed from exposure to this lilac flame; the heavy vibrations of the church were starting to weigh on me a bit. The lilac flame burned all that away.

Later I got debriefed by Blaise on this little episode, which, it turned out, was central to the eventual reactivation of the Dog for the Glastonbury zodiac. 'Feel the lilac flame of transmutation awakening the Dog's creative energies. They have been blocked for a long time. We place the dancing lilac flames at this spot and send the Dog our Love from Above. As you are aware now, Joseph of Arimathea came to the landscape temple you know as Avalon. He was aware, and indeed recognized when arriving at the port of Langport, that the guardian of the temple, the Dog, was here. Joseph brought the Christ energy to this area. He initiated the Dog as the zodiac guardian with the Christ light.'

Glastonbury legend holds that Joseph of Arimathea, one of Jesus' main sponsors and defenders, came to Glastonbury after the Crucifixion with the Holy Grail (a chalice bearing drops of the blood of Christ) and founded a church here. He landed on Wearyall Hill, planted his staff which blossomed, and, as a master geomancer with an imprimatur from Blaise and the Christ, evidently got down to business and started tidying up the Avalon temple for its future epiphany. 'Joseph brought the Christ here in his thought body,' adds Blaise.

'He brought a chalice from the Last Supper and other vibrations, points in his personal awareness which related to his personal practice.' In a sense, I'm retracing his steps through the Region of the Summer Stars while at the same time trying to acquaint myself with this remarkable story in the landscape.

My next stop is the church of St. Andrew at Aller, about a mile straight overland from Wick, provided you thread your way expertly between the rhynes, dips, gulleys, and other foot-focussed treacheries of the fields. I perch under the lovely lime tree that faces the moors and looks back towards Wick. I feel myself into the Dog, its landscape form, its starry body. I begin to feel like a dog myself, sitting calmly on my haunches, observing activities in the zodiac. The Dog's heart is happy, still, glad, loving, wise, contented, compassionate, and his service to the zodiac is unhesitating, unrelenting, faithful. He knows the zodiac can be a nuthouse at times, but it's okay; he can handle that.

I have one more Dog stop today. It's a place called East Lyng, situated a few miles past Burrowbridge Mump. When I roll into East Lyng, I head for St. Bartholomew's Parish Church. You can pretty reliably count on the old churches and chapels in the British Isles to accurately mark the geomantic sites; they serve as an architectural mnemonic for the ancient geomantic knowledge that's essential for this kind of work. Sometimes the churches themselves get up my nose, but I'm always grateful to them marking the page for me in the land-scape.

There's nobody in the church so I have my pick of the seats. I park myself close to the altar and after a few minutes of quiet breathing to the star, aspects of East Lyng's earlier days and life as part of the Dog come into focus. I see a stone beehive-cell oratory, safely elevated above the soggy marshland. Several men step out of a coracle and enter the chamber, which seems about fifty feet wide. I imagine myself in the chamber with them. I want to know what they're doing.

This seems to be a place for final preparations for entering the zodiac. This is where the Dog reviews your knowledge and experience so far and counsels you on the next step. I like to think of this place as the Dog's Bone. Here the Grail Knight gnaws on the bone and sucks out the marrow of star knowledge. Here you get the big picture; you see the Dog in its entirety as guardian and psychopomp. I have the impression that the Knights spent the night here in the oratory, praying, meditating, shivering, whatever – getting ready for their immersion in the confusing fantastic spectacle of the Summer Stars.

There is a fascinating statement from a ninth century Irish text called the *Glossary* by Cormac. He says 'The *fili* [seer] must chew the flesh of a dog in order that his gods should show him the things which he desired they should reveal.' Who knows if they were talking about real dogs? For me, Cormac is referring to the landscape Dog. It's not so much a matter of me eating the Dog, as assimilating it, becoming one with it – becoming the Dog itself.

After all, if the ancient Hermetic axiom of *As above, so below* is true, then what is up there is down here, the Dog-Star in the galaxy, and the Dog-Star in the Grail Knight. And of course, as you learn early on in the Grail Quest, the full statement is *As above, so below, and in the middle too*, which means the Earth has a Dog-Star too. 'Many, in fact,' says Blaise. 'Several hundred. One for each zodiac. The Earth has hundreds of zodiacs like this one.'

For a few moments, doglike, I feel myself occupying a five-mile stretch of landscape, my body full of bright stars, criss-crossing lines of light, spiraling light lines, thimbles of color and pulsating knobs of energy, churches, chapels, vanished stone circles, former stone rows, a few dolmens, menhirs, and other megalithic features. I sense gnomes scurrying around my body; fairies tending the plant life; undines in the streams and ponds; sylphs zipping through the air like barn swallows; salamanders sparking just above the ground like fireflies; angels standing ineffable and majestic atop the bright hills; even some of the dutiful Dead making themselves useful, tidying up the energy fields.

Amidst all this, men, women, children, dogs, cats, cows, rabbits and birds going about their lives, oblivious to the slice of heaven all around them. But who can criticize them? A few weeks ago I had no idea any of this existed either.

When I stepped out of the church, I was surprised to find it was already dusk. I'd lost track of a few hours, and now I'd have to ride home in the dark. Naturally my bike had no lights and I was wearing dark clothes and there were no street lights on my home route. Not to worry: Blaise had in mind another episode of what I fondly call Blaise On My Head.

With a clash of cymbals, the six Blaises appear on my head, smartly outfitted with goggles, crash helmets, lilac scarves, leather bomber jackets, and golden gloves. As I alternately barreled and wobbled down the dark lane, the Blaises shouted with glee, their scarves streaming out behind them like wind socks. They swoop off like a flock of swallows then wobble down the air under parachutes to land on my head whose interior now resembles a well-equipped livingroom. A sign announces, 'The Blaises spend a quiet evening at home in the Grail Castle.'

One Blaise watches television; one listens to music with earphones and nods his head continuously; one types on a keyboard, using only two fingers, and surrounded by stacks of books; another slurps a cup of miso soup; another meditates and pokes a dull sword into a teacup; the sixth Blaise rides an exercise bike, working up a sweat. Then as fast as a finger-snap, the scene changes. Now the inside of my head is an orchestra pit.

Five of the Blaises have formed a brass quintet, and the sixth conducts them. I've been chanting *O Michael uplift us*, a little ditty I picked up somewhere and apparently in reference to the Archangel Michael. My pedaling has fallen into synchrony with my intonations. Evidently Blaise thinks a little musical accompaniment will perk things up.

So, from left to right upstairs, there is Blaise on the trumpet, tuba, trombone, French horn, and cornet, playing something Mozartian that perfectly meshes with the pedaling, chanting, grunting, and puffing coming out of me. Everything seems under control, so I climb upstairs and hang out in the pit until we reach home. God knows who's pedaling now.

Russell and I have a good laugh over the Blaise antics. Then I wonder if I've been a bit over the top, fantasizing Blaise in acts beneath their angelic dignity. 'Not so, Grail Knight,' they tell me later. 'We inspire angel jokes. They're all right. They keep you happy. If a man or an angel cannot laugh at himself, he is of no use.' However, when we were done with the laughs, we got down to business which in this case was a trip to Glastonbury Tor.

It was fairly late in the evening and the Citröen was already tucked away in the garage, and none of us felt like driving into Glastonbury, so Blaise offered a lift. As they should – they're the ones who wanted us to be on the Tor tonight. So without lacing up my sneakers, pulling on a sweater, or even rousing myself from the comfortable lounge chair I was ensconced in for the night, Blaise whisked the three of us to the top of Glastonbury Tor.

We weren't out of body, it was more like traveling on a star. You focus on the star, which is Blaise, and they transport you in your mental or visionary body, and there you are, else-where, with them, in some twilight intermediary between the spiritual and physical worlds. In this case, we were looking out upon a very different Glastonbury and a landscape filled with stars and angels.

Russell saw six angels linked together, then a dozen behind them, and an ocean of light behind them. They made a ring around St. Michael's tower and enfolded us with their multiple wings, he said. Blaise directed my attention to the top of the stone tower. There stood a tall angel with outstretched hands, singing or orating, or whatever angels do when they 'say' things in their realm. Berenice reported she saw a pale lemon light encircling the Tor, a blue diamond above the tower, and a blue dove above that. Outflanking all that was a single majestically tall angel.

'The Archangel Michael is pleased to see you all tonight,' Blaise said, letting us know we had all been glimpsing bits of the presence of this great archangel. 'Michael would like to show you something. Focus your attention just above the tower.'

Russell and I scratched our heads and wondered what the thing was Blaise wanted us to see, but Berenice caught it. The archangel, she said, was raising his hands over his head and his fingers were channeling the celestial light like lightning rods into the hill from which it ran like spring rivulets into the landscape. Somehow seeing this opened a door for us and new, remarkable sights appeared all around us down in the flatland about the Tor.

The place was lit up like a major airport runway at night, but the lights were the living figures of the zodiac. The bull, the lion, crab, goat, the centaur – the familiar constellations of the zodiac and their stars were the source of light. The Gemini twins looked like two infants overlighted by a pale sun. The whole zodiacal circle was ablaze around us with living, animate, three dimensional figures whose bodies were made of hundreds of stars.

It was as if Katherine Maltwood's two-dimensional map of the Glastonbury zodiac had suddenly been inflated, the way a preshaped balloon assumes its intended form after you blow air into it, and what had been but a strange concept was now an almost palpable reality. The zodiacal creatures were so seemingly real, so tangible, so illuminated, you felt you could enter their otherworldly domain as you would an amusement park or a mystery temple.

Then I saw something unusual on Wearyall Hill. It looked like a complex crystalline form about one-fifth the size of the hill. It had a cubic base and contained dozens of icicle-shaped shafts or pillars. Then I saw the same thing at Pointer's Ball, less than a mile from the Tor, and another on a hill called Dundon Beacon, several miles from Glastonbury in a different direction, near Lollover. I peeked inside the giant crystalline shape at Wearyall; it was like a beehive. 'These devices were placed here long ago from Lemuria to store records,' Blaise explained. 'You might think of them as libraries.'

That reminded me. I had been seeing a lot of crystalline shapes in the landscape. I mean crystals the size of shopping centers, as big as the hills, and one of those hills was Dundon Beacon. It was on one of those deliciously lazy afternoons I spent on Lollover Hill that I first saw the big crystal over and in Dundon Beacon.

On the physical level, there was Dundon, a breadloaf-shaped wooded hill, full of brambles and stones and gnomes; but on another level a huge crystalline shape resembling an inverted umbrella occupied the same space. Down through the upright handle, which faced the sky, flowed a rich current of pure light, then this spumed out through the umbrella spokes, which were like glass ribs. It was like frozen water in which you could see the movement of light yet it had also congealed into a describable shape.

I asked Blaise about this a few days later. Our world, our bodies, everything in our physical reality, is making a transition from being based on carbon to silicon. As a result, the crystalline structure of Earth's matrix is starting to become apparent in the subtle or what we think of as visionary aspects of the planet. There's also a consciousness angle.

From Blaise's viewpoint, water and light, or consciousness are synonymous. When the domes came and settled over the landscape, they summoned up the water from deep within the Earth. The water rose up and formed the characteristic underground water domes that dowsers often report.

'It's inevitable: one above, one below. Light in one form above, as the domes, light in another form below, as water,' Blaise said. 'Illumined consciousness is dependent on the state of vibratory resonance in any organism of the water element. The water that exists in these places is what creates the crystalline pattern.' So these crystalline forms are solidified light, both a memory of what originally happened and a potential we can claim as we become aware of the pattern.

I had to leave the sublimities of solidified light and illumined consciousness for another day, for I was expected at South Cadbury Castle the next day for a spot of jousting. That was the part in Malory's *Le Morte d'Arthur* that I always thought was silly, over the top, best skipped over. Here were these bone-headed, macho guys weighed down by thirty pounds of armor, long lances, shields, and obliging horses going at each other on open fields, seeing who could unseat the other first, like billy goats knocking each other unconscious.

I always thought this bit was an embarrassing residue of medieval behavior or fantasy best left behind. That is, until one afternoon, seated comfortably on the edge of the hill at South Cadbury, I suddenly became aware of a knight, lance raised and fewtering, visor lowered, shield raised, coming right at me. I madly rolled over a few times hoping to escape his attack, and even started to tumble down the embankment only breaking my roll by grabbing on to a thick tuft of grass. So what's this all about, I fumed, feeling both ridiculous and ready to get some payback.

I climbed back up the embankment and resumed my seat. No sooner am I seated than the mounted knight is at me again. He's got the whole outfit, like he ordered it from a medievalist's catalog: big mail clad horse, crimson sashes, glinting helmet, pennoned lance. He charges me in a furious pummel, and shoves that six fix long lance straight through my chest. I am a skewered mushroom. Before I can catch my breath, he yanks the lance out, recharges, and skewers me again, and then he does it yet a third time.

Technically I should be dead from all this thoracic perforation, but I'm just mad and perplexed. Where's my shield? What is a shield in this kind of business? Where's the handbook on jousting? I ponder all this on the ninety-minute bike ride back to Wick. If we're going to play medieval games, I'd rather be carted home, supine, the noble groaning wounded Grail Knight conveyed in a hay wain through the admiring villages.

You know, one thing you can count on with angels is their tact. Blaise could have said, or even insinuated, I was a blockhead when I asked him that night what I was supposed to use as a shield. But he didn't; the Blaises were the epitome of gentlemanly reserve and circumspection. Don't hurt the Grail Knight's feelings, even if he's a bit ... because we don't have a lot of other candidates at present to take his place. That's probably how Blaise was thinking.

It turns out my shield is a meditative image I'd been using for weeks. We flippantly call it the Blaise Image, because they gave it to us, and they probably thought it up. Here's what my shield was to be: a six-sided emerald in my chest with a blazing star inside it, a sapphire blue sphere around my body, on the periphery of which burnt orange and red flames, a lilac flame that rises up from the ground through and around me to flame high above me into a single point of brilliant light, and another smaller lilac flame burning from my head up to that same star. So if I could remember to get my shield up, I might escape another perforation the next day when I was to return to the jousting fields.

I should mention that South Cadbury Castle is one of those anomalous, grass-topped old hillforts you find all over the place in England. Who knows what the 'castle' was, but archeologists cautiously propose this might have been King Arthur's fifth century Camalate, complete with the legendary Round Table. Local legend has it that South Cadbury is one of those enigmatic hollow hills England is famous for, and that King Arthur and his knights are in fact sleeping deep within it waiting for their next engagement in human culture and history.

This hill, hollow or not, rises 500 feet above the quilted Somerset farmland and affords an expansive view, including Glastonbury Tor which from here is a nippled misty knob. As I walk along the outer ramparts of this old hillfort, I become aware of a Round Table that is the size of the greensward itself. It's as if the hill were a great circle that had been divided up into a dozen wedges.

A different astrological sign marks each wedge, and at the outer, fat end of each wedge sits a Grail Knight. But the Round Table doesn't stop at the edge of this hill. The wedges actually extend for a great distance straight out across the landscape for at least a mile including other hills and fields in the Round Table. Each of these wedges has its own Round Table as well giving you a vast sports stadium with 144 different slots for gladiatorial prowess, or fecklessness.

So this is the jousting field, but what do I do next? 'Joust your sign,' Blaise whispers from the sidelines. My attention is drawn to the Scorpio wedge. This was November, the month of Scorpio, and that's my rising sign, astrologically speaking, so I thought I'd give the Scorpio knight a shot. Sitting cross-legged on the grass, I put up my shield and pull out my Grail sword. It's not as long as a lance, but it would prove well suited to the work of jousting, which as you might suspect by now, is not quite the way Malory described it.

I nod to the mounted knights. Okay, fellas, give me your best shot, you miserable punks. I seem to have learned how to do this overnight, because when he gallops toward me, all I do is focus my sword at the emerald I see sparkling in his chest. I grab a gold coin from a pot of coins in there, withdraw my sword, and give him a wallop on the butt for good measure as he steams past me.

A second knight, smartly outfitted in silver armor and a scarlet sash comes at me and surrenders his coin and gets a whack on his thigh. The third knight doesn't budge. He sits motionlessly on his horse like a noncombatant. I get up and stomp over to him, slap him around a bit, verbally abuse him — still nothing. I shove my sword into his emerald, collect the coin, and he falls over inert.

I joust like this for some time until the greensward of South Cadbury Castle is littered with the corpses of thrown knights as if they were toppled manikins. Come to think of it, the minute I inserted my sword into them — which is to say, probed them with my mind — they lost all their spunk and died. Maybe the whole point of this is to collect the coins; knocking them off their mounts and giving them complimentary wallops is merely a pleasant bonus.

I examined one of these coins. I shouldn't have been surprised to see that it wasn't a coin at all. That was just a way of indicating compression. Each coin contained a scene, or a series of images more like a movie, of a past time. It was like having a stack of videos to watch each of which was an action film starring me in some secret other life filmed God knows when. I was the villain and the hero, the wimp and the jock, the Cary Grant and the Arnold Schwarzenegger. I was the perennial star of my own horrorscope as Berenice jokingly referred to her astrological birth chart. I was every point on the Round Table, the 144 positions – all of me over time was laid out, skewered perhaps, on the Table.

As I ride home to Wick I have the fleeting impression of standing before a majestic Arthur and Guinevere standing at the center of the Round Table, and presenting them my coins and my interpretations of their contents. I could see other knights, men and women, in different time periods, doing the same.

In fact, for a moment I could see people all over the Glastonbury zodiac, this great turning wheel of stars, sitting in the landscape, having visions, following gnomes, being guided by angels, immersing themselves in the light. 'It's all about transmutation,' Blaise said. That made sense: changing what is stuck, freeing the energy, allowing things to change, move on, grow, mature.

On the ride home, Blaise explained how King Arthur's magus, Merlin, had selected the knights for Camalate based on horoscope considerations. And he used the Glastonbury zodiac, and other zodiacs elsewhere, as a training ground. Merlin sent the knights to specific places in the landscape zodiac so they could get to know their own inner obstacles through the astrological mirror the star point presented them. I had seen a little of that in my Scorpio jousting. Each knight had to work through the oppositions, squares, transits, and other problems in their psyche as indicated by their natal charts, Blaise said. The goal of course was psychological integration, or what the Jungians call individuation.

The next day I was sitting on Wearyall Hill, staring indolently out across the Glastonbury landscape, eyeing the Tor warily half expecting it to morph into a new shape as I watched it. I remember one of my first impressions on coming to Glastonbury and standing on the crest of fish-back Wearyall was that in an odd way the landscape between here and the Tor resembled a sprawling giant. Wearyall and Edmund Hill are this figure's legs, the Abbey is his lower abdomen, Chalice Hill his stomach, the Tor his chest, while the upper torso curved off to the right through Pointer's Ball, Park Wood, and out to Lugshorn.

As I looked over this landscape figure, I saw a half dozen Blaises and the towering Archangel Michael making a feathery, almost frolicky circle on the Tor. Then they lifted off like a flying wreath and settled on Chalice Hill, spun themselves around a few times, and drifted down to the Abbey, and did it again. They made an elegant pirouette at the fish pond then like a gang of angelic frogs hopped over to Park Wood, then back to Pointer's Ball, then to Wearyall Hill. In those days I wasn't sure whether it was reassuring to see angels be so whimsical or worrisome – shouldn't these guys take their responsibilities more seriously?

'What was that all about?' I asked Blaise when the peripatetic angelic hoop seemed to have settled down for a few moments. 'Oh, not a lot. Just having fun. Dancing the energy spots, aligning the centers, loving Albion.' Something about this word, *Albion*, went through me like an electric shock. I *knew* that word, somehow. I knew what it referred to. Albion!

As if the mere mention of that word had been a magic incantation, the landscape before me was transfigured. It no longer resembled a supine giant human; it *was* a vast winged human spread-eagled across Glastonbury. Its wings were filled with hundreds of stars, extending for miles in equal arcs to either side of Glastonbury like an apple sliced in two. I realized the Glastonbury zodiac was twice as big as people thought because it has two halves, two wings.

Points of light glinted brilliantly up the central shank of this figure like chakras, and energy pulsed regularly up this channel and out through the wings which grew ever brighter with each pulse like an auric field for an intensely alive being. Albion: A Light Being in Our Neighborhood, and we're living and walking in it. Albion, said the English mystic poet William Blake, is the 'Human Form Divine,' the 'loveliest Son of Heaven,' the 'Angel of My Presence,' an image of spiritual beauty expressed in human form as a giant who is the antecedent of us all.

For a moment I felt I was this being, that my consciousness was occupying his magnificent landscape body, that I was winged, miles across, encompassing towns, villages, and all of Glastonbury, scintillating the points of light, a current pulsing up through the center of my form and out to the wings, down to my feet, and up again, continuously. Looking left, looking right, all I see is stars, and this pulsing light feeding them, making them ever brighter.

I say 'I felt I was this being,' but there was nothing special about me in this identification. Anyone can identify with Albion; in fact, that's the point. Albion is there for all of us. This outer, seemingly huge Albion is a geomythic mirror of the Albion that each of us is. You work with the outer one so you can see the inner one, to remember you are the inner one, only to realize they are two aspects of the same being; in fact, both are mirror images of a third.

So this is what a zodiac is all about, I marveled. To yield an Albion. Connect all the dots and you get this giant in the landscape, his body full of stars. I understood that Albion is a much larger version of the 'me' that the Round Table at South Cadbury comprised. That one was all the bits of myself over time and through the horoscope, collected and, sooner or later, individuated. This one, the Albion, would embody all the bits over time of everybody who had lived within it in this 35-mile wide double star wheel called the Glastonbury zodiac. Collect and connect all the bits in this figure and you get a kind of collective individuation.

'It's not about just yielding an Albion,' said Blaise. 'Albion needs to be awakened. All of the Earth's Albions need to wake up, and be healed.' That explained Blake's rather dark vision of the giant Albion in *Jerusalem*: 'In a dark & unknown Night/ Outstretch'd his Giant beauty on the ground in pain & tears.' Blake painted an image of a doleful Albion, slumbering and groaning, chained to a desolate rock on the edge of the continent, abandoned, forgotten, apostate, 'sick to death,' his back turned away in despair from the celestial vision.

So this isn't the only Albion, I asked Blaise. 'No, there are others, but they are all one. Each is an aspect of Albion, but they are all one. They become involved in a process of reciprocal maintenance and are energized as the Glastonbury Albion awakens.' So if the Glastonbury Albion is only one of many such landscape figures and they are all aspects of the one Albion, where is he?

A couple of days later I was enjoying a respite in the late fall weather, lying on the chaise longue in the garden at Wick. I was thinking of all the things the Dog had shown me. Sometimes I get clearer visions when I don't try or don't care. Maybe that's the same as detachment. I noticed my star was getting bright, insistent, almost throbbing with light, and enlarging. Inside it I could see the Earth like a bluewhite marble.

As I breathed to it, the image grew larger and it was as if I was seeing the Earth from space, a bluewhite beachball over which a remarkably limber humanlike figure reclined. There's a yoga pose that looks like this. You lie on your stomach, grab your feet from behind, arch your back, and hold. In the arc formed by the legs, hands, and torso lay the globe of the Earth. I busied myself in the yoga comparison until I pulled myself up and realized what I was seeing.

This is the one Albion, Earth's Albion. That freed me up for more clarity. His body was filled with stars — no, not only stars, and myriads of them, but temples, lines of light both straight and curving, domes, pillars, labyrinths, golden rotundas, coiled dragons, silver eggs, white heads from whose eyes shot out fierce rays of light, orchards of apple trees with golden apples, troops of celestial musicians and dancers, rainbow bridges, translucent castles, crystal cities, white lilies, spinning golden wheels, all of which was attended by troops of angels, and dozens of miniature versions of all of this inside identical but smaller Albions all over the planet. All of us, everyday, whether we know it or not, are walking in Albion, inside this celestial being who is the soul of the planet.

I found myself spiraling down a vortex to the center of the Earth. I landed in a large open chamber. On a large marble table lay a human. He was tied down with stout ropes and wrapped in many layers of winding sheets like a corpse. He couldn't move a muscle; he couldn't open his eyes; he couldn't speak. He could only moan in his sleep. I used my sword to cut all the ropes and sheets. There were many layers of binding covering him, but eventually they came off and the figure lay on the table without any restraints. He was a beautiful figure, not male or female, though human, like the perfect idea of a human, the original mold. He was still sleeping, but he had stopped groaning.

My attention returned to the Albion draped over the Earth, his body full of celestial temples, devices, and presences. I realized this Albion was looking upwards, adoringly, at a mirror image of himself. There above him, in the galaxy, as the galaxy, was the same magnificent humanlike figure, his body the spiral shape of the galaxy itself. As above, so below. The Albion above, the Albion below. 'Albion is the Light Bearer brought to Earth,' said Blaise. 'Albion is the essence of the Essence within Gaia,' her secret lover, her spouse in waiting.

Yes, I was sure of it, even though I didn't fully understand it. We are always walking in Albion. Inside the big giant's star body. 'Walking in Albion,' said Blaise, 'means walking consciously, step by step, contacting the essence, making an imprint in the energy matrix of the Earth, producing a tangible effect in the consciousness of Gaia that the initiation of Christ in the Buddha Body may come to a positive practicality and a recurrent possibility. Walking in Albion is the same as the Christed initiation in the Buddha Body. One day not too long from now you will see this in your own experience.'

6

The next requirement for the Quest may sound a bit odd. You will need an egg with two eyes. I never knew you could obsess about eggs, but for a while I came close to driving Russell and Berenice batty with my constant ruminations about eggs. Not breakfast eggs, mind you, but landscape eggs.

It all started with a queer little dried up stream called Magotty-Pagotty. The name was right out of Tolkien, something you'd encounter in the Old Forest a few day's journey out of Hobbiton, but then I suppose Tolkien got a lot of his inspiration from the British landscape and its eccentric place names.

One morning Russell and I were having morning tea, going over the grocery list, when he said Blaise had dropped a nursery rhyme in his head during his shower. 'You take the path from Magotty-Pagotty/Through Copley Wood to Worley Hill/The Cosmic Egg/Magotty-Pagotty, come and play/We bring to you a brand new day!' Blaise was like that: gnomic to an extreme, a lover of clues, subtly dropped, never sufficiently explained, just enough to whet the appetite.

Something about that name, Magotty-Pagotty, sounded familiar to me as well. I'd heard it somewhere. It turns out there's an old stream, so hoary with age it's lost almost all its water, that flows through Copley Wood between Kingweston and Littleton, about an hour's bike ride from Wick. According to the topographical map, the stream is called Magotty-

Pagotty. So I was off. The weather was geomantically appropriate too, grey sky, brisk wind, intermittent showers. It wouldn't have felt like the Quest if it was warm and sunny out. My mission impossible was to find the cosmic egg in Blaise's nursery rhyme.

Once I got there, it took me another hour tramping across stony fields and through the woods to find the stream and then a suitable perch alongside it. In fact, I went there every day for a week, but I won't bother you with all that. Sometimes it takes a while to get *it*, for the percolation from the higher to the thicker self to take place, so don't be dismayed if you have to keep at it for some time before you get it right. I was fortunate I suppose to have the time to screw up a lot before I understood what I was trying to do.

The stream had so little water running in it you could barely hear the characteristic trickling and gurgling you'd expect from a woodland brook. Maybe Magotty-Pagotty gets a little more water action in the spring. To its credit I must say that this nearly moribund stream bed exudes an unmistakable ancientness, an insinuation of primeval joy and an undisturbed stillness. If a stream has an aura, then you could say Magotty-Pagotty's aura is a vibrant, rich stream flowing at the height of its vigor, despite the dried-up shell its physical self has become. I can work with that.

I struggled for a while, trying to figure out what to do. I breathed to the star; I focussed on the Grail chalice in my chest; I daydreamed about what the gnomes and fairies were doing; I strained to hear a gurgle from Magotty-Pagotty now and then. Nothing much happened.

Then somehow I felt warm, fatherly hands on my shoulders. My neck tingled as a radiance illuminated me from behind. I turned around to see who was there. It was me, what you would call a higher, translucent, light body version of myself. No matter; I'll take help from whatever quarter it's offered today. Then the I behind me said, 'Find the divine seed in the Great Stream.'

Now I feel like I have some focus, some direction. I see myself standing amidst a great flowing stream of light, the 'higher self' version of Magotty Pagotty. The water flows through me like a continuous beam of light. I make sure it particularly flows through the Grail chalice in my chest. I do this for about four hours.

I realize that what's flowing through me is not so much water or light as a deep continuum of consciousness, an awareness from before Time began, before incarnation became an addiction, before humans were even a glint in the Old Man's eye. 'It is a secret, most ancient of ancient. *Mahati Prahati*,' whispers my better half, keeping the meaning of this arcane phrase to himself.

Suddenly something remarkable happens. A blaze of light flares in the Grail chalice like a pearl bursting into flame. It is a seed on fire. It took a long time to kindle it, but we have flames.

When I got home and related the day's events to Russell he said he had figured out what Magotty Pagotty means. 'It's Sanskrit originally, *Mahati Prahati*, which means 'Great Stream,' the great flowing forwards. You could say it's the river of the wisdom of the magi, the flowing together of all the mysteries since and before the beginning of Time. It flows over that which is deeply and secretly buried in the ground of the psyche and the world.'

That night Blaise explained a few more things. 'You are now at the point where you begin to see the essence of Magotty-Pagotty. The Stream flows into the Grail. The Great Stream fills the blaze of light, the seed, in the Grail. The Grail has at its center the seed of the flame of immutable love. The river Magotty Pagotty fills the Grail with light to kindle the seed of the immutable flame. It is represented, inner and outer. The Stream unfolds. The Grail Knight gets his toes wet.'

Then Blaise let me know they expected me at Magotty Pagotty tomorrow. I still had no idea what a cosmic egg was or where I'd find one.

The next day after I stowed my bike in the bushes, I sprawled amidst the stones in the field abutting Copley Wood to recover from the long ride over. From where I lay I could see all of the wood and the top of the rise which was known as Worley Hill. Maybe this wasn't here yesterday or I missed it, but a giant egg of light sits like an ovoid dome over Copley Wood and Worley Hill.

It's more accurate to say the wood and hill sit within this massive translucent egg. Is this the long-lost cosmic egg? If so, I've been stumbling and meditating and streaming through it all week, never even suspecting I was already in the thing I was looking for outside me. The Archangel Michael looms magnificently behind and toweringly above the egg, almost protectively, while a couple dozen Blaises fly loops around it, wrapping it in a sevenfold lilac ribbon. Inside the egg stands a humanlike figure, seeming both new born and eternal. His body is a blaze of light, and one eye is golden, the other silver.

There seem to be a variety of trails that lead up the hill from Magotty Pagotty and I take the one that seems most traveled. I cup the flaming seed of immutable love in my Grail bowl like it's the only lit candle in a dark mansion under siege by the wind. I'm not alone in the woods.

Midway up the hill I encounter a ghostly procession of Knights Templar; the leader of the procession bears a large banner showing a white cross against a red background. Every one of the three dozen men in his troop is cupping a flaming seed like me. Some ten minutes later I cross paths with another spectral troop of Knights and each of them cradles their flaming heart seeds like the most fragile of eggs. I abandon the trail and follow them to the top. 'This is the Hill of the Whorl,' one of them says to me. He points to his heart seed. There is a sevenfold spiral of red light inside it.

I reach what appears to be the top of Worley Hill and ask the gnomes to point out a suitable place to sit down. The three of us perch next to an old oak: me, the cosmic-egg questing Grail Knight, the translucent paternal higher me, and the flaming seed itself, antecedent and parental to us both. The gnomes sit in a crescent around us, and a clutch of Blaises stand in a winged arc behind that. Those many dozens of Knights Templar are also arrayed in concentric circles around me. Before us all stands the Archangel Michael, seemingly waiting for me to prepare.

I breathe Love from Above like a blowtorch to the flaming seed in my Grail bowl. I visualize I am once again standing in the Great Stream with its waters of cosmic origin flowing endlessly, vivifyingly through me. The blazing white seed in me swells and soon becomes twice the size of my physical body so that I am inside it. It is a membrane of fire, a flaming eggshell around me, a cocoon of fire.

Michael lowers his sword, its tip blazing fiercely with angelic light, and touches the egg membrane around me. Fire to fire, and only fire remains. The egg burns even more brightly, almost blindingly, explosively, like a moment before the legendary Big Bang that scientists think precipitated the universe. Time passes, though I have no idea how much. When I return to my physical senses, the ceremony is over; everybody has dispersed. Inside my chest a luminous membrane like an eggshell envelops the flaming seed.

Around me I sense a maternal presence, not a mother, but the Mother, the omnipresent Mother of everything. All of us who were here on the hill today, the gnomes, Knights Templar, the birds, ants, trees, the higher me — we're little sentient bubbles of awareness rising out of the deep still lake of Her being. I don't see a mother of any kind, but images of a partridge, a white goose, a lovely dove, a solitary swan floating on a serene lake pass fleetingly in my mind.

All this has energized me unaccountably. I run down the hill, through the woods, and out across the stone-drenched field back to my bike in what seems like only minutes. As I'm about to ride away, I look at Worley Hill again. The egg is still there with Michael, but he seems to be standing inside it now. 'In his breast, see the Great Initiator,' Blaise tells me. 'See Christ the quickener in his heart.'

There was a golden humanlike figure inside the chest of Michael which resembled a wheel of light. The figure Blaise identified as the Christ seemed to be strapped to the heart wheel, his arms and legs outstretched as in that famous drawing by Leonardo Da Vinci. Or maybe the Christ was voluntarily filling the space with his form and consciousness so as to permeate the whole wheel. This image seems to be a palimpsest, because now I see a Christian cross where the Christ figure on the star wheel was, and then a living green tree in its place. Then all of this appears within Michael's shield which he holds before his chest.

Now the form of the Christ appears again in the midst of these superimposed layers like a blinding sun. A golden jag of light like a sudden lightning strike connects this sun with the flaming seed in my Grail. I can feel the impact in my chest and almost fall over.

As I start to pedal down the road, I look once more at the Worley Hill egg of light. A female figure many times the size of the egg, her face hidden by a shawl, stands behind it protectively, maternally. Now she's holding the egg and everything in it, almost prayerfully in her hands. For a second, I see her holding my egg in the same way, my attention rapt on her.

The scene reminds me of one of my favorite creation myths. The Greeks say that in the beginning, Eurynome, the Mother of All Living Things, assumed the form of a dove and laid the Universal Egg. At her command, Ophion, the cosmic serpent, wrapped itself seven times around it and kept the Egg warm until it hatched. When it did, out tumbled everything in creation, the stars, planets, galaxies, gods, angels, nature spirits, animals, plants, people, Grail Knights.

'The Mother is one way of describing all that cannot be known,' says Blaise later. 'The Mother is what brings you and all beings in human form into this world. From within Her darkness you came as a star down the tunnel through the lesser lights. You will grow until you become the Mother. Then all who know Her will return, but you cannot fully know Her. She is always dying, always doing what needs to be done, always suckling Her children.'

I got a clearer sense of that when I got involved with my next egg. You may remember I told you about how a golden infant got released from my chest when the sword at Burrowbridge Mump miraculously cleaved it. I say 'miraculously' in the sense that I got open-heart surgery without anesthetic, stitches, or pain, care of those masterful cosmic doctors, the Elohim. It didn't happen at the Mump, but that's where I became aware that it had happened.

I'll admit up front that at the time, which is to say, during the time I lived in Glastonbury, I didn't know there was a golden egg at the Abbey. It wasn't until years later when I encountered the same energy configuration and saw it better and understood it a bit more that I looked back to Glastonbury and realized I had first encountered it there, if unknowingly.

But that's how it is when you're in the thick and fast of an initiation that has no familiar edges, when it's not another copy of a standard recipe out of some well-rehearsed tradition. This one was a freelance initiation off the metaphysical tourist's map. It was certainly off mine.

I had always been drawn to the Abbey, not the buildings, what remained of them, but the ample, parklike grounds, entirely framed by a massive stone wall. The Abbey grounds take up most of downtown Glastonbury, and before the Abbey was dissolved by King Henry VII during his great purge of 800 religious houses between 1536 and 1540, it was a major player among cathedrals and their ecclesiastical administrators in England's churchly affairs. Today it's 592 feet of stone ruins enveloped by a 42-acre green lawn, lots of trees and paths.

Abbey tradition says the place is the repository of lots of saints, or at least their relics, that King Arthur and Queen Guinevere were buried here, and that some of the monks from an earlier time occasionally talk to the living, sometimes to their detriment, which is what happened to architect and excavator Frederick Bligh Bond in the 1920s. When he admitted that a group of deceased monks calling themselves the Company of Avalon was revealing secrets of the Abbey, even the location of vanished chapels, he lost his job and reputation for the heresy. Today he'd be on *Oprah* discussing his best-selling account of the monks.

Once known as the 'Holy House at the Head of the Moors Adventurous,' the Abbey hosts an annual pilgrimage of Anglicans, and has done since 1924. 'Christ has died, Christ is risen. Christ will come again. Let us proclaim the mystery of faith,' so intones a priestly voice over the loudspeaker to the thousands of assembled pilgrims with their banners, crucifixes, and Bibles.

My interest in walking the Abbey grounds coincided that June midday with the pilgrimage, and I had to retreat to the far corner of the grounds, to Almoner's Pond, a small ovate stonelined fishpond, to have a little peace and space to myself. 'Hail Mary, full of grace, blessed is the fruit of thy womb, Jesus,' the minister continues. I like this place, but I could do without the church.

That's what I thought then, but since that time, I see it was the perfect place for a Christ-dedicated church, in fact, for one of England's first, said to have been inaugurated, in its earliest guise, by Joseph of Arimathea, the unofficial thirteenth apostle and Jesus Christ's traveling companion and Glastonbury's prime geomancer some two thousand years ago.

The golden egg is something you approach in stages. It's a big mystery temple, typically spread out over many acres and often several miles long. It's meant to be walked, visited, meditated in, many times, over a period of time. It has three parts: a base or introductory foundational steps; a central egg-shaped interior space; and protective, nurturing outer membrane. That's putting it a bit abstractly. More vividly put, it's a landscape version of the Madonna and Christ child, or the Egyptian equivalent of Isis with infant Horus on her lap. The Christ child, born within the golden egg, is held at the breast of the Madonna.

If you were to stand a fair distance behind the Abbey, in the back part of town at Beckery or even out in the moors, you would perhaps notice a giant egg of golden light set on the Abbey grounds as if in an eggcup. It's hundreds of feet high, taller than the Tor. You might catch a glimpse of the glorious golden embryo, what the Hindus like to call the *Hiranygarbha*, the golden seed, the Christ yolk inside this egg. This golden embryo seems to pulse, like a continuously running current, endlessly looping in an oroboric circuit.

The part of Glastonbury that lies directly in front of the Abbey gates is like a mandorla out of which this golden sphere is pushed into the landscape, like a single golden pea in a split-open pod. This part of town is the support for the golden egg, the base of the eggcup. It's like a set of hands delicately holding the egg, presenting it to the Abbey for affirmation. You enter the egg at the Abbey gates. If you want to talk in terms of chakras, you could say the Christ child's first two chakras lie before the gates, and the rest within.

Don't expect to find a golden Christ infant somewhere inside the Abbey. And don't expect to have a stunning vision of a Christ child of light either. It's more like swimming. Get in the water, float, look at the sky, relax, forget about it. Let the child find you. When you immerse yourself in the amniotic fluid of the golden egg, it's like a magic wand that will gradually manifest the child. Man or woman, you will be impregnated, and you will deliver on term – your term, however long it takes. Months, years, decades, lifetimes – whenever. Don't they say the Christ comes like a thief in the night? You won't know it's happened until something acts as a mirror and you realize the child is already born.

You spend time in the golden egg to get in the mood, see how it feels, have the child modeled for you, to get in resonance with something outside to evoke the same thing inside. Think of it as a manger for the inner birth. Here your blazing seed from Magotty Pagotty will transform itself into a wonderful child – the incarnation of the Higher Self expressed as the divine infant.

Here's where the geomantic elegance of the Glastonbury temple becomes irrefutably apparent. You see how well thought out the setup is. First, who's looking after the newborn? The Madonna of course. Chalice Hill, which rises directly in front of the Abbey as you look up the grounds from the gates, serves this function. Admittedly, the hill has a gorgeous, delicious maternal vibration.

But energetically, or I should say geomantically, it has the effect of encircling the golden egg just the way the Madonna is always shown cradling the Christ child. It's as if in another layer of reality where Chalice Hill stands the Madonna enfolds the golden egg with her long, loving arms, reaching down to the base of the egg beyond the Abbey gates. I once visited a golden egg elsewhere in England where the Madonna part of the golden egg temple was known locally as Maidenwell. It was perfectly apt, for the Madonna's energy is like a baptismal well of the Maiden's consciousness, another version of the Mother such as I mentioned with respect to Worley Hill and the cosmic egg.

That's the subtle level of baptism, but the Child – you, me, any of us, really, as a newborn consciousness – needs a more palpable baptism, right? Just a little distance beyond the top of the infant's head at the far end of the Abbey is Chalice Well, the physical baptismal fount for the newborn Christ awareness. I often went there to chill out after a Blaise outing in town or in the Grail Outback. Sometimes I drank the water; sometimes I anointed my head with it; sometimes I imagined it flowing through me.

Sitting there one afternoon I realized that the child's crown chakra gets a perpetual baptizing by the spirit from its mother from her inexhaustible well at Chalice Hill. One of the benefits of this Mother's milk nourishment is to open the child's clairvoyant faculties and with it the possibility of remembering its origin.

Both the Fisher King and myself took a step towards remembering more of our cosmic origins when I got involved with a silver egg, the third of my egg quartet. Like with the golden egg, this is something I became aware of *ex post facto*, after the egg had been hatched. Actually in the case of Glastonbury's silver egg, it had been brooded and hatched a long time ago, but the silver egg I cut my teeth on was in Sedona, Arizona, and that one had not yet been hatched.

It was some years after my initial Glastonbury incursion. I was in Sedona for almost two weeks leading up to and including the Epiphany on January 6. Geomantically, this date is a big deal because the Christ as a cosmic being sends a focus of his attention to a single, pre-selected sacred site somewhere on Earth.

If you think of this as a ray of light, it gets progressively bigger, stronger, brighter in the week leading up to January 6, when it peaks. The individual site gets the initial hit, then the Christ energy gets distributed globally through the Earth's energy body. The January I was in Sedona coincided with the Epiphany being focussed on that site. That was good news for the silver egg.

I spent several hours a day meditating at a nondenominational church called the Chapel of the Holy Cross. It abutted a tall rock face a few hundred feet high. Curiously, towards the top this rock face carried an unmistakable imprint of a falcon's head as if somebody carved it out of the stone or, my preferred theory, it magically appeared out of the ethers as a mnemonic for something. That something was one of the reasons I was sitting in the chapel.

Occupying the same space as the rock face next to the chapel was a giant egg of light. Something was inside it but I wasn't sure what it was. The rest happened quickly, as I was ushered briskly around by Blaise who knew the way.

First I went to a place I would casually describe as a massive crystal city; it had a physical reference to a part of the Sedona landscape called Cathedral Rock. While I was in this city of crystalline light, I followed an inwardly winding spirallic passageway to its end where stood a yellow translucent pillar filled with hollow crystal shanks, each about two feet long. I took one and left. Then I 'flew' up to the top of the silver egg beside the chapel and inserted the crystal shank like a sword or perhaps more aptly, like a computer disk.

Within fifteen minutes or so, the egg flushes luminous white as if to explode, and soon the shell cracks, falls away, and dissolves, and a giant silver hawk emerges, standing upright, at least one hundred feet tall, probably more. *Horus!* I hear the word echo in my bones and cells and whatever body I was in when I 'flew' up to the egg with the shank. Streams of different colors rush up the cliff face behind the silver bird, like a double vertical rainbow. 'The Ray Masters have arrived,' said Blaise.

Before I wrap up all this business with eggs, the golden child, and silver bird, I have to tell you a few stories about dragons. You wouldn't think dragons would play much part in this egg business, but they're central to the picture. And there are dragon eggs, too, which was the fourth type of egg I obsessed about.

The second time I ever saw a dragon in the landscape was when I climbed Silbury Hill in Wiltshire. Silbury is that odd, cone-shaped mound across the fields from the Avebury stone circle in Wiltshire, some 30 miles north of Stonehenge. A fair number of crop circles get produced in the fields around Silbury and Avebury every summer, and lots of people climb Silbury to get a better look at them. Like most of Britain's megalithic heritage, most people don't know why these structures were built, what they did, or why they're still around. The same goes for Silbury Hill.

The first time I saw the hill, as I walked across the fields from Avebury, I understood why it had been built and why it was still there. Silbury Hill is the site of one of the planet's 13 dragons. These were brought here long ago when the Earth's energy body and the astral temples were set up. As I walked closer to Silbury, I saw the dragon, coiled massively and magnificently not so much around the physical hill but in the same place as the visible hill, its head like the central jewel in an exquisitely crafted torc.

I *know* this dragon, I realized. I climbed the Hill with the odd feeling I was clambering up the flanks of a living being, an old friend. It was a queer sensation, two sensations meeting like meteorological fronts. On the one hand, I thought, how could I know a dragon – I barely understand what a dragon is; on the other, I *remembered* it, and stuff we had done long ago. Yes! Hello again, good to see you – how could I have forgotten about you.

I walked counterclockwise up the hill, following the dragon coils in reverse, winding myself back to its center, the head with eyes that regard the landscape, that sees far and wide and deep. For a moment I see the world as the dragon sees it, and I become one with its might and vision. His coils fill all the space around the hill, all of the visible landscape, spiralling out for miles to the horizon.

Standing on the top of the Hill and effectively on the dragon's golden crown, I felt remarkably exhilarated, reconnected with an ancient aspect of 'my' planetary past. You know what I mean: the somebody that is the origin (and to blame) for this long incarnational saga for which I am merely the most recent and occasionally obtuse lineage holder. I stand as if I'm hundreds of feet tall, holding a sword of light, not to subdue, certainly not to slay, but to activate, to energize, to release this dragon energy into our world. I saw myself doing precisely this in earlier times, wearing different bodies and costumes. This probably sounds odd, but it was a treat to reconnect with this old friend.

The third time I saw a dragon I already told you about — that picaresque affair with the gnomes, the jewel horde, and the sword. But the first time was in Glastonbury. I was on a Blaise assignment, early one morning when the tall grass behind the Tor in Glastonbury was still sufficiently wet to thoroughly soak my sneakers. I was walking meditatively (when I wasn't fixating on how *wet* my feet were getting) from two very old, mostly moribund oak trees known locally as Gog and Magog up the back flank of the Tor. It turns out those two pre-diluvian oaks were the first of a total of 144 oaks planted in two rows, 72 on each side, and once blessed by Glastonbury's master geomancer, Joseph of Arimathea some 2,000 years ago when he came here to fine tune the Glastonbury temple.

On one level, I was walking through wet grass across a field up to the base of the Tor. On another level, I was walking (in memory, I suppose) along an oak-lined promenade in a ritual procession heading towards the Tor. In this memory, I saw hundreds of Celtic men and women standing amidst the oaks, watching our procession, the 'our' being myself and three others. There was something regal about our outfits and manner of being, as if we were demonstrating or even exemplifying something. There was a fair clutch of angels about too adding to the festive atmosphere.

The point of this reminiscence, however, is to describe what awaited me at the end of this processional. A dragon of course. Flaming, crowned, winged, alert, animate. This one lay in coils far bigger than the physical extent of the Tor, and its tail coiled casually, almost indolently, across miles of landscape, far out to the levels and moors. Behind this red dragon you could see hundreds of lovely apple trees in perfect spring blossom on the Tor, pendant golden fruits hanging off every limb and silver leaves sparkling in the rich sunlight.

Golden apples guarded by a red dragon; how deliciously mythological. This is right out of the eleventh labor of Herakles, I thought, where he had to sneak past Ladon, the fearful dragon guardian of the orchards of the Hesperides in the Far West, and grab a golden apple. But why should these golden nuggets of spiritual wisdom be guarded by a dragon?

I got another insight into dragons when I visited Mount Haleakala, the massive volcano on the island of Maui in Hawaii. I was trying to get a sense of what Pele, the Polynesian fire goddess, really was and what 'she' did in relation to volcanoes. The question led me to dragons, in this case, to *the* dragon. The Norse mythographers had a name for the singular planetary dragon: *Jormungandr*, the Midgard serpent, cast into the Sea by Odin, chief of the gods of Asgard, to encircle the Earth like a necklace. This serpent, the myths tell us, got so big that wrapping itself entirely around the Earth it could bite its own tail.

I saw *Jormungandr*. The first thing you have to realize is that at this level of expression, serpent and dragon mean the same thing. I suppose it's easier to imagine a snake encircling a globe than a dragon with cumbersome wings, but dragons can and do and don't complain about the athletic imposition.

Picture the Earth encircled by a single planet-sized dragon, like the jewel in the torc image I mentioned above. The dragon's head is somewhere in the South Pacific, and the many islands of Hawaii and the hundreds of Polynesian islands are but mere charming freckles on the great beast's scaly skin. One of this singular dragon's functions is to distribute the fire element for the planet, specifically through volcanism, and that's where Pele the Fire Goddess came in. It's a fascinating image to picture Pele flying around inside this vast planetary dragon, bringing up threads of fire to the surface, initiating volcanic eruptions that flare up like boils seen over time on the dragon's skin.

The whole dragon set-up is a hologram. This one is the mother of the 13 dragons I referred to earlier, which include the one at Silbury Hill and Glastonbury. Each of these is in turn the mother of 81 more dragons, which comes out to be 1,053. These dragons, and the 13 and the one, are all copies – holographic projections – of the original dragon known as Draco, which is a constellation of at least 13 major stars in the form of a dragon, coiled about the Pole Star at the 'top' and 'center' of the galaxy from Earth's vantage point. Draco probably isn't the original one either, but for the Grail Quest, it will do.

Now I'll tell you about the adventure at Walmsgate. Even the name is redolent of the dragon presence at this obscure site near the village of Tetford in Lincolnshire – the Gate of the

Worm. This dragon guards the northeastern entrance to a geomantic temple complex with at least a dozen features. Another dragon guards the southeastern gate in the city of Lincoln, some 20 miles away.

The Walmsgate dragon is at least a mile wide, from the left tip to the right of the massive coils, its crowned head in the middle of all this. In a sense, all the temples in the greater Tetford landscape – Grail Castle, other eggs, including a gnome egg, another copy of that puzzling crystal city – lie within the dragon, in the dragon realm, you might say. The proper entrance to this geomantic domain is through the gate of the dragon's mouth: the Walm's Gate.

Physically the place I'm referring to now is the ruins of a miniscule medieval hamlet, somewhat hidden and tucked away at the end of an unmarked farm lane a few miles from the village of Tetford. There's a very old, hoary beech tree, the outlines of an old chapel, and a lot of sheep-grazable field.

What draws my attention are two raised mounds about six feet high and thirty feet long; they seem to flank the entry to a cave, but there is no cave, just the grassy bank at the end of these two parallel mounds. They look like two chubby green fingers, like the index and middle, lifting up the sod from underneath exposing the central cavity between them which is seemingly a dead end. But only seemingly, because at this seeming *cul de sac* is the insinuated Gate of Walms. There is a golden archway and under it a vast dragon. Even more interesting is the fact that this dragon is sitting like a mother hen on a nest that must have thousands of eggs.

I walk through the gate, into the dragon, and enter his realm. It is an immense spirallic dimension, like being inside a living spiral that is constantly expanding, as if perpetually unfolding itself in an ever larger spiral yet at the same time remaining the same size. I suppose it's the old paradox of pi, the quest to know the circumference of the circle from the vantage point of the radius. I stand outside the dragon again, on its head, and probe my sword into its brow. This is a vortex of interlocking plates, and I pass through this, like spinning down a tunnel, tumbling out into a land of obsidian crystals and dim light, a black land.

Coming back through the gate to the land of sheep and meditating Grail Knights, at the Walmsgate dragon's invitation, I collect several baskets of dragon eggs, largesse from my outing and presents for Russell and Berenice.

About this time Blaise had a few words of clarification on the matter of dragon eggs. 'The egg is one of the few forms which is entirely healthful to human consciousness. Each egg has a potential for insight into its function and nature according to the level of the egg which is concerned. Within each dragon egg is the seed of something to be transformed through the cooperation of the elemental, human, and angelic kingdoms. When this trinity of forces comes together at a dragon egg, then the force latent there can be diffused within a center of a section of the grid matrix for the unfoldment of consciousness within the elemental and human kingdoms, depending on the energy preset in each dragon egg.'

It was getting so I needed a chart to keep track of all the players in this dragon mystery. One big dragon wrapped around the planet; then 13 major dragons, big, highly impressive, very old, each at a major sacred site. The Ray Masters deal with these guys. Then more than a thousand second level dragons, still impressive, maybe a little smaller, placed at the larger dome caps that came out of the domes, and the big shot mythic heroes like St. George, King Arthur, Siegfried sort these worms out. Walmsgate is one of these dome cap dragons.

Now, dragon eggs – the key thing to know about this is that there is a ridiculously large number of them, some 33.2 trillion. That's our bit. The idea was to have enough eggs so every sentient soul that would ever incarnate on Earth could have one dragon egg – even souls who never bodily incarnated but still had some focus on the Earth plane. Why do you need a dragon egg?

'A complete person would have assimilated the energy from at least one dragon egg and integrated the seven levels within Man and the seven aspects within each level,' Blaise told me. Basically, it's another opportunity for a mystery initiation that will benefit you and the planet. When you assimilate these energies, it affects all the dragon eggs and their existence in our world, and all these levels have to do with the chakras and their secondary aspects. In other words, the dragon egg is *your* designer mystery temple.

The game is to activate a realization of the dragon inside you and to illuminate it without becoming an out-of-control fire-breathing monster, dead, irretrievably afraid, or running pell mell from it thinking this will save your sorry ass from its heat. The key thing to remember is don't try to kill the dragon.

Of course there was a dragon egg with my name on it waiting for me. I found it at a tiny parish church in the village of Somersby, near Tetford. It was right across the street, incidentally, from where Alfred Lord Tennyson grew up. I could see the baby dragon inside the egg. First it seemed to be blue, then red, then gold. I insert my sword into it and instantly I am the dragon. My body starts to twitch quite dramatically as if somebody were running an electric cattle prod up and down my back and across the back of my neck. I feel like a skewered dragon, which is funny of course because I did this to myself.

The dragon's thickly, scaly skin starts to slough off as if it's spring molting time. The body starts to break up, fall apart, crumble into fragments. Where the dragon's body formerly was now lies a luscious golden apple, as if it had been the secret pearl inside the dragon's carapace. This is a twist on the myth: not only does Ladon guard the golden apples, the orchard is inside him.

But finding the golden apple was not the end of my mock dragon-slaying. I clove the apple with my sword and there was a newborn golden child, the infant solar hero, awake, and regarding me. Inside the child was the Grail.

Don't get the wrong impression. Dealing with your dragon takes longer than one fun-filled morning in an English parish church. Those were shots across the bow, an opening parley, a fast-forward preview of my coming misery. You deal with the dragon slowly, in stages, at whatever rate you can transmute the poison; after all, assimilating the energies of 49 levels is a bit of a task.

In fact, it's not far off the mark to say once you meet and enter the dragon, you remain in this dragon egg until you're finished with the transmutation, even if that takes ten or twenty years. You are always still inside the dragon. So over the years my dragon egg at Somersby is quietly and steadily feeding the local geomythic landscape in Lincolnshire. Every time I assimilate another of the 49 levels of my dragon, the Somersby dragon egg takes a little step up in awareness and geomantic utility. As for the other 33 trillion dragon eggs, it's a reasonable bet that some are hatching and maturing right now, that many have already been completed, and that a great deal await their time.

But the initial foray into the dragon realm helped me understand why you need an egg with two eyes, one golden, one silver, and what this egg yields.

Remember I mentioned Horus earlier? The Egyptian myths tell us that Horus slew the fierce dragon Apophis, or Typhon, as the Greeks called it. One of the meanings of this encoded mythic statement is that, as Blaise told me later, 'the lower nature which is Typhon is transmuted into the awakened one, which is the silver child as the inner being of Horus.'

This fits the Glastonbury setup. At the Tor you have on one level a big fat dragon; at another, a mature silver egg – hence the mythic tableau of Horus 'slaying' Typhon. The silver child, it turns out, is the clairvoyant aspect of the golden child, its other psychic half, making the two child beings parts of a Gemini twinship of sorts. The Egyptians spoke of the Elder Horus, who was the hawk, and the Younger Horus, who was the infant in Isis' lap. Both were aspects of Horus.

One of the Hindu creation myths says that in the beginning there was nothing but an egg called the Egg of Brahma, or *Brahmanda*. That was the cosmic egg. After a year it was split asunder, and one of the eggshell parts became silver, the other gold. Those were your silver and golden eggs. Horus was the chick inside both eggs.

To the Egyptians, his right eye was the Sun and his left the Moon, or from a different perspective, the Sun was an 'Eye of Horus' and the Moon was an 'Eye of Horus,' part of a cosmic Face said to look down over Egypt — all of which explains why he was called 'Horus of the Two Eyes.' In one text it is said of Thoth, the Egyptian Hermes, that he has seized 'the two Eyes of Horus, the White Eye [Sun] and the Black Eye [Moon].'

'When the silver and gold aspects come together, then the all-seeing aspect of Horus arises,' Blaise told me. The Egyptians spoke of Horus as a high-flying falcon who soared far above the world, surveying everything. I think this was initiate's code for saying he was super clairvoyant. 'The falcon image is the teacher who sees all aspects of a situation from above as Love from Above,' Blaise said.

The reason we need to care about this funny business of golden and silver eggs, silver and gold children, and trillions of dragon eggs is that it affects the lives and destinies of two big time beings: Albion and the Fisher King. Everything is connected in this Grail business, everybody knows everybody, the key players are on the Grail Knight's speed dial.

'Albion is now unchained and awaits his healing,' Blaise explained. 'The Fisher King as you know is the representation of the wounded one. Part of healing Albion is through the reintegration of the thirteen parts of the Fisher King. If Albion is to be healed, then what needs to take place is the balancing of the Moon at the brow of the Fisher King [that's the silver child of the silver egg] and the Sun in his solar plexus [that's the golden child of the golden egg]. These are two of the thirteen parts that need to be restored. The silver child and golden child in Albion's heart may then walk together under the Sun behind the Sun.'

Hatching a silver egg opens the doorway of perception for the human world, awakens the far-seeing one inside the Grail Knight. Hatching a golden egg gives this clairvoyance a body. Both help restore the riches the Rich Fisher King lost when he became the wounded one. You do it outside to get it inside.

Everything is continuously turning inside out. I am the Wounded Fisher King, I am a hologram of Albion, the one who hatches golden and silver eggs, who deals with the dragons, and so are you, and your friends, and my friends, and their friends. I'm beginning to get the picture. You heal yourself through the Earth and its geomythic mystery temples and through that you heal the Earth. The Grail Quest is about finding those temples, those mystery mirrors, and learning how to use them on behalf of yourself, the world, and the planet.

I was riding my bike out of Glastonbury late one afternoon when I saw it, the combined Horus, the bird and the child. First I heard the phrase, 'I am the one who was in the beginning and will be in the end.' Then I saw the golden child with a silver falcon at his brow chakra; then the golden child was riding the silver falcon as it soared above and through Glastonbury and the Seven Heavens.

The silver bird gives the child the clairvoyance of the deep, antique past, all the vision that the Fisher King desperately seeks to remember. Horus the Elder is consciousness in extension, moving, seeing, putting it all together. The golden child gets to see everything, in the most distant past and most arcane future – he sees the riches the Rich Fisher King once had, once saw, and is wounded for lacking. The golden child sees what the Wounded Fisher King would see if he were healed, and *will* see again when he is healed.

The Elder Horus who sees and the Younger Horus who rides — together they are like Vishnu's Mount, the far-seeing, high-flying bird of Vishnu, the bird the Hindus called Garuda. Vishnu and Horus the Younger, Garuda and Horus the Elder — it's the same story, same relationship. And the child, the golden embryo, Brahma's *Hiranygarbha*, is the perfect expression of existence, the flawless manifestation of the creator god's idea of perfect existence.

The golden child is the freshly born, immaculate, virginal, perfect Albion, the seed of Albion, his beginning, end, and model, a child because he has just entered the scene of existence like a blank slate, like a brand new year, with not even the first second having yet elapsed. The golden child is the perfect expression of Brahma, the creator god, of the Supreme Being, a golden pulsing current, containing the planets, stars, constellations, all the galaxies and zodiacs, the realms of the angels, everything that ever will tumble out of the cosmic egg, everything that will ever comprise the awakened human, all the agencies of consciousness.

Like a single drop of God essence, that cosmic egg and its falcon-browed golden child dwells within each of us, an inconspicuous but universe-creating drop, like a stowaway from the first millisecond of existence hiding amidst our tired cells and their karmic baggage, like a stealth virus encoded to deliver apocalyptically invigorating memories and information of why we're here and how to be here.

7

Another thing you'll need for the Quest is a willingness to travel, which is to say, you'll need to find the location of some of the doors out of this world.

Here's how I found the first one. I woke up one morning with the phrase *Who is that Blazing Star?* running around my mind, a question demanding an answer. As soon as I was awake, though still comfortable under the duvet in my room, I noticed the star at my belly was brighter than usual, almost insistently bright. I turned my attention to it and it started to expand, slowly, then more rapidly, rushing towards me. I felt the usual flush of Love from Above, that glorious melting feeling, no doubt a species of bliss, envelop me, smothering me in more exalted consciousness, until the star exploded before me or I walked into it in a blaze of light. Whatever way I put it, I was somewhere else.

It was a vast flat green lawn on a country estate, at the end of which stood a huge multistoried mansion. It was as if I were on the grounds of the prototype of the best outfitted, most elegantly landscaped, most spacious of English estates. I entered the building and stood in the center of a large circular room on whose periphery stood thousands of closed doors. Somehow I knew I could enter any door I wished to.

I opened one door and entered. It was like walking into a movie. I was a Hindu male with long beard, dark skin, rings, white sarong, walking among thousands of other Hindis at a prodigious religious festival. Living gurus, larger than life size, sit on pedestals before which people bowed and prayed. I am looking for my own guru, but somebody says he has already left the fair.

I opened another door. I am with young Christian monks dressed in baggy brown robes. We carry Bibles and sing hymns in the cloisters of a church. A third door shows me with hundreds of Jews at the Wailing Wall in Old Jerusalem, swaying, rocking, chanting. A fourth shows me having my head chopped off. A fifth shows my body on a butcher's block, cut into many pieces, while a jeering crowd watches. A sixth has me as a Native American chief, dying of thirst and injuries on a steep cliffside some 400 feet above a river. A very large man comes up and heartlessly pushes me over the edge.

Each door, another lifetime, another heartache. You get the picture. I sampled a couple dozen of these doors until I'd had enough. This is like the Wheel of Fortune card in the Tarot deck. You could go round and round this wheel forever, opening the next door, hoping in *that* life you had the epiphany and not the disaster.

I walked out of the white mansion and down the expansive lawn to a lovely white gazebo. It had six white pillars, a few steps up to a small circular area, and a transparent round table in the center. Architecturally it was more like a free-standing rotunda than a garden gazebo, but in any event, I'd like one of them in my back yard. I'd never seen such vibrant, living, green grass as this. I walked up the steps and entered the rotunda.

Blaise is there with me, surrounding me and the table. It's as if they stepped out of the white pillars, or perhaps they are the pillars and momentarily congealed into angels in the guise I've become accustomed to. Eight feet tall, majestic, each Blaise has a sun in its chest. They all seem to be chuckling at a joke one of them must have popped just before I arrived. I've learned by now not to ask them what the joke is. Too often it was me, or something I did or thought.

I sit on the crystalline round table, surrounded by six Blaises. A thick leather-bound book lies before me. A name is inscribed on the cover. I suspect it's mine, but it's in a strange language, certainly not English, and not one I recognize. About four-fifths of the pages have entries. At the top of each page is a different name, presumably the name of the person in that lifetime.

When I focus on the contents of the page, again, written in an unfamiliar script, it transforms into a single gold coin, the same type of coin I pulled out of the knight's chests when I was in my jousting phase of the Quest. I look at the coin. It presents an image of stopped time, but my viewing it seems to animate its contents, and as it was when I walked through a door in the white mansion, each coin is a movie.

'Coins, pages, doors – they are equal aspects of looking inside the star,' Blaise said. It seemed as if all six were speaking and as if just one of them was speaking, but I left sorting out this paradox for another day. 'We are the Nimitta, the point of absolute light. All emanations arise from that point. Here is the first cell, where the two became one. The potential of who you were yet to be was born from this point.

'The knowledge of all the beings you have been before and all the beings you are yet to be in the future was locked into this single cell. If you access the diamond, the Nimitta, you access the cumulative knowledge of all the beings you've been in the past and are yet to be in the future. The deeper you access the diamond, or Nimitta, the closer you get to the star. The star is like pure being, original being, stuff that was locked within you that began you on your journey back to the Star.'

'What diamond?' I asked Blaise.

'Look at the center of the table again,' Blaise said.

The book was gone from the table. In its place was a diamond, but it had more facets than I could count. More facets, in fact, than you would think technically possible to exist on a crystal this small. Thousands? No, more than that. The more I looked at the diamond, the more facetted it became, the larger it became.

I lost awareness of the table, the Blaises, the pillars, the rotunda, the green lawn – all there was everywhere was this vast diamond with *millions* of facets, each one a doorway. All I had to do was walk through one or allow it to blissfully engulf me like a tsunami. I passed through a facet, there was a pop of light, and the next thing I knew I was back in my bed, still under the duvet.

Over the next few days, I kept my attention on that diamond, waiting to see what it would do next. Actually the diamond and the star kept trading places. I would breath as Love from Above to the blazing star at my belly, marveling at how exquisitely tiny it was, almost too small to see or imagine, then it would swell up and become discernible as a multi-faceted crystal, the Nimitta form again, then it would condense into the tiniest of pinpricks of light.

I remembered meditating in the mountains somewhere – it

seemed like the Andes of Peru — and watching as the Blaise rotunda delicately descended, like a globular feather, on the cliff face before me. I entered the rotunda, and it seemed to zip itself up, the six white pillars melding into one in a flash of light. We went somewhere, but I couldn't remember where. I just knew we did.

Later Blaise had a few more comments about the size of the star. 'We come as we are, as a pinpoint of light that is an atom of bright space within permanent blackness. We place a star at the center of your being so small you would need the most powerful atomic microscope to see it. It's even smaller than that. It's half that size. It's even tinier than that. We just can't express how tiny it is. It's beyond tinyness, yet it contains the known universe.

Then Blaise threw a marvelous, slow, endlessly curving curve ball, which I am still waiting to catch. 'God is always very small. That's how God crushes that which is very big. The big expands beyond itself, dissolves into darkness while the small contracts into itself and becomes the brighter.'

One of the things you realize on the Quest is that you get things by degree. Swords, Grail bowls, insights, under-standings, visions, details. It helps greatly if you persevere, take notes, remember your questions, and keep trying. Maybe you'll see only a few edges at first, a couple of surfaces, or only its outlines will appear as if in a fog. Keep trying: eventually, you will see more of it, and be able to put together a reasonable working image of what it is.

One of the most intriguing and for me, useful, things Carlos Castaneda said in his body of work was that it took him many years — twenty, I think he said — to reconstruct, to remember

everything he had seen, said, and done in the 'second attention,' which is to say, having wild and inexplicable adventures
with Don Juan. You find that you remember details out of
sequence, that causes seem to have preceded effects, and
you're not sure if in your latest vision you have experienced a
new dimension of an old mystery, or merely remembered
more from your original immersion in that reality. Practically,
it doesn't matter.

That's how it was with the crystal city, as we first named it,
because it looked like one. It's a place – a dimension, I suppose – I have since visited many times, and now, I believe, see
more clearly than in the beginning. No doubt what I think I am
seeing is still but a vivid metaphor of something more multidimensional, more real, but it's enough and enables me to get
my Grail business done.

We were visiting Hamdon Hill, a heavily quarried, mostly
treeless hill now made into a public park some ten miles or so
from Wick. Russell's interest had been piqued by a book he'd
encountered in which the author claimed Hamdon Hill was
the 'Pyramid of Albion' and a Grail Castle within a complex
geometrical overlay he had traced over the topographic map of
Somerset. We had become a bit like firemen, acutely sensitive
to every nuance of smoke, every insinuation of heat, always
wary – in our case, desiring – of suggestions of fire.

It was a typical Blaise outing. The weather was atrocious,
the special effects were impressive, and the vision was slow in
coming but worth the trip. Then the three of us sat down to
tune into whatever Blaise had in store for us. Afterwards we
pooled our visual impressions to build a composite image.

It was as if we had been looking down on Hamdon Hill from

a great height. It was topped by a dome, and from the dome a great shaft of light went straight down to a city. It was what we would call futuristic, as if all the buildings were made of crystal or light shaped into pleasing, harmonious geometric forms that seemed to vibrate and shimmer as if cycling back and forth between form and light.

No city on Earth looks that good, that balanced, that symmetrical, I thought at the time, and I remembered some correspondence I had had from a friend in the North of England. He had written about a dream vision of visiting a city of light that existed several thousands of years in the future, and said he had entered this city from several different locations, one of them close to London.

In my next encounter with the crystal city it was as if the city came to visit me. It was some years later and Russell and Berenice were living in Lincolnshire. We were drinking tea in the Pendleton's tiny living room about a week before Christmas when Blaise visited. That night they had an unusual agenda which of course they were not going to explain to us until after it had been completed.

After the preliminaries, which included reviewing a new visualization they had given us, and their introductory remarks about the ineffability of a tiny pinprick of light that was almost too small to see yet brighter than all other stars, they began. 'We bring a being in front of you. Would you please describe him.'

First I saw a gorilla wearing a mask and carrying a club, then this same gorilla appeared upside down holding a baby. I knew this was rubbish, and sat there for a while breathing to my star as Love from Above to clear the fog. 'I see a very bright sun, and within the sun stands a being that looks like the sculpted face of the Greek god Apollo against a pale blue sky.'

'Good. This is what we hoped. This is the first ray, also known as the Master El Morya. Again, focus on the space in front of you and describe what you see,' said Blaise.

Next I saw a beautiful, majestic image of a golden Buddha, like a giant wall ornament with tall peacock plumes for a head piece against a rich orange background. 'This is the second ray,' Blaise said. 'You have just seen the Maitreya, otherwise known as the Master Kuthumi, John the Baptist, or St. Francis of Assisi. Again, focus and describe what you see.'

This time I saw a Mother Superior, but a young one, her hair short in a braid or tied back in a bun. The cowl sweeps low over her forehead and she is not looking at me. She is very pretty, solemn, powerful, familiar to me, her complexion is pristine, and she has large dark eyes; there is the sense of vibrant pink about her. 'That is Master Lady Nada, the third ray. She is also known as Mary Magdalene, the consort of the Christ, Aphrodite, Bridgit, and Joan of Arc.

Next I saw a pale green Tibetan *heruka*, which in their vast iconography is a fierce, wrathful deity said to protect the Dharma from corruption. 'This is the fourth ray manifestation. It belongs to Ray Master Hilarion.'

A bright white misty flame appeared before me next. Inside it stood a woman in her fifties wearing a golden crown; she had short hair and grey eyes. 'That is White Flame, or Master Serapis Bey, Ray Master of the fifth ray.'

A red rose of especially bright, almost scarlet redness appeared next. Inside stood a human man holding a dagger or what the Tibetans would call a *dorje*, a religious instrument like a dagger with blades at both ends. The man is shaking this dagger of light as if to emphasize a point. 'Who is that?' I ask.

'Master Jesus, the sixth ray, carrier of the Christ, and also known as Hephaistos, Santanda, Mithras, and many others. Tell us what you see now.'

This one was somewhat amusing. Basically it was a handsome, virile, forty-something male greatly resembling Clark Gable, seated at a table like a European noble with a hint of roguishness. 'This the seventh, lilac ray, and the master of the seventh ray, Prince Rakoski, also known as Saint Germain, Francis Bacon, William Shakespeare, and the Eastern master Harakhan Baba.'

So it went for another hour until I had stumbled through some fairly primitive and embarrassing identifications of fourteen Ray Masters, as Blaise called them. What does a god look like, anyway, in its full expression, as Blaise would see them? When Arjuna got a good look at Krishna in his full ontological regalia, it nearly blew him out of his chariot. The same of course could be said of God, even more so, although I suppose the angels develop a capacity for continuously beholding the magnificence of the presence.

Of the Ray Masters, some were known to me by name through mythology, others through history, others not at all: Pallas Athena, Lao Tzu, Quan Yin, Djwhal Khul, Portia, the Mahachohan, the Venetian master. Take the basic seven rainbow colors and divide them again, so you have a light blue and dark blue, an orange and a gold, rich green and light green, a red and a pink. There are your fourteen rays with a master or administrator handling each.

Then Blaise gave us a glimpse of what we had been doing.

'We stated when we brought you over to England this time that we would be commencing this implantation through your consciousness. It is now complete, at least in the initial phase. We have been implanting the threads of each of the fourteen rays into the top of the dome over this village. These rays have to be anchored by a grid engineer and facilitated by us and by a certain amount of sympathetic resonance by Russell and Berenice. All domes, to be fully activated and active again, must be similarly wired to the fourteen rays of the Great Bear.'

But I said above that the crystal city came to visit us. This is what happened. It turns out the fourteen Ray Masters are the crystal city; that's where they live; that's their headquarters and it's located in the constellation Ursa Major. Projecting the fourteen rays which are each a beam of color and consciousness, a whole pathway and parameters for a particular stream of evolution, soul development, and portion of total consciousness throughout the planet and humanity is what the Ray Masters do. The crystal city might as well be called Ray Master city, and it has other names too as known in mythology such as Mount Olympus and Asgard, both called the home of the gods.

'The fourteen rays are standard,' Blaise continued. 'There is nothing special about them. Light has fourteen major subdivisions in manifestation. The rays are the qualifications into qualitative form of these manifestations of light. We are specifically speaking, when we speak of rays, as to the quality of light.'

How do you guys attach these rays to the domes? 'A dome is an energy matrix imprint from the fourth dimension. The light facilitates the activity of this energy matrix. The more rays that are connected to a dome, the more the energy matrix becomes effective. We would never activate them all as this would be a negative effect, like eating too much chocolate pudding. We are preparing several sites simultaneously, of which this is one, but we are limited to the probability or possibility of a few humans coming together who are prepared to do what we wish that we may facilitate these projects.'

So what is this crystal city, Blaise, I asked next. 'The crystal city, as you call it, exists in the future and is not yet in manifestation,' Blaise said. 'It is an aspect of Shambhala and pertains to the Great Bear, two rays from each of the seven stars in what you call the Big Dipper. We place its date of future manifestation at around 3,000 AD. It is possibly both a new dimension and a new realm for humans today, but it is an unknown aspect because humanity has not evolved enough yet. Home is where the heart is. The heart is the *Ananda-kanda* chakra, the home within the Great Bear.

'St. Germain of the lilac ray and Lady Portia of the gold ray are particularly active with us now in our work on behalf of the Earth energy matrix. Master St. Germain brings the transmutative energy of the Christ. Master Lady Portia brings the discriminative wisdom of that transmutation. Both are involved especially with our dome activations because within this time period the gold and lilac are sympathetic resonances within the sphere.'

Over the years I gradually became more aware of these Ray Masters and some of their involvement in our work and adventures. Once I was on a mountain in Southern California with a few colleagues. We had finished leading a geomancy workshop there and were talking shop when I became aware that a couple dozen Blaises were flying around the top of the dome over the mountain trailing long colored ribbons.

I realized they were wiring the dome with the fourteen rays of the Great Bear because I was there. They had told me that once our being bodies were 'wired' or introduced to the rays, those rays would always be implicit in us, which was advantageous to them. They could only rewire the domes to Ursa Major through grid engineers (actually, that's too complimentary: apprentice Grail Knights would be more apt) present at a site.

Somehow it didn't require me to do anything for them to use my pre-wired condition to wire up the dome, although I suspect it's the horse with a feed bag and rider situation. The rider can very well be off conducting what to the horse, happy with his feed bag of oats, would consider arcane business without knowing, or needing to know, or wanting to know, anything more about it.

Here's how Blaise put it, rather tactfully I thought. 'You're like a battery. A battery is still a battery whether it is connected to a light or not. If there are wires coming out from the terminals of a battery to a lamp, there is light. If the battery has enough stored energy, the image or energy matrix surrounds your being, whether or not you are conscious of it.'

One time I was meditating in the woods on one of the constellations of a small landscape zodiac in the United States. For a moment I was aware of the Ray Master Portia approaching me in a golden rotunda; she settled down around me — I think, technically, or spatially, I ended up inside the rotunda — and I noticed she had Rudolf Steiner on board.

Another time I was in the French Pyrenees working on

another landscape zodiac; it was dinner time and I was fussing about the restaurant fare. I didn't like it; it was weird French food – you know, the kind of things you end up mumbling about to yourself when you're traveling alone and are a little cranky from the work and in this case a considerable lack of consensus reality. St. Germain appeared before me in the restaurant, as nonchalantly as an expected diner seating himself at my table. He grinned, and said, 'Stop griping about the food. I had to live on nothing but pig's feet for a week once.'

Then the day came when I had a more coherent impression of their city. I was in Virginia at a holy site; in fact, I was in Thomas Jefferson's former backyard at Monticello outside Charlottesville. Monticello is a small hill facing another, larger one, called Brown's Hill; local legend has it President Jefferson fancied the taller one but had to settle for the smaller hill.

Sitting on the edge of Jefferson's lawn, I saw this huge humanlike being, hundreds of feet tall. He had a horn, a sword, and wore shining white armor, and he seemed to be guarding a bridge of rainbow colors that spanned the brief valley between the two hills. On the far hill, was the crystal city – to be precise, a copy of it. There are actually more than one hundred of these around the Earth, each one the same crystal city. I guess you could say these are multiple doors into the same place.

A rainbow bridge – that's a new touch. There are only a few myths that speak of a rainbow bridge, and one of the most conspicuous of these is the Norse description of *Bifrost*, the Rainbow Bridge into Asgard, guarded by Heimdall. The Rainbow Bridge in a curious way is made of the fourteen Ray

Masters who also live in Asgard. You could even say the Bridge is the Masters, is Asgard.

I crossed the bridge and entered the crystal city. This time, however, it was less of a city than a massive, sprawling round white cathedral with a very high central domed ceiling. It could have passed for a magnificently opulent art museum, the kind with immaculate marble floors and pillars and lots of space. There was a central circular opening from which like spokes on a wheel opened out fourteen sections. Each was framed by a large sculpture of the god of that section.

As I looked at each statue, it seemed to come alive, animate itself into color, resemble the particular Ray Master it was meant to resemble. I began to see the (to me) familiar features of St. Germain, one of the Ray Masters I had been particularly involved with on account of the Earth energy matrix work with Blaise. All fourteen statues faced into the central open space, so that their backs were to their own sections. I could imagine the fourteen of them springing to fully animate presence when Zeus or Thor, the chief of the gods, was present.

I could imagine – this part was fun – Hephaistos, Pallas Athena, Apollo, Aphrodite, Ares, and Artemis, striding out of their respective sections into the central meeting room. All of these Greek Olympian gods were Ray Masters. It gave me a new and I admit exciting way of looking at mythology too. Remember the *Odyssey* where Homer constantly said grey-eyed Pallas Athena was the champion of wily Odysseus? She was his specific initiatory Ray Master. Or Homer's *Iliad* where he recounted the comings and goings of the gods at Troy in support of their favorite human heroes in the ten year battle?

Again, the open secret of the presence of the Ray Masters has been right before us for centuries in this widely read saga.

Looking at the individual statues of the Ray Masters, you could almost see the figures morphing through the catalog of mythic and human incarnation these gods had undertaken over the vast length of planetary time, and even before that, in previous universes and cycles of cosmic existence.

I looked for St. Germain's lilac section, found it, and entered. It is as if he had painted a section of the planet lilac to indicate every place where his influence extended. In the St. Germain subdivision of Asgard you could see the world, and in fact, the galaxy, from his perspective, from his points of entry and activity. These are the thousands of places into which his particular ray has extended and is working. Like angels, the Ray Masters can multiply themselves into thousands of copies and be present simultaneously at many places, appearing before many people in different locations at the same time.

In fact, the Ray Masters each have their own dedicated temples or openings into the Earth plane throughout the planet, and I saw a few of these, such as Newgrange in Ireland (for Apollo), Ephesus in Turkey (for Artemis-Kuthumi), Mont-Royal in Montreal, Quebec (for Hilarion), and the Parthenon in Athens (for Pallas Athena). They were like reservoirs in which the Ray Masters pooled their specific energy, presence, and consciousness, releasing small amounts into the landscape through the energy lines at various times.

There were other gods to meet, gods with different functions and residences, and over the years Blaise facilitated my entry into their realms. The next one first caught my interest when I kept seeing this lovely dancing girl inside a piece of Indian music. I certainly was not the first to be entranced by an apparition of a charming spirit dancer beheld in the refrains of music, but for a while I had no frame of reference for what I was seeing.

Every time I listened to one specific piece of Indian music (a raga played on a guitar) I saw her, and she saw me. Of the 'her' in question all I can say is that she looked like a winsome young Hindu woman of anywhere from 16 to 20, and she loved to dance. I could easily have gone off with her, or spent the day and night watching her dance, if I knew how to get to where she was.

It's funny, but one of my favorite characters in the Arthur myth did know how to get there. Merlin, King Arthur's magus. The stories say that young Vivienne le Fay, also called Nimuë, and sometimes equated with the enigmatic Lady of the Lake, lured him with her beauty, youth, and talents into an enchanted realm, then sealed him up under a heavy stone slab, keeping him out of our world. Or she locked him in his own crystal cave. Other versions of the story say Merlin got stuck in an apple tree and had only his pet pig to converse with in his isolation. Perhaps.

But by this point I'd learned not to take the stories at face value, and I'd learned the name of that dancing girl: *Apsara*. Actually that's the group name, *Apsaras*, the celestial maidens who dance to the intoxicating music of the *Gandharvas*. The Apsaras are said to be beautiful, fairylike beings whose charms bewitched all the hosts of Heaven; some say they were created solely to tempt humans so as to distract them from their spiritual path, to prevent them from gaining so much saintliness that they would rival the gods in their purity.

I was sitting at the base of Glastonbury Tor one day, not doing much of anything, just lollygaging on the grass, watching the clouds, chewing on straw. For a second, I saw that *Apsara* from the music dash past me, through the white archway over the dragon, and into an expansive orchard beyond. I decided to follow her.

I'd already made friends with this dragon so slipping past the big beast was not difficult. I entered the orchards, the trees laden with golden apples. The Tor is much bigger in this level of reality, more like a considerable mountain. Its slopes all the way to the top were covered with lovely apple trees with golden fruits and silver leaves. Each apple looks like a living, sparkling sun.

At the peak of the Tor stood a massive white marble palace shaped like a four-leafed clover. Inside innumerable people were feasting, laughing, talking, enjoying the music and dancers. Numerous fountains spumed water; statues of Ganesh, the elephant-headed god abounded; reflecting pools girted with lilies were everywhere – the place was unrelievedly, deliciously, perfectly opulent. Its essence is delight.

It's like a genteel cocktail party in Heaven. If this place rented out rooms, I'd book one today and stay a year, I thought. It seemed like the ideal place for reverie, fantasy, creativity, for wishing for one's heart's desires. It felt to me as if I were reclining on a fabulous celestial swan boat gliding through the starfields.

That suddenly brought back a memory from childhood that until that moment I didn't know I'd ever registered in consciousness. I was six, at recess, out in the large field next to my elementary school, a three story brick building. An angelic conveyance much like a magnificently huge swan boat sailed over the school and stopped long enough for me to climb aboard. Winged horses pulled the pleasure yacht which was packed with angels and other delightful beings. The boat itself seemed to be a swan of light, as if the constellation of Cygnus had grown suddenly, inexplicably animate and was in service to this angelic party.

Meanwhile, the musicians – these were the Gandharvas, and there were thousands of them – drifted through the many spacious rooms of this palace playing flutes. Except for not having blue skin, they all looked like Krishna, shockingly healthy, pure, radiant, with pearly white crowns rising from their foreheads in tiers. The Gandharvas are known as the fragrances or celestial harmonies, the angels of song who reveal the secrets of Heaven and the divine truth, and they are connected with Vac, the Hindu goddess of speech.

In some way I couldn't explain it seemed to me their music was structuring reality, generating the elementary vibratory field that holds our physical, mundane reality together, and they were all enjoying doing this.

As for the golden apples, well, you don't eat them so much as enter them. You enter their field as you would an enclosed or defined higher dimensional space. I found myself inside a tall, arching chamber. As I walked through this chamber – through the apple, technically – the shape of the interior space kept changing, assuming new forms.

One form resembled a huge hollow golden head, or perhaps the inside of a hot air balloon with a small pale golden circle or seed set in a base in the floor directly under it. This hollow golden head (or hot air balloon – shall we amuse ourselves by proposing the gods are fatuous?) fits over my head like a nimbus and fills my consciousness – that is, my field of awareness *here* – with gold. The golden light is so intense, it so saturates my awareness, that it pops and disappears and I am shifted to another space.

Perhaps the golden apple is an induction device, or perhaps I fell asleep and missed the good bits. 'The fruits of spiritual practice are often called traditionally in certain cultures of the Middle East and Western Europe apples of insight,' said Blaise. 'These apples are fruits sometimes gained at an inner astral plane. Each apple is a stroke of wisdom. They are the keys that can sometime corrupt the practice of true spirituality as shown in the myths of the Garden of Eden, the golden halls of Ogygia, and the Garden of the Hesperides.'

As for Merlin, 'he helped to create the Cabala as you know it,' Blaise added. 'Think of the apple tree as Cabala's Tree of Life. Within the system in which you are being trained, there are paradises in which adepts get stuck.'

And Nimuë? 'The Lady of the Lake is a figure of authority. She is the guardian of the astral realms from the lowest astral rubbish to the highest astral orders. Nimuë is one of three aspects of this guardian.'

Whatever the golden apple truly is, it sheds a new possibility on the meaning of the famous 'golden bough' by which the classical heroes, notably Aeneas, were admitted into the Underworld. Other mythic heroes would return from the Land of the Living, or the Irish paradise world, *Emain Ablach*, or the Celtic Avalon, with a golden apple as a trophy of their otherworldly adventures.

For it was Avalon, the legendary Summer Country, into which I had dashed, following the Muse, as it were, in the guise of a lovely dancing maiden, the *Apsara*. Avalon, that same land of enchantment into which the besotted Merlin was led, and Avalon, that land of rest, rejuvenation, and patient *waiting* into which the mortally wounded King Arthur was ferried after his disastrous battle with Mortred, his 'bastard' son, at Camlann, according to Thomas Malory's version of the story.

Waiting — they wait in the sense that the myths say King Arthur and his knights are sleeping even today in the hollow hills, waiting for that summons from our world to leave Avalon and return to Logres, the Wounded Fisher King's blasted land, where we — and he — live and suffer and wait for healing.

But there was more to Avalon, a lot more. For one, the name itself is an invocation to the realm it describes. The word *Avalon* is a phonic key that opens the door to perception of the astral plane. Chant it quietly for twenty minutes every day for a few days and see what happens.

For another, Avalon is a metaphysically encoded word, a word that carries a secret, a description. Take out the two letters *al*, and you get *nova*, a star which suddenly increases its light and energy output tremendously. As for *al*, that is the pre-eminent god-name and suffix in Hebrew angelologies, as in Mich*al*el, Gabriel, Raphael, and in *Al*bion, and for good reason: it refers to the creative forms of the Elohim (or *Al*ohim), the prime creator gods of world and humanity. Avalon — unlimited co-creativity

within the expanding star. The Lake of endless possibi-
lities, of the limitless luxury of light.

'*Al*,' said Blaise, 'is the essence of creation. It is the in-drawn
breath, the birthing of something, the point of light, the star,
the essence of Mind, the forgiveness in [He] forgave. The
Elohim are the forms of *Al*, the projections, entities, or forms
which are acceptable to conscious perception of this essence.'

But it still doesn't end there. Even the planet is implicated in
the apple of Avalon. 'The apple has an inner core, two halves,
and a surface that is green and red,' Blaise said. 'That is how
we see your Earth. The apple is from the ultimate inspiration
of the creative divine source and is the ultimate symbol. It is
the closest image of the Earth for us. The apple as a hologram
is the same as the Earth energy web and is a light receptor. It is
also the approximate shape of the zodiacs.'

The apple is also related to an angelic being known as
Sandalphon, described in some detail by William Blake. 'The
Adept Master William Blake was the first for a while to note
the Earth's connection with the being Sandalphon,' Blaise
commented. 'Sandalphon can appear in any material form
though his essence closely resembles or relates to the essential
structure of an apple. As you might guess, this bears on the
Avalon myth.'

Sandalphon is one of the great angelic princes, the master of
heavenly song, and he's said to be one of the tallest angels in
heaven. Standing on Earth, his head reaches heaven – he is a
500 years' walk tall. He gathers the prayers of the faithful,
making a garland of them, and brings them up to Metatron as
a crown of glorious fire and great splendor to be presented to
the Supreme Being.

Not long after my trip to Avalon, Blaise took the three of us to a place seemingly off the Grail map. Russell, Berenice, and me were sitting around the living room, having a cup of tea in the middle part of a Sunday evening when Blaise arrived. Without much of a preamble or monologue, they announced they wished to take us somewhere, if we wished. We did. What we didn't know was we had an appointment, at least in memory, with the Hyperboreans.

'We take you back within the star. We remind you of a room with crystal sides, pale blue in color, with a table of clear quartz. It is a large room with many people in it. If you wish, bring your consciousness within the star to this room. The room is full of light. Feel for the energy in your spine....'

As Blaise inducted or transported us into this other place, I saw a long silvery greenhouse attached to or perhaps morphing into a Greek-style marble temple set alone in a barren landscape. Then we were inside this odd greenhouse. It seemed to be underground, maybe in an abandoned salt mine or inside a high peaked mountain. In any event, it seemed recessed from the rest of the world, arcane, busy, vital.

I had an impression of a large room full of industrious people, leaning over drafting tables, making calculations, studying figures, planning things, like the intellectual core of a successful engineering-architectural firm. For a moment, I was seated at a drafting table, deeply engaged, deeply enjoying my work. I was calculating how many of, I don't know what – something – a local setup could handle without blowing the circuitry. I was working on parameters.

We worked with high concentration inside this drafting office, but I had the feeling there was nobody outside, for hundreds of miles, or at all. No people at all. It was like we were the people hired to set up the party — one of the Great Gatsby's blows in West Egg if you like — and nobody had arrived yet. Weren't even expected for a few days. We had the run of the place to ourselves.

I saw a man juggling a slinky of light behind his head, somehow bouncing it off his neck and occiput like a little beachball. The bouncing created a series of changing geometric shapes. He had a bright red star in his lower back.

'Each person in the room has a task in relation to the Earth energy grid,' Blaise was saying. 'Each has the possibility of completing an inner and outer circuit within the energy matrix. On the crystal table are geodesic solids. Each is made of different minerals. They represent the different energy matrices of the time period of this being, Gaia . . . .'

Then again my attention shifted to examining the curiously all-blue room. I noticed that crystalline table Blaise had pointed out. It looked like a miniature glass version of part of Stonehenge, the two massive uprights, the even bigger lintel straddling the two. It resembled the Greek letter pi — π. The table seemed about twelve feet long and four feet wide, and the more I looked at it, the brighter it grew. Those geodesic solids looked familiar. Yes! They're the Platonic Solids, the cube, tetrahedron, dodecahedron, and the rest. Indispensable to the Earth grid — its essence, really.

'Now you have connected with this room within the star, within yourself. You have accessed it for this incarnation. You may visit it for energy or information as you wish. There is much now that you can access through this experience. We have indicated many different aspects of this room to you in the past. Having now access to it again, you also have the possibility to remember the times you have accessed it before. We leave you to discuss your experiences.'

As usual, we were a bit mystified, flummoxed, and exhilarated by yet another look behind the curtain. 'So what's with this blue room?' I asked. This, incidentally, in later years, became our accustomed way of referring to the place, the Blue Room. 'Well, Russell, what have you got to say for yourself?' I sometimes had to pump old Russell to extract even a few syllables on a topic.

'I saw a fellow holding a spiral tube down at one end of the table. On the table, the geodesic solids were vibrating. Each had its own special type of energy, and its own color. Each was placed, by somebody, didn't see who, really, over or in a hologram of the Earth which was projected over the surface of the crystal table. The guy at the head of the table seemed to control these geometric forms with his mind. He was trying out the effect of placing different solids in different places on the Earth, to see how it changed the overall energy pattern and how it affected consciousness. I noticed all the walls were translucent and vibrant, yet you couldn't see through them.'

Berenice offered her observations. 'There were lots of people standing around in this room, and they all seemed to have red and gold around their heads. Maybe they had red and gold uniforms, too. They also had rather large, elongated ears. One person had a brilliant red light in his backbone. It settled around his sacrum. Some of the others wore green clothes and had a device attached to the top of their head and neck, like a tube of wires. I had the impression they might be trying to program people through tape recorders, or maybe those tube-wire things were a storage mechanism for information needed in the future. Each person stored what they would need later.'

As if listening offstage until we had laid out all the pieces of the mystery so that they could, triumphantly, nonchalantly, Poirotlike, re-enter the room to explain and resolve things in a single masterful reconstruction of the crime scene, Blaise returned. 'Are there any questions about any of this?' Can angels be coy?

'So Blaise, when was this experience in terms of Earth epochs?' I asked.

'This was when the Hyperboreans first established a space within the Earth's crust,' Blaise replied, stunning me in a single sentence. 'It was pre-Lemurian, prior to the first dome presence. The place was a dome in Siberia.'

The reason I was stunned by that single sentence, that single word — Hyperboreans — was that it had been one of those niggling enigmas in my research. God, the Greek historians would be elated to learn this. Only a few of them, like Herodotus, Pliny, Pindar, Pausanias, and Diodorus of Siculus, most notably, made any mention of the Hyperboreans who lived in the far north and to whom the Greeks sent their first fruits as offerings, appeasements, who knows. Apollo was said to regularly sojourn with the Hyperboreans for years on end, no doubt enjoying their music, which they played continuously, and excellent health. Some guy named Abaris the Hyperborean was said to fly around on an arrow. Of course nobody knew what any of this was really about, or if it had any truth.

'From your point of view, Blaise, who were the Hyperboreans?'

'The Hyperboreans were travelers, wanderers. Their origin is lost in time, but they were originally resident within the Pleiades star system. That name means just what you know it as.' (Indeed: the Pleiades, said the Greeks, were the 'wandering ones', from *plein*, 'to sail or wander'.) 'It was a world culture affecting the entire globe at one point, with its culture centered first in Lemuria then subsequently in Atlantis. The epicenter of Hyperborea was what is now the British Isles.'

'What was going on in that room? I asked next.

'Certain Elohim and Hyperboreans were sent here to Earth by the Most High Architect of Supreme Existence to lay down certain energy matrices over the surface of this planet that it might support beings with higher being bodies.'

'In other words, designing the Earth grid at the beginning of the planet?'

'Correct. It is a multidimensional and interdependent pattern. Most of it dates back to the time of Hyperborea, or earlier.'

'Please tell us what was that red star in the man's backbone,' said Berenice.

'This was an energy transmission that brought a creative impulse into the inner and outer natures of that being and simultaneously into the planet through one of the geodesic solids on the crystal table. When we said, 'focus on your spines,' he harnessed the creative energies in the group there and transmitted it into one of the icosahedrons for future use.'

'How about the guy juggling the light forms?' I asked.

'This was the being that originally brought or summoned the oroboros dragon impulse around Gaia. He was working with that visualization.'

'What was the crystal table?'

'When you witness something which is inherently inter-dimensional, that penetrates the fourth dimension, then its third dimensional manifestation is always open to discussion. We will say, for now, it is the energy matrix between the archangelic hierarchy of Oriel, Raphael, and Michael.'

We'd barely unpacked our bags from the trip to the Blue Room when a few nights later Blaise showed up with tickets for another outing. As per usual, they revealed nothing about our destination, or why we were going there. Other than to say, 'We wish, if you wish, to take you somewhere you haven't been before. Breathe to the star as Love from Above....'

We breathed. It grew brighter, we were inside it, and suddenly it was moving, as if a vehicle of conveyance, a little faster than light, an angelic *tigle*, like that benevolent traveling soap bubble around Queen Glenda, the Good Queen of the West in *The Wizard of Oz*. We hover above a vast island dominated by a single monumentally large mountain, with numerous other majestically huge peaks surrounding it like jeweled points in a crown.

We descended to ground level. There were hundreds of people around the beach and lots of boats of various types, sizes, and capacities, moored at the harbor. In fact the range of boats was fantastic, from ancient Celtic coracles to futuristic transparent globes. I noted a golden dome under which stood a building made of eight globes, each a different color, piled in several layers. The blue globe interested me, so I entered. Immediately I was being cleansed like a car in a car wash with bright blue light that flowed and splashed like water. Then I was back at the beach, feeling wonderfully refreshed, even better than I would had I been swimming in the ocean. What ocean, anyway? Where is this place?

'Some call it Mount Meru,' Blaise said when we had seemingly returned to the living room and our bodies at Wick. 'Some call it Mount Analogue. It goes under many names.' Ah: Mount Analogue — Rene Daumal's 'symbolically authentic ultimate symbolic mountain', inaccessible, invisible, protected from human visitation by 'a ring of curvature.' As Mount Meru, the home of all the gods, the entire hierarchy, the singular cosmic mountain for the Earth.

I asked the obvious question. 'How come we got to go there, Blaise?'

'It is for your inspiration in the months to come. And because you're lucky, Grail Knight. It will give you all a firm foundation of spiritual wealth. The temple the Grail Knight visited was a healing temple. Each of you saw your part in the development as it is for this time.'

'I saw a group of people on the beach,' Berenice said, 'as if they — actually, we were part of that group — were waiting for something.'

'Friends of the Sangrail, you have only just begun,' Blaise said. 'You have not even contacted your group yet. You know some members of it but you have not started work together yet. Therefore your position is indeed on the beach.'

'What do you mean by Friends of the Sangrail, Blaise? You mean like-minded people to do with the Grail Quest and all that?'

'Correct. It is a soul group. Such a group involves the same people, but they evolve and change places. Each learns more by being in different relations to one another. Each soul group gathers more information for itself and its component parts by reenactments of the same myth in varying relationships in different cultural settings, by going backwards and forwards in time, and by being able to replay particular settings.'

'You said the 'same myth.' Do you mean the Arthur myth?'

'Yes. There have been fifteen similar periods in world history in which cultures have resonated with this myth system. This means there have been fifteen King Arthurs, not always Celtic, but known in different languages and cultures, such as Tibetan and Mayan. But it is always according to the same archetypal formula. Arthur, the once and future king — remember? Think of it like a wave. An Arthur wave, if you like. Like waves from a radio transmitter they travel from the Arthur vibration through time and space, coming more and less into matter. This is the peak of one such wave now.'

Late that night I was still awake. I had given up trying to find a third side to toss to and finally go to sleep, and I was exhausted from using the two I had. I was thinking of waves. Big waves. Tsunamis. Full of Grail Knights and angels and chalices and round tables and jousters and swords and stars, and King Arthur himself, bright as a sun, cresting continuously, flooding the beach not so much with water but cosmic light. I was surfing the wave, swept up in its undertow, watching calmly from the beach, one of the Knights, angels, jousters, and stars in the breaking wave. All at once.

And just as the wave was about to crash tumultuously on the expectant sand, I was over Mount Meru again, as we had been earlier, before we descended. I saw something I had missed the first time. Surrounding the magnificent peak were six, no, seven — eight similar mountainous points of light, spaced equally in a circle at the outer edge of the cosmic mountain, like satellites or celestial cities.

8

This is the bit where you have to become comfortable around swords.

It all started late one night at a place I'd never been to before called Ivy Thorn Hill. It was a special occasion — namely, the appointment was for 1 a.m. — so I got to drive the Citröen which of course had headlights which my bike doesn't. To be fair to my bike, though, the old Dawes is a lot easier to handle because you don't have to drive left-handed on the wrong side of a road you've never been on and which has no signs or names that I could see.

When I got there, turned off the car lights, got out of the car, and allowed my eyes to adjust to the darkness, it was still pitch black and I couldn't see anything. Except the gnome. Him I could see vividly. He offered his hand, I took it, and he guided me through the brush and brambles down the slope and into the woods, then stopped and pointed to a spot. That's where I was to sit. I had been grumbling a bit about how come I always had to do these assignments, especially and often late at night, and how Russell and Berenice got to sleep. And where are all the other Grail Knights anyway? The Brits would call this whinging.

To be fair to Blaise, this was the fall equinox and I guess they can't be blamed for it happening at 1.45 in the morning. They also said, but I didn't understand it at the time, that Russell and Berenice would be joining me in their dream or sleep bodies. Blaise also gave me a little speech to rehearse. It was, actually, a bit uncharacteristic of Blaise, a little more florid than their usual style, and certainly more formal than my wise-guy preferences in diction. Here's how it went: 'O Knights of the Grail. O Knights of the Grail. Be with me now. The time is right for a blessing to come on. I write a book. Help me to sharpen my sword that I may speak the truth from this, the Ivy Thorn.'

I was to say this aloud at least eight times as soon as the equinox kicked in. I told Mattingley, my gnome friend, rather sternly, not to laugh at me as I said it. To pass the time, I practiced one of the Blaise tricks I'd recently learned. You put your attention on the Blazing Star at your belly and see it in the center of a big pale blue sphere. You breathe to your star until it gets gigantic, so big it engulfs you like a supernova, and it's gone and you're in it.

Then you're in this empty vast pale blue sphere. You pretend you're lying on your back in a salt water lagoon in the South Pacific and that you are the entire blue sphere. You allow the bottom half of the sphere to become a shallow concave blue dish or saucer. Then you lay this blue dish under something, like a house, a hill, a mountain, a sacred site, a standing stone, a whining Grail Knight and indifferent gnome in the middle of the woods on a dark night in September.

Blaise had once given me a glimpse of the Earth in its earliest days, after the Hyperboreans had completed their grid installations. The planet was floriated in blue dishes — many thousands of them blooming on the Earth like morning glories, which they were in a poetic sense, because that was the morning of the world and the dishes were a glorious sight.

They were also essential to the integrity of the energy exchanges on the planet, and they still are.

'To be receptive, the blue bowl catches the light from above,' said Blaise. 'Each blue dish is a receptor of cosmic rays coming to this planet, linking to the dome caps which have the Master Rays connected to them, making a circuit within the grid. The fourteen rays penetrate the dome and are dripped into the bowl. The blue dishes or bowls are the receptacles for all that has been in the past and all that will be in the future.'

It was another example of how something you think is part of your personal practice, specific to your Grail Quest, turns out to benefit the planet. It starts to benefit the planet the minute you can do it. 'When after considerable practice the blue sphere is able to open and receive, it becomes the blue bowl.'

It was showtime. A huge stillness flushed the woods like the hush before a stage performance. I saw Russell and Berenice arrive by Blaise taxi, and I was amused to see they were not in their pajamas but respectably attired for the Ivy Thorn show. Lots of Blaises arrived in fact, probably in the thousands. Then I saw the Archangel Michael in the midst of a large circle of men and women, including me, Russell, and Berenice.

We walked down a staircase of golden steps, then passed through a golden courtyard into a temple made of gold, then through that into a vast open space. We were in some kind of amphitheater filled with lots and lots of faces, none of which I recognized yet all of whom I sensed were unintroduced colleagues. At last. Grail Knights!

Michael raised his sword in our midst, and this was the cue for all of us to upraise ours. I was a little nonplussed when I compared my sword to Michael's. The tip of my sword blazed impressively with light, but the edge was blunt, soft and ineffectual like a butter knife. Then either we all pulled out our swords again or I rewound the scene of my having just withdrawn my sword and saw that I had pulled it out of a stone in my chest as easily as pulling a knife out of butter.

There it was again, that gesture: we pull the sword out of the stone in our chest, then brandish the sword aloft, copying Michael's gesture. We obliging Friends of the Sangrail did this a few more times, then on the last go, an explosion of rainbow light enveloped all of us and the thousands of swords. It felt like we were at a company party, or a stockholder's meeting, and were toasting the chairman of the board who had made us all rich last year. Hail Michael, chief patron and protector of Grail Knights. Hail Michael, rich in Grails.

It was quite a sight, the thousands of Grail Knights, swords upraised under a rainbow rain of light, making a nimbus around the towering archangel. Somehow all of us pulling the sword out of the stone in our chests has produced the round table, as if the amphitheater was transformed in an eyeblink, in a single decisive sword-brandishing, into a vast round table big enough for us all. All our swords for a moment blend with Michael's magnificent sword, then we get them back. Mine is as if reforged, its tip diamond sharp and gleaming. Then we hammer our sword edges against Michael as if he were an anvil. When we finish, he dubs each of us with his sword, as if conferring knighthood afresh.

There is a pause as we sit in this celestial tableau of knights and sponsors. Then a female figure of astounding beauty and majesty appears in our midst, seemingly in the center of the round table. Her form is robed in emerald, her face is veiled, and her being exudes warmth and love. I don't know who she is: the Lady of the Lake? Lady Venus? Dante's Beatrice? The Gnostics' Sophia?

(You end up wishing, and you know it's jejune to ask it, that these celestial beings would, at least for a while, wear clearly readable name tags for the neophytes like me to make correct identifications. I've spoken to Blaise about this.) The emerald-robed figure anoints our swords with what looks like an emerald wand. The tips of all our swords flush a brilliant emerald green in response, and then the event is over.

I drive home elated that I have finally met some colleagues, even if they come from God knows where around the planet and I didn't get any addresses. I wondered if any of them remembered the Blue Room; were with us on the beach at Mount Meru; found Blaise funny . . . . Would I ever meet them in person?

The next evening when Blaise visited, it was clear they had brought a new hoop they wished us to jump through. 'We come as a diamond point of light surrounded by the sapphire blue of Christed consciousness, encircled in gold, the ray of solar splendor, and all of this within the stable sphere of consciousness. We bring amid you the Sword in the Stone. Breathe as Love from Above to this, if you wish.'

Five minutes passed in silence, then Blaise said, 'Now discuss this among yourselves, if you wish, until we return.'

I went first. 'There was a sword pointed straight at the diamond, then the diamond became a rectangular slab of grey stone, like a big piece of unshaped stone a sculptor would start to sculpt something with. Like a Grail bowl. There was a concave spot on the side of this stone, a little shallow depression. The sword was half inserted into this. Then I realized all of this was in my heart chakra, and the stone had become the round table, but the sword was still in it, half way. Or half pulled out, depending on how you look at it. The sword came out and drifted in space in front of me. The round table disappeared and in its place was a golden infant.'

'The sword in the stone was a golden blade,' Berenice began. 'Then the sword and stone grew bigger and so much brighter until the sword was removed. An angel held it, kneeling. The hilt was at his brow and the tip touched the ground. Another angel faced him, and he held something – I'm not sure, maybe a book, or something round, or perhaps a baby.'

'I saw a stone but it looked like an egg,' said Russell. 'Inside it was a golden sword with jewels on its handle – a ruby and two emeralds, I think. The scabbard and the sword hilt were inside my body, vertically. I noticed my heart center was shaped like a stone, and in it, somehow, was a tiny golden child. It had a sword through its head and middle section, coming down from the top. An angel appeared and dubbed a man with this same sword, and all of this took place in a pale green light, something like the emerald sheen you saw at Ivy Thorn, Grail Knight.'

This did the trick for Blaise who seemed to be waiting politely in the eaves until we had shared our impressions. They were among us again at once. 'Good. Each aspect you have each revealed is your information given to you at Ivy Thorn. You were present there by your will to witness an event in consciousness. We revealed the Sword in the Stone. Each of you had a different aspect revealed, and each of you will remember more of this aspect as time goes by. This is the first time we have revealed the nature of the Sword in the Stone.'

The Sword in the Stone as many of you may know is high end myth, prime Grail real estate. The basic story goes like this: King Uther Pendragon dies, and the way to get the next Celtic king is to have him draw a sword out of a stone. Merlin has contrived the test because he knows who the designated king will be. Arthur of course, who happens to be Pendragon's son, though he was raised in obscurity and oblivious of his lineage. Arthur is young, still in the jackanapes category, but he pulls out the sword effortlessly, almost by mistake, so casually as to barely remark upon the marvel of his deed, and becomes king.

I knew I had more sword business at Ivy Thorn so I returned there in the daylight a couple days later. Mattingley is there to greet me and he shows me to the same spot where I previously sat in the dark. I do the Blaise preliminaries: let the star go supernova, float in the saltwater sea of the blue sphere, and lay down a blue dish under the hill like slipping a saucer under a tea cup. I'm the saucer.

Then I allow the six-sided, double-terminated emerald to appear as it were above me, because I am, for the moment, a shallow blue dish. I'm looking straight up the sides of this towering, sparkling, skyscraping emerald set like a jewel in the center of the blue dish. I allow my attention to float up to one of the facets of the emerald and pass through it as if it is only a curtain of light. Inside is a vast open space, like a Gothic cathedral, but hundreds of times bigger.

A figure suddenly stands before me, a male; tall, large, regal, kingly. He has a gold crown, his eyes sparkle, his white hair is clipped short, he bears in one hand a shield on which the Pendragon image is emblazoned – rearing dragon encased in lilac flames – and the image of the Mother of Christ with infant, and in the other hand a long glinting sword, also encased in lilac flames, or perhaps emitting them. In his chest I see a golden Grail chalice, and inside the Grail stands the Christ in human form, crowned, looking at me.

Then two things happened in quick succession. The man held a mirror before me and I saw myself in it, a bit older but sporting the same regalia as this figure. Then he lowered the mirror and shoved his sword into my chest, right into the Grail bowl. I gasped, saw the brilliant flash of light, felt something quicken in there, and then it was over and I was back at Ivy Thorn Hill. But I heard something in that milli-second after the sword went in and I returned: *Go to Megrez.*

The directive would have been even more enigmatic if I had not already known that Megrez is one of the stars in the Big Dipper, also called Ursa Major. In the familiar image of the seven-starred dipper, Megrez, from the Arabic *Al Maghrez* ('Root of the Tail'), is the star at the junction of the dipper and handle.

The star is said to rule the other six stars in the constella-tion, all seven of which are traditionally known, at least in India, as the Seven Rishis or in China as the Seven Elders or the Purple Forbidden Enclosure of the Celestial Emperor. We – meaning our little Blaise group and the Blaises – know them as the home of the fourteen Ray Masters. But Megrez is 65 light years from Earth, so how am I supposed to get to Megrez?

As clever as I thought I was about star names, I had for-gotten one bit. Russell pointed it out. Another name for the Big

Dipper, especially in the British Isles, is Arthur's Wain. As in King Arthur. Where do you go for the epicenter of Arthur in England? You go to where he was born: Tintagel in Cornwall. Then the rest of the linkage fell into place: Tintagel must be the Earth dome for Megrez. As Russell and I exchanged this thought, we could see Blaise nodding, lots of Blaises, hundreds of angelic heads nodding affirmatively at our insight.

The three of us drove down to Tintagel the next day. It's a little tourist town on the western tip of Cornwall, and the Arthurian part is a cluster of stone ruins out on a windy promontory barely accessible these days up a steep, wet, and potentially perilous series of steps carved into the abrupt hillside. The myths say Arthur was born here, conceived by King Uther and his mistress, Igrayne, as a result of machinations by Merlin who saw the future and took steps to make sure it happened, namely, that Arthur would one day be King of Britain.

The assignment is simple: I am to circumambulate the Tintagel headland for several hours every day. I'm accompanied by a host of gnomes and Blaises so it's more like a parade than a solitary stroll. And I feel another presence with me continuously: strong, large, sunny, confident, masterly, infinitely creative, as if the crowned figure with sword and shield from Ivy Thorn were with me. I noticed other things at Tintagel: a dragon, like the one at Walmsgate, a cosmic egg, like the one at Worley Hill, and of course the dome overhead for Megrez. But I wasn't there to do anything with them, at least not on this trip.

At one point, the Elohim appeared. There must have been twenty of them standing unperturbed in the Atlantic Ocean making a towering crescent around the Tintagel headland, each Elohim angel hundreds of feet tall. One of them presented me with a sword, its blade adamant, its handle glinting with jewels. I take the sword, and in another body made of light and much taller and larger, stand in the middle of the headland and hold the sword aloft. Excalibur.

I had a fleeting vision of sitting at a stone circle nearby called the Merry Maidens, which comprises 19 stones in a circle 78 feet in diameter. We had stopped there for an hour before arriving at Tintagel. The story goes that nineteen maidens had been turned to stone for dancing on the Sabbath, but I think the Maidens were Elohim. I see the stones become beacons of light, flashing laser beams into my head from all directions. I think their dance had something to do with the crown chakra, with producing clairvoyance.

My head, now golden with a silver crown, expands to be the size of the stone circle; the contents of the circle itself and the stones are like laurel leaves around my skull. The rest of my body, seemingly underground, beneath the circle, is much larger now, no longer physical, but rather a cone of purple light through which rises like a barber pole a caduceus of gold and silver with a pillar of pure light straight up its middle. The Merry Maidens dance inside my cranium, pulsating, strobing, creating a meshwork of celestial light, a grid for *seeing*.

It was as if the stones, the Merry Maidens themselves, had walked overland to stand in the ocean as the Elohim to present me with this sword. From out of the inside ceiling of the dome came lights of many different colors, like rain, like swooping swallows, like arrows, creating a framework around the sword, almost a scabbard of moving, weaving multihued light.

It was the Ray Masters, I was sure of it, but what were they doing?

I flashed on a curious exchange in *Le Morte d'Arthur* where Merlin questions the young Arthur on the sword and the scabbard, asking the youth which he thought was most valuable. Arthur said the sword, but Merlin said, no, it is the scabbard, which, appropriately, was the part Morgan le Faye stole when she was trying to make trouble for Arthur, her brother. Later Blaise clarified the matter of Tintagel, the scabbard, Arthur, and the sword, when they gave a three word definition of the place name, Tintagel: *Tints of Angels*. Ah. The Ray Masters. The tinted ones.

Arthur claims his sword by degree, Blaise told me. 'Each aspect of the Round Table as it is revealed within its various tints and hues reveals something for the insight to be gained. Excalibur is the symbol of insight. It is a Gnostic word which means insight. It is the point at which human insight is able to perceive the angelic realms. Excalibur is also a mantric sound. The Pendragon is the force that surrounds the sword.'

'Well, Blaise, why do they say King Arthur was *born* at Tintagel?'

'Arthur in the etheric and astral sphere of Gaia is always present there to be birthed. Arthur is the element of growth which is governed by higher energies and linked to Gaia.'

'What about Arthur? What's your take on him?'

'Arthur is between Adam and Man. His name means 'Sun-Star.' Arthur came from the Great Bear but he was their ruler. Arthur was the physical manifestation of the Christ impulse within the tradition of the warrior. Now Arthur is the point in the metamorphosis of the psyche that balances the twelve aspects of the self from the fourteen rays of the Great Bear. King Arthur is a collective image of something transcendent between the Christ and the warrior tradition. It is the beginnings of the upright path, the path of those who are prepared to stand up for what they believe in.'

'Will I ever meet King Arthur?'

This question brought down the house, and the Blaises retreated from the scene in a flurry – dare I say, a fit – of laughter. Some weeks later I'd get the joke.

A few nights later back at Wick Blaise returned with a visualization. The topic was swords, especially Excalibur. 'The sword here is insight, the penetrative aspect of the air element, that which is closest to the spirit. At that time Excalibur came as a particular form of penetration and insight. It came after many generations of usage of a particular practice for a particular purpose, and was given to Arthur by Merlin.'

Then Blaise gave us Excalibur, or at least its blueprints. Like the Grail, you *start* with the sword, or the Grail, then learn how to use it and make it your own.

Visualize a sword pointing down through the top of your head. The sword tip touches the base of your spine. The sword rests inside a jeweled scabbard, and its points, which contain the sword's handle, come out at your shoulders. 'This is the means of self-defense and protection,' Blaise said.

There is also an activating force, which is another sword. This sword's handle sits at the base of your spine, in your pelvis, the top point of its blade passes up through your spine to just above your head. It has no scabbard. The two swords are parallel to each other, one facing up, the other pointing down. Finally, surround the whole of this image of two swords with a lilac flame. 'It is the flame of transmutation that also lies above the Grail bowl,' said Blaise. As they told me at Tintagel, lilac flames burning around Excalibur is the Pendragon.

'We hold the sword above you, pointing down your spine. We point the sword towards your heart. It lies in front of you. You have a sword in your right hand. Above, reaching from out of a cloud, a hand offers you a sword. All these are different perceptions at different levels of different aspects of Excalibur.

'For instance, the hand holding the sword out of the clouds is the root of the power of air. When the sword is held in your right hand, it is the sword of intellect. When it runs down your spine, it is the sword of healing and transmuting, the clear channel before the kundalini rises. When it points to the heart it is the sword of detachment.'

I worked with this image for some weeks, pulling out my sword, flashing it around for good effect, poking it into things, putting my attention at its tip as an aid to clairvoyance and inserting myself into objects, ideas, places. At times I thought of myself as a pincushion, a repository of swords inserted at all angles. I wondered how I was able to pass through doorways with all the swords in me. No doubt the gnomes found it amusing. They're happy with just one sword, as maybe I should be, that lovely heart-shaped green gnome sword I got from the gnome king, but here's this ambitious Grail Knight with six armsful of swords.

I mentioned the Blaise laugh heard clear across the galaxy when I asked if I'd ever meet King Arthur. I came to Glastonbury looking for Arthur. It's as if I woke up one morning in the United States and had to know who he was, why he kept showing up in so many stories, why he was the once and future king. It made no sense at all, but I felt my life depended on it, on finding that answer.

For a while, in the early days I spent in Glastonbury, it was as if I were tunneling diligently, feverishly, eagerly, chipping away at the hard rock of tradition, history, speculation, distortion to reach the real, living truth of Arthur. In some inexplicable but encouraging way, I sensed that Arthur, for his own arcane reasons, was similarly tunneling towards me, and that one day, our shovels would clang as they made contact. There he'd be, and there I'd be, and the search would be over, and I'd *know*.

There's an old story in the Grail literature that King Arthur once stayed in Glastonbury, on Wearyall Hill, of all places, and was invited three times by an angel to visit Beckery Chapel just a little distance beyond the western base of the hill. Once a small chapel dedicated to the Irish saint Bridget was said to stand at the small mound in the back of Glastonbury called Beckery.

It was known locally as Little Ireland and St. Bride's Island, by the Saxon name, *Beokeri*, and also as Bee-Keeper's Island, which might have derived from *Becceriu* or *Eo Beocere*. Today, physically there is nothing there at all, certainly no bees or keepers, just tussocks that are treacherous to walk across and the town sewage works across the street from an abandoned sheep skin factory. Almost nobody comes down here, certainly none of the sacred sites tours of the town, and it's barely on the Glastonbury maps. Even so, it's one of Glastonbury's most important places.

The story goes that on the third nudging from the angelic

emissary, Arthur finally roused himself at dawn to sit in Beckery Chapel. He entered and found a holy place 'adorned beyond compare,' as the 13th century *The High History of the Holy Grail* recounts. The Virgin Mary appeared before Arthur, bearing the infant Jesus in her arms, and presented the divine child to the priest at the altar.

The priest ate the Christ child as he would the Host, and as soon as Communion was finished, the Christ child reappeared hale and whole on the altar, 'unharmed and entire, the spotless paschal Lamb.' Mary awarded the astonished Arthur a crystal cross in commemoration of his witnessing the divine office and the Mystery of the Eucharist. Arthur left Beckery 'mightily rejoiced' and 'visited by manifold joy,' so much so that he immediately changed his armorial bearings to include a silver cross and an image of the Virgin Mary and Christ child.

Early one morning, as a result of a nudge by Blaise, I set out for St. Bride's Island to meet the Bee-Keeper. It was just before dawn as I sat down on the dewy tussocks, but I could make out the filmy outline of a white chapel, either the ghost of the original physical one or its astral counterpart. Inside the chapel are four golden candles, lit and set into tall candlestick holders. Each of the four candles burns at one corner of a sarcophagus shaped like a human body. Behind the sarcophagus is a giant wall hanging, a *bas-relief* of some kind, seemingly in hammered gold, of a rearing dragon framed by a golden sun. But it was the woman who riveted my attention.

Honestly my first impression was right out of J.R.R. Tolkien, when he first introduces one of his near celestial women to a character, such as Arwen, King Aragorn's intended bride or Galadriel, Queen of the Elves at Rivendell. Or maybe I should invoke The Lady, the hushed humble perception of the celestial and luminous female figure that the adolescent seer, Bernadette Soubirous of Lourdes first beheld in the grotto.

A figure more than human, almost godly, but still seemingly approachable by humans of either gender who don't mind a little ravishment — her dark hair was tied in a bun under a Moon-white bonnet with slender chin straps. Her sequined white gown flowed like the Milky Way down to her ankles. A gold crown rested on her head, while her eyes were dark, animate, loving, wise, pools of knowing beyond me. I don't know if she talks to me or not, but somehow I sense her voice sounds like the buzzing of bees.

She gestures for me to climb into the sarcophagus. I do and she closes the lid. Sometime later she opens it and I leave and go home awed, stunned perhaps, in a way I can't explain.

I knew I hadn't stayed awake during much of my Bee-Keeper's Island vision, and so did Blaise, so they asked me to return to the island in a few days. The celestial woman was there again, but what I had taken to be a modest white chapel was this time a substantial white marble temple with a huge recess in its center, much like an indoor Olympic-size swimming pool.

In the center of this dry pool is a golden wheel with sixteen spokes that radiate out to the sides of the enclosure. In the exact center of the golden wheel was the sarcophagus. Except you could also interpret this shape as a Christian cross, as in the Crucifixion, as a Round Table with hand and leg straps. In any event, you lie in the body-contoured hollow and await the experience which I assure you is not one of torture but illumination.

I sensed a stream of energy, laser-focussed, was piercing me, particularly my solar plexus and heart centers, coming down from above. It was as if a golden blade were steadily, deeply, seemingly perpetually, piercing my chest, infusing it with light. It's an intense yellow, gold, orange, and combinations of these colors, flushing in waves or pulses of color. There is a golden-yellow bore, spindle, or pin the height of the silo, and it spins rapidly inside the silo.

Now I'm inside this golden spindle as it rotates ever faster, and I become one with it. I am like a corkscrew, drilling the land with golden light. 'You are a living solar cell,' Blaise says. Then just before it's all over, I see that face again, more Celtic than before, the older man with sword, shield, crown, and, finally, I know who it is. Arthur. *King* Arthur. King of the Sun.

Like a man momentarily giddy with insight and bereft of manners, I speak out loud, to the celestial woman, to Blaise, to anybody listening, what I've discovered. Arthur not only initiates you by inserting his sword in your chest, he is the sword. The Arthur current is the Arthur sword, and Arthur and sword are one, as far as Grail Knights go. Arthur comes from the Sun. He is the King of the Sun. The sword is the Arthur stream being born in you, and you are the stone into which Arthur plunges. Arthur *is* the sword. The Arthur current creates the sword in you, and when the sword comes out, the stone disappears and the Round Table is born. . . .

I left Beckery that morning a little dizzy — some would say overwrought — with revelations. But it didn't last long. The next day I realized how much I didn't understand about this experience, where all the holes were in my new theory of the Grail Mysteries. Anticipating this, Blaise had scheduled a lengthy debriefing for me that evening and they tactfully refrained from referring to my madman on St. Bride's Island episode.

I started with the easy stuff. 'Blaise, who was that gorgeous woman?'

'Someone important to you, in fact, to all of you and your work. Her name is Nada, Master Lady Nada. Her name means 'sound.' She is master of one of the celestial rays of the Great Bear, and as the Magdalene worked closely with the Christ during his Earth mission. You could say she administers Beckery, and sites similar to that, and the process associated with them.'

'What was the spinning golden bore I experienced? Somehow it was connected to King Arthur at Beckery.'

'We are pleased you have made this identification,' Blaise answered. 'The Solar Logos was present at one period of time within that dome. What you describe as the spinning bore is one aspect of Arthur as the Solar Logos.'

'What's the Solar Logos?'

'The Solar Logos is the Word expressed through the Sun. The Word spoken without being filtered. Not words as you speak them, but the Word as sound.'

'Like that odd sound I heard, like somebody chanting Arthur's name?'

'Correct. The syllables *AR-THUR!* are the sounds of the attunement to the Solar Logos, the manifestation of the Word in flesh. The first syllable, *ar*, is the Sun or solar aspect, which means change. The second syllable, *thur*, is the Word or Logos aspect and means growth. Arthur: growth and change.

'The third syllable, HUM. The third is about the grounding of the sword or the direction of Excalibur, the grounding of insight within. When the fourteen rays are earthed into a dome and there are humans within it who have activated the Christ in the Buddha Body, then the Solar Logos can manifest through them.'

'What's the connection with this Arthur current and the Round Table?'

'King Arthur is an aspect of the Cosmic Heart. He is one of twelve of the knights about the Round Table of the Cosmic Logos. The being known as Sanat Kumara is an aspect of the Cosmic Logos as are all six of the Kumaras.'

'*Where* are all these guys, Blaise?'

'The seat of the Cosmic Logos is at the Great Bear. The star Sirius focussed the energy from the Great White Lodge on Sirius before it came to Earth. The energy of the Great White Lodge originated within the Great Bear and was first focussed within Sirius. Then after its focus and the beings within the Sirius system became sufficiently developed, the focus of the White Brotherhood or Lodge moved to Gaia.'

It occurred to me that maybe all this business of a Cosmic and Solar Logos had an application in the landscape, maybe even at Beckery. So I asked Blaise.

'If you have a temple that has all seven levels or a complete system of chakras, you could call this the Cosmic Logos. At the heart of the Cosmic Logos there is the Solar Logos, spreading between the heart and solar plexus centers. That too is a complete system with its own Cosmic Logos and Solar Logos within it. Basically, just imagine whenever you think in terms of scale, that there are three aspects. First, the material, physical Earth. Second, the solar, Christ, transcendent Sun. Third, the cosmic, Holy Ghost or Father. All temples have these three aspects.'

It didn't seem likely to me that I'd get much sleep that night. I was buzzed, wide-awake, ready for more. Blaise has that effect on you. You can easily spend most of the night following a visit in a kind of hyper-awake state, happy, clear, *ready* — as if you could figure out the next three cosmic mysteries to come along. That particular night around 3.30 a.m., with no interest in sleeping in sight for me, it was as if a door into the deep past suddenly swung open, and there was a vista of the Earth's antique geomythic landscape.

My attention was drawn first to a golden man of considerable height. In fact, what height he was I couldn't tell. The height was more an impression of stature and presence. He was, let's say, ten feet tall, entirely golden, as if he wore a skin-tight suit of golden armor, crowned, bearing a sword and shield. It was as if the Sun were shining out into the world from within a man; so bright a Sun that it illuminated every cell in his body, flushing it golden, radiant, burning. A Sun in the form of a golden man.

Then I was with him and I also was him, and he pointed to a golden mound in the center of a huge circle of standing stones, the largest I'd ever seen. Inside the mound was the beginning of what proved to be an inward-winding spiral. I followed it around until it wound itself into a central chamber which was intensely golden and with a much higher domed ceiling than I would have thought possible given the apparent outer size of the structure.

Standing before me was a griffin, lion-torsoed, eagle-faced and winged. At his feet a heap of molten living gold, like puddles of congealed sunlight. I remembered the baffling comment by one of the classical authors that the griffins guarded the gold of the Hyperboreans. You read it, know it means something important, but can't for your life figure out what that is.

Now here was the answer in front of me. The griffins guarded the gold of the Hyperboreans. The griffin offered me a handful of this living gold. I daub my brow and crown and back of the neck with the gold, and suddenly it's turned into a lovely golden helmet.

Then it conveyed the thought that it was the oldest creature on the Earth, put there by the Pleiadians in the morning of the world to guard the wisdom in the grid. I understood from the griffin that during the Hyperborean days, the griffins were designated the guardians of the gold, which is to say, the wisdom encoded in the geomythic matrix as well as in the temples of Hyperborea.

The griffin pointed to one of the round golden walls of his chamber. It was like looking into another world, another level of reality. I stepped into it. I walked into a pale gray-green land, a light green without any yellow in it. There was a green stone of this same color with a *bas-relief* image on it of a griffin with a white pyramid at its brow. I entered this pyramid and found myself standing on a cliff overlooking a vast starfield extending in all directions around me. In an odd but exhilarating flash of understanding I realize I am a star in this starfield.

I see a figure seated in meditation out in this pale gray-green landscape. I'm taken aback by the impression that it's myself, in a different body, in fact, a different *kind* of body, with a bigger head, more luminous torso, and no hair.

Now I am this other me, meditating in a pale green world, my awareness extended throughout this planet and onto other planets as well; Earth, for one. I am seated on a small depression in the ground in a circle a few feet across. A pillar of light arises from the base of this tiny circle like an illuminated tree. I am this tree and I reside inside it; perhaps the light pillar is just another body form.

It's a queer, unsettling feeling, but this me on this olive-hued world is in connection with still other versions of itself, mostly on the Earth. I see one in Peru; one in Greece; another in Mexico; one in England. Each of these 'copies' is similarly seated inside a column of light rooted in a small circle in the landscape.

It's a special Grail Knight device I call an Earth circle, something Blaise taught me in the beginning days of the Quest and the training, and which I'll tell you more about in a moment. The urgent point I want to make here is that one of these similar points of connection this otherworld me was making was with my Earth circle out in the woods near Wick. My sense of time and space started to spin: What is my primary reality? Where am I right now? Which of these circles is the original one, linking with the others? And what day is it? What eon?

The proverbial rug got yanked out from under me and I experienced myself being in half a dozen places at once. What cheered me, I suppose, was a quip Blaise had once made, knowing, no doubt, it would come in handy one day when I reached maximum perplexity: There never was a rug, Grail Knight.

It didn't stop with six linked Earth circles. I started to see dozens more, and it wasn't always me, or even a semblance of me sitting in them. I saw other men and women — O Knights of the Grail from Ivy Thorn Hill — occupying them.

Then I'm back at the huge stone circle and the griffin is outside, in the center, surrounded by megaliths ten to twenty feet tall. The griffin itself stands at least one hundred feet tall. There is a pale blue dish underlying the stone circle, which must be almost thirty acres in extent. The griffin spreads the living gold like a carpet out over the blue dish so that the gold is thick and resplendent. It rears majestically on the blue-gold dish, his figure framed by billions of stars.

The Earth circle at one level is a simple, straightforward affair. You make a small circular depression in the land, its diameter based on certain body measurements. The gnomes show you where to do it; the archangels give you a light seed to plant in it. Then you grow the circle by breathing Love from Above to it and by meditating in it regularly. The whole thing is not unlike gardening.

All the Grail Knights throughout time have had such a circle, though what else it's been called I've yet to find out; I did once see an Australian Aborigine making a circle in the Outback on the same day I made my first one. I just looked up from my digging and saw the guy on his knees, doing the same thing. So those guys know about the circles. Once when I looked back at the wooded hillside where my first Earth circle resided, I saw hundreds of former circles there, landscape memories of the efforts of my Grail Knight forbears.

Here's what Blaise told me about the Earth circles: 'It is a way for you to ground your consciousness within the Earth sphere. As you create these Earth circles, you harmonize with the Earth and bring your consciousness in line with the Earth and its form. When you harmonize your vibrations with the Earth, then you effectively connect with the subtle energies of the planet.

'When the Earth was created in the beginning, then the energy matrix of the Earth was implicit in every particle. As your consciousness within each particle contains the same energy matrix, then as you evolve consciously, you harmonize with that of the Earth. If you take the circle, and you harmonize your consciousness with that circle, you harmonize with the Earth itself. As the angels wish to communicate with the elementals, it is only possible through humans. It is only through humans that the angels may assist the elementals in healing the grid and loving the Earth.

'The relationship between the body of the Grail Knight and its blueprint at the genetic level has a resonance with the blueprint laid down in the temple of the Earth. When the Grail Knight treads the temple, then a symbiotic relationship is formed that arcs across time and space, seeding the Grail Knight and the Earth with emerald and star and the Source.'

In an almost shocking way, the Earth circle is one of the most direct ways to connect with the Earth and do it some good. To say it's a matter of resonance hints at the connection, but it's much more profound and immediate than that. Blaise said the whole point of the Earth grid matrix — the entire geomythic ball of temple structures – was to emphasize the energy aspect of matter.

'The blueprint for the landscape zodiac is synchronous and symbiotic with the blueprint of the Earth and the genetic structure of the Grail Knight. The relationship between the body of the Grail Knight and its blueprint at the genetic level has a resonance with the blueprint laid down in the temple of the Earth.

'As your consciousness within each particle of your body contains the same energy matrix as the grid, then as you evolve consciously, you harmonize with the Earth. This has repercussions both for you as an individual via your RNA-DNA encoding and for the planet via its coding. Your body measurements are instantly translated into that of the circle. If in the Earth circle you harmonize your consciousness with the circle, you harmonize with the Earth.'

Another benefit you get from an Earth circle is it helps you remember. God, did I want to remember, deep things, events from shockingly long ago, from the beginning of things, stuff the Wounded Fisher King had forgotten. Somehow the circle gives you more traction on deep recall, and I used this circle, and the ones I had in later years, partly for this purpose. I used it to revisit and deepen Grail adventures, to see what I had done in the dark, my dark. To look into subjects, topics, objects, places, relationships, to connect places and experience, even to probe the outer edges of the Akashic Records.

I saw myself in other times, at other Earth circles, with other men and women with Earth circles, and us meeting, congregating regularly in temples. I began to think: why couldn't we do this again? If it worked before, it could work again – it's the once and future idea again, but not just Arthur, but Arthur and all his colleagues, the Knights, the Round Table companions, and Blaise. Camalate.

It's funny but for the next couple of days I couldn't get that old, odd word out of my head. It's as if it were alive, communicating with me, impressing itself upon my awareness, both conscious and subliminal, as if trying to deliver a message to me. The word came to feel like Avalon, mantric, invocatory, bearing secrets and invitations. My attention on this word also seemed to bring Blaise in brighter and closer, as if they were, finally, hearing something they had hoped against hope to one day hear in our cluttered, noisy, multidirectional brains.

'The purpose of Camalate,' Blaise commented, the next time they visited, 'is to encourage, ruthlessly and without mercy, people to uncover and take responsibility for the star they are.' Blaise let us know that there had been 26 such Camalates in the Earth's history, situated in different continents and cultures, and that the Blaises were hoping for a twenty-seventh. I had already remembered two of them, one at Cusco in Peru, another at Mycenae in Greece.

'So Blaise, how come the name Camalate has been buzzing around my head like some kind of mantra I can't turn off or forget?'

'In this word you have a sacred name with numerological correspondences that form patterns of light. These represent a reciprocal matrix that surrounds this cosmic sacred name from a divine source. That name takes on a focus for people who use it. Camalate is the place to which came a lot of people for the purposes of the realization of light, understanding, humility, truth, love, sincerity, spirituality, integrity, and compassion. If, in this context, people come together synchronously, anything is possible, provided those people are working towards a process of individuation.'

As they were leaving us for the evening, Blaise asked us to focus our attention on the star. We did. And at once the star rushed towards us, as if with arms outstretched, ready to welcome us back to its fold. I took the embrace and entered the star and floated deliciously in limitless luxury on the buoyant seas of the pale blue sphere. I indulged in this sensation for a few moments, then established the blue dish and immediately was aware of the emerald above me. I entered one of the six facets as easily as walking through an open door. That got me into the vast cathedral where my attention was drawn to the Round Table.

I found my place at the table, and noted Russell, Berenice, and others seated there as well. An intensely bright point of golden light started to form and pulse at the center of the table. As I breathed as Love from Above to this tiny golden sun, it grew larger, *much* larger, and became so bright, its light engulfed the entire table, and I was inside the sun. Everywhere was golden; there was no place that wasn't golden, including where 'I' was. Obviously my body wasn't in this space, but even the mental space where I sound the 'I' all the time – that was suffused by golden light as well.

As if my eyes were starting to adjust to the brilliant golden light, a shape started to form out of the gold. A chalice, with two handles, a base, and an empty space in the center. I wasn't looking at the Grail: I was the Grail.

This Grail shape had congealed itself out of the field of

golden light, and my presence was distributed throughout the chalice. It was everywhere: in the handles, the rim, the gentle slope to the bottom. I felt like I was zipping around to every conceivable point in this chalice, at all points simultaneously. Where I would expect my body to be was a hollow, empty space; where I would expect the outer world to be, there I was. Everything was inverted, turned inside out.

A point of scarlet light started to appear directly above me. I watched it fall, a single drop, like a bead of blood, coming towards me in slow motion, growing ever bigger as it descended, more deeply scarlet. I was but a piece of absorbent blotting paper, ready to be stained scarlet when the drop touched me, when it filled the Grail chalice. The drop did in fact fill the chalice, or so it seemed to me. Everything flashed scarlet. As with the gold, there was nothing, no place, that was not scarlet. Reality was scarlet. The Grail disappeared; my sense of self got eclipsed. I heard the words, 'Not I, but the Christ in me,' over and over.

That's good, I would think in later days, because I would sure need it.

9

Now we come — at last? too soon? — to that unpleasant night when the demons interrupted our fireside visit with Blaise. You'd think, wouldn't you, that a close association with high-ranking, fun-loving angels would exempt you, indeed, protect you, from inimical influences; that it would be wall-to-wall revelation, bliss, joy, and delight for the rest of the incarnation, after which there would be even more of the same. Not quite, though it's not out of the question.

But you have to spend some time with Klingsor. There's no way around it. In this space, now, I'll share a few notes from my years with Klingsor.

Klingsor was the villain in Wagner's *Parzival*. He was the Fisher King's enemy, the opera's bad guy. He originally was one of the Grail Brothers, or wanted to be, but failed to purify himself and ended up being their enemy. He lacked the strength to slay the sins within himself, Wagner wrote. Furious, Klingsor turned to black magic and strove to snare, distract, and corrupt the Grail Knights, and he stole the Fisher King's spear or lance, which had touched the blood of Christ, and thereby destabilized the Grail Castle and its holy rites.

Since Klingsor held the spear, Anfortas, the Fisher King, could not be healed; he languished, wounded, awaiting the Christed knight, Parsifal. The story had a happy ending, though: Parsifal arrived, got the lance back, and healed Anfortas. But it took a few years. The interesting questions to ask are these: Was Klingsor really the bad guy? Who was more wounded, Anfortas or Klingsor? Were they perhaps two aspects of the same king, rich and wounded?

Questions like these of course never occurred to me in the early days, especially in the aftermath of the demons' first incursion into the Blaise circle.

We were upstairs in Russell's and Berenice's spacious bedroom. Blaise was just walking us through a new visualization and handing out assignments. It felt good, but I was a bit unaccountably edgy, irritable, on guard against something. Blaise was saying, 'If you wish, please breathe love to your new images for a moment...' When something interrupted us, burst into our awareness from a strange place.

Russell and I looked at each other in alarm. We both saw them. I started to perspire and shiver at the same time. I hadn't felt alarmed like this in a long time. Surrounding us was a circle of ugly birdfaced semi-humans with piercing red eyes, pointed noses, and unarguably ill intent. They glared malevolently at us, oozing hatred and opposition. My mind was flooded with fearful thoughts: I'll go mad. I'll jump through the window to get away from this. I'll kill myself.

I got up, walked around the room a bit, did a few deep knee bends. I was trying to ground myself, get back into my body from wherever I had jumped to. I am not by nature particularly histrionic in the tone of my mental processes, so these expressions of high drama that just ran through my head like papers urgently awaiting my signature didn't feel like me, even though they were dressed up in my 'voice' — you know, the radio announcer we all have in our head, that amazingly indefatigable monologuist who never runs out of commentary and declarations about the tragicomedy we call our personality.

The shock of this intrusion shook loose a memory of an event from that afternoon. I guess I had been only peripherally aware of it at the time. I was returning at dusk from my Earth circle, sauntering across the fields. I wanted to saunter, but in truth I felt uncomfortable, as if watched by neighbors who didn't like me walking past, who, if I pushed it, didn't want to see me or know I existed. Except there were no houses in sight for any neighbors to be in to wish me ill.

I had just walked past a derelict old stone cottage, mostly fallen down, and a couple of antique, rusted out farm trucks. Prime ghost country, I suppose. I felt something sinister breathing down my back, as if its hands were squeezing my shoulders. I spun around, but there was nothing there, except a jagged red energy line that crossed the field behind me. I had just walked over it. That's where the creepy sensation came from.

As if climbing out of this red line, like a knife slash across the skin of the physical world, there was a line of demonic faces leering at me, ugly, deformed, subhuman faces, horned, drooling, their skin leathery, their teeth pointed, their breath foul no doubt. They were textbook devils. Hieronymous Bosch couldn't have improved on their bad looks and nasty mood. That was my mind being fearless. Meanwhile my body ran like hell across the field to get back to Wick.

'There are now energies at work that are as yet unprecedented in your experience,' Blaise commented. This was before the demons interrupted us. 'You picked up something out there that has already produced some unfortunate consequences.'

That was Blaise being polite about how I insulted Berenice and her son, Edmund, very efficiently in about two sentences before dinner. I hadn't quite felt like myself when I was talking to her, but who else could it have been, I thought at the time. 'Do you mean the devil figures I saw at the red ley line in the field?'

'Correct. That was your conscious assimilation of something already attached to your being bodies. You were made to be unprotected today, with no chanting, no image, by energies you have not experienced prior to this occasion.' I did everything wrong this afternoon: I went to my Earth circle around dusk on a waning moon, forgot to chant on the walk out, forgot to put the Blaise image around me — basically left my back completely exposed. 'We have much opposition, as you will discover,' Blaise added, on their way out.

Thus began my many years of opposition, of lunching with the devils. Perhaps I should say, being lunch for the devils. Once that door was opened, there was no closing it. In fact, I had to move into that dark room and live there. If dealing with your Shadow were fun, it would be a spectator sport. Everybody would be doing it. It isn't fun. It's appalling. Not the dealing with it part, that's just hard work, but the contents, the bogeyman and his extended family and the myriad of relationships you have formed over time with this family — let me simply say, I was grateful I had no idea what I was getting into at the beginning.

At first it was like having an atrocious case of fleas. You feel as if you've been bitten all over, and still the bugs find fresh skin to irritate. And they bite you all the time. I called them 'entities' in those days because, frankly, I couldn't tell them apart or classify them into types or species. I thought at the time they were attacking me, invading my space from outside. Here are some typical examples.

I was with a few Grail colleagues on an Epiphany assignment in central England. Energetically, it was as if the town didn't want us there. It was like a sweltering rain forest teaming with invisible biting insects. Everywhere I went, in stores, in the woods, down the lanes, I was jumped by entities who slimed me with negativity. There I was, trying to be as Love from Above, but boilingly irritable, grouchy, argumentative, captious, ready to rip your head off if you looked at me the wrong way.

I'd retreat into the star for some relief, but the minute I came back out again, there they were, the pain-in-the ass entities. I walked around the town muttering, 'I never want to come here again'. The whole town seemed to be infiltrated with dark beings, a horror show of negativity making everyone angry and off center. Or maybe it was just me. The painful part of this work is sometimes you find nobody else experiences the entities the way you do. You feel like a freak, an aberration — how come it's just me they're picking on?

I asked Blaise why the place had seemed so virulent with entities. 'There are many agencies from many different levels of what you call experience interested in preventing your progress at this time. Particularly at this place.'

Another time we were in Sedona, Arizona. God, I hated that place. We were there for two weeks in January and it rained 800% more than usual, no exaggeration. I don't care what they say about the amazing vortexes there. To me, it seemed appallingly polluted. Especially a place called Airport Mesa. A friend and I were making our way across the field past the airplane strip on the mesa, to get a better look at the crystal city out in the valley at Cathedral Rock.

As we walked across the field, ever closer to the edge of the mesa, we both felt attacked. My friend experienced it as nausea, and she vomited. I just got more irritable – that's my speciality, but it's also a kind of dowsing rod indicator of the presence of entities, when your mood suddenly shifts from calm and amused to irritable and frowning.

I started feeling petulant, whiny, then furious. I felt like I was going to pass out, faint from hypoglycemia. I started to rant out loud about how I hated Sedona, how I was wasting my time wading through this muck, that Blaise was a jerk for making us come here, and that if the aliens, ETs, or goddam Space Brothers were calibrating my emotional body and adjusting my goddam DNA I'd kick their light body heads back to Andromeda. What can I say? You know the angels will forgive you for being a loud-mouth, ungrateful jerk; maybe they find it all amusing or tragic or a little of both.

We managed to complete our goal, which was to make a connection with the Ray Master enclave out at Cathedral Rock, but by the time we returned to the motel, we were exhausted. The further I got from the airport area, the less irritable I grew. Eventually I even felt like myself again.

Some days later, Blaise commented: 'As you experienced, when energy is heightened, then opposition is significant. You were well prepared. You know what is not you. To clean things out they have to come to the surface. Ask the Archangel

Michael to bring his sword to clean out that which needs cleansing that the Michael Light may illumine those areas that are not cleansed.' We did, and he did, and all I can say is I wish I knew what he did about cleansing places.

This stuff was merely introductory. Then I started getting the entities wholesale. I lived for a couple of years in a house infested with them. It seemed to have its own direct line to entity headquarters and we got a truckload delivered every day. We never ran out of them. Everyday I had to deal with them. People came to dinner and left their entities with us. My roommates were infested as if with lice. I had heaps of them. The land seemed to attract them.

I suppose things were heightened a bit by the fact that the house was situated in a small zodiac which Blaise, me, Merlin, and a few of the Ray Masters were fixing up, making a long, slow, gradual turn on the zodiac's dimmer switch. That was probably like a neon invitation to the entities to come make me miserable. I say 'me' because my roommates weren't aware of the problem.

Occasionally a Grail colleague visited and confirmed the degree of astral pollution, and together we'd ineffectually try to cleanse the place. We tried whacking the entities with our swords; we called on the Archangel Michael to 'clear us;' we tried clearing each other; we put salt on our chakras; we exorcised the house; sometimes I pleaded with Blaise to free me from them, and when I was really pissed, I demanded it.

We'd feel relief for a while, then there would be another wave of entities and the negativity would engulf us again. I felt sorry for schizophrenics: nobody believes them when they say they see awful things like this, and they think they're crazy.

They're not, because these things are there, but having to deal with entities every day can certainly start making you wish you were crazy. Because if you were crazy, you wouldn't have to fight them anymore. No, I never felt I was going crazy; it wasn't even an issue. But I did feel enmired.

Around this time, I asked Blaise why this house was continually overrun by these negative entities and what could I do to definitively flush them out. 'They are food for angels. The angels transform the negative entities and do not need your help. Know we are quite able.' Interesting viewpoint, I thought at the time, but it didn't help me on a practical level.

On another occasion I was working with some people. One of them was an entity warehouse. I'd been there for a few years, and things had gotten difficult. One day I walked into my office and was hit with an oppressive, whiny, tremendously resentful vibration. It hadn't been there when I left the last evening. I told my staff to take an hour off at the coffee shop and I found a place to sit about fifty feet from the building to see what kind of mess I was dealing with. Naturally I called for backup, Blaise and the big boys who knew something about cleansing. A friend, who was psychic, also lent a hand.

I saw a huge brown gorilla occupying my swivel chair at my desk. I saw another twenty of these in my colleague's office. She wasn't physically there, but a residue of her was, sufficient for me to see these gorilla beings completely covered her aura so that there was none of her to be seen. They weren't really gorillas, but that's the way my mind interpreted the energy data. Gorillas are big, they can be violent, they can dominate or control a space, and they can be scary if you're standing next to one.

I rummaged through my Blaise toolbox to see what I could use: swords, Nimitta, Blaise rotunda, golden spindle, Grail, Christ. Things felt a bit desperate. I had to do something. I couldn't have my staff come back into the office with that kind of toxicity still present. I didn't care for it either. So I gave the gorillas some of all of this, my best shot, so to speak. I torched them with the lilac flame; I spun them in the Grail bowl; I blended them in the golden spindle; I asked the Christ to please come and save my sorry ass.

This backed the gorillas off a bit, but then the rats came. As if through dozens of holes in the floor, hundreds of black astral rats streamed into the office, running over everything. You could barely see the desks and computers. They kept streaming into the office, as if they were invading from another dimension through some mini-wormhole under somebody's desk.

My friend's observations were interesting. Where I saw gorillas, she saw long dark slugs. She said the woman in question was a kind of portal or magnet for this shocking level of negative entities, siphoning them from another dimension into ours due to some bizarre 'agreement' she had with them. She also said the whole building was filled with a big black sphere of walled-in grief and anger, a heavy dark ball with many layers of pain and deep hurt and other negative emotions. This ball, like the woman, drew the dark energies to it.

During our work, she said, we ignited the ball with light or flames arcing from the tips of our swords, and the whole place burned up in a conflagration of lilac flames. Angels were now visible all around us, standing at the four corners of the building like freshly installed security guards. Eventually things calmed down enough so it was safe for everybody to return to work. But I never really liked being in that building anymore after that episode.

I knew I was missing something, but I didn't know what it was. Throughout my years with Klingsor, Blaise was always what I thought was aloof. I couldn't understand why they couldn't just protect me better. I didn't see why they had thrown me to the wolves with hardly any survival skills.

Things between me and the entities kept getting fiercer, more intense, with no definitive resolution in sight, just more misery. But Blaise didn't seem too concerned, other than to remark one day, 'When we pull back the curtains in your mind we see monsters from the past. We see that there are ghosts living in the present.' I thought at the time that Blaise wasn't helping me, but these two sentences, to me then, irritatingly enigmatic, would be the key to freedom.

It was time to get some perspective, as the question I'd been running away from, the big picture question that any sensible person diligently avoids, now had to be asked.

'Well, Blaise, I take it that the reports of there being a negative hierarchy are true?'

'Yes, relatively true. Satan, Leviathan, Beelzebub, and others form the first ranks of servitors to the dark side. Each of them is part of the hierarchy of that side, just as Michael, Raphael, Uriel, Gabriel, and others are equivalent parts of the light side. What you are concerned with is the Light, not in relation to the dark, but the true Light.'

'You once referred to the opposition we faced, that you face. What's that?'

'Make no mistake, there are forces at work that are attempting to corrupt what you don't. Fear is what lets them in. We must help you to become aware of this whole situation. There is a cosmic conflict. There is an attempt between two opposing forces to usurp the power of light on Earth. This is only apparent now at the end of the Age of Darkness.'

This opposition thing, the cosmic conflict – it got so everywhere I looked there was more of it. One night Blaise could only visit for a few minutes. They said they would be occupied until daybreak sorting out a problem in Sirius. 'The suns within Sirius are being manipulated for the wrong needs. Therefore our energies are needed to concentrate these back into their natural pattern.'

One time they wanted me to go to a particular place in Norway, only they wouldn't tell me where. Supposedly a French group was going there to wave at the UFOs as they landed, but those boneheads never cited the actual place. They referred to it only by nickname and nobody in Norway called it that. I got to Oslo and hung out for a few days, but I was wasting valuable time because it was the Epiphany week and if I didn't get to the right place before January 6, I might as well go home. Russell found out at the last minute and I dashed for the train.

Naturally I wanted to know why Blaise couldn't tell me where the place was since they urgently wanted me to go there.

'Massive interference. Because of certain Pleiadian karmic forces, we sometimes have trouble with facilitating a smooth communication with you. It is also difficult because around the energies that we are and others are focussing in this area, there is much military interest. Therefore it would be foolish to reveal too much about its location.'

'But surely you can reveal it to me?'

'You are still vulnerable. You could be penetrated by the other side. You remember what that's like. If they know you don't know, then they won't bother.' As it turned out, nobody showed up except me, and the opposition. The UFO people never made it out of France.

'Blaise, what do you mean by Pleiadian karma? I thought they were the good guys.'

'It's to do with certain karmic forces that are with you to do with your lineage in the Pleiades. As you know, there are many forces interested in the outworking of energy on this planet. The forces against us, specifically, are from the Pleiades and the constellation Euripides. In a sense, the Pleiades is part of you. Then it is karma you have brought here with you.

'There are many Euripideans who would not like this planet to consciously evolve for they only come here to seek pleasure. Euripideans are bound to the karma of their race and its working out. Only by descending to the material plane as such on Earth can they fulfill any pleasure. Therefore their interest is in maintaining low level consciousness on this plane. The figures in black you have seen at various sites were representatives of this manifest on the planes of experience as interpreted by your consciousness.'

All of this raised an unsettling question in me. Was it all my fault? Was all this interference produced by me in some way, by my karma?

'Everything that happens is a direct result of karma, positive or negative. Positive karma is interference of a positive nature, therefore opportune. Negative karma is interference of a negative nature, therefore experienced as destructive. Everything that you experience at the dualistic level is karmic, initially personal, but as you grow on the path, collective. You only become of interest in terms of clearing past and future karma when you focus on the star. It's impossible for any karmic interference outside your karmic sphere. Most of what you have experienced so far was personal karma. You brought on all that stuff yourself. How else?'

Just when I was starting to feel okay with blaming the constant interference on Blaise's cosmic enemies, that they were picking on me because they didn't like Blaise or his friends. . . . So it was my fault after all!

'Throughout the rainbow mists, many beings arise. There never was or never will be a separate one. When you have difficulties, remember this. When you are happy, remember this. There never was, there never is, there never will be, a separate one. Any physical, mental, or emotional problem of any sort stems from the nonunderstanding at some level of this conceptual framework. Disease is what happens in parts of the being that do not rest in unification.

'Faith is that which knows beyond any doubt that reality which is beyond separation. Faith is that which knows that it is, therefore it is able. The star within each of you is the property of the angels. As a man plants wheat and rice and other seeds, so angels plant stars in consciousness, in sentient beings. If they are not realized, if they are not brought to individuated consciousness within the unified field, then the crop bears no fruit and the seed has fallen upon stony ground.

It is difficult, apparently, for you to remember what we say to you.'

No doubt, but there was something about the way they pronounced that word – individuated – or maybe it was merely hearing the word again in this context, that opened a door for me. Of course. Individuation. Assimilate all the parts, including the Shadow. So I began the long feast of the Shadow, the slow-motion encounter with the Lesser Guardian of the Threshold. This is a term Rudolf Steiner mentioned. When you start to enter the spiritual worlds, if you're going to do it properly, you need to meet this Guardian, and I guarantee you'll hate every minute of it and prefer to run screaming in the opposite direction.

This Guardian, Steiner said, is the repository of everything you've repudiated, turned away from, denied, suppressed, thrown away – forever. Not just stuff you don't want to remember or claim from this life. But *all* your lives, this planet and elsewhere, terrible, weird, painful, nasty, strange stuff you couldn't conceive you'd ever been involved with or had been dragging along behind you like a big heavy sack all this time, as Robert Bly says of the Shadow.

Everything that had happened to me up to this time had been merely kitchen smells, whiffs of the foods spread out at the banquet table. But I was yet to step up to fill my plate from the smorgasbord of the Shadow. Now I would.

Years passed, and still I ate. The funny thing is, in some respects, it all gets easier when you stop resisting, stop trying to flee, to deny, to blame it on somebody else. When you just say, with a deep exhale, okay, give it to me.

It's far too big to see at first, and you wouldn't want to. God no. Only in retrospect, some years later after months and months of steady eating and heavy drinking at the feast of your Shadow, your appalling past deeds and egregious pain, can you form an image, and only if you care to. It's not required.

Picture yourself, your body, as you know it, and its energy field, which maybe you don't know, but imagine it as two or three times the size of your body, or ten times if it's easier. It is a challenge to the imagination to conceive of how your astral body can store so much detritus from your vast past, so many beings, and pictures, and demons, and aliens, and past life traumas, and more. But when you get a glimpse, you make an unforgettable discovery: you're a monster. In fact, the only monster worth being frightened of, if even then.

Your parents and family are there, and grandparents, uncles, aunts, cousins, and hundreds of generations of family lineage, all there, all hooked into you. You may see their faces, all looking at you, judging, evaluating, controlling. There are hundreds of cords, some as thick as tree trunks, plugged into you, front, back, sides, and top, connecting you to these family members across the generations.

Hundreds of more cords connect you to people you've known, loved, hated, killed, screwed, hurt, helped, healed, injured, abandoned, rejected, talked to, ignored, and to people you still know and haven't but might do any of these things to, people you walked past on the street and who threw a thought at you. You have so many cords coming into you – or leaving you, hooking you into scores of other people – it's a wonder you can walk through a door, or even take a full breath, or not fall down laughing if you could see yourself *this way* in the mirror.

Innumerable strange, even terrifying beings are packed into your astral body. Hundreds of snakes, coiled or extended, some the size of your torso. Snake eggs, some dormant, some hatching, multiplying the snake presence. Spiders by the dozens, twisting your muscles, injecting psychic poison into your system, and their brood of eggs, waiting the designated moment of hatching. Strange birds with long beaks, black pelicans, dark crows, harpies. Fallen angels, black cherubs with darts instead of trumpets. Devils by the busload, big ones, little ones, ones with darts, pitchforks, spears, lances, prods, arrows, honey-coated tongues to convince you they're not there and it's you you're hearing.

Remember the gorillas I mentioned? There are dozens of these, probably hundreds, big, hairy ill-mannered beings forcefully controlling your space. And human-like beings who seem to be mostly obsidian head and long taproot, growing like parsnips in your torso, having penetrated all your chakras, major and minor, their dark visage protruding just above the top of your head.

Aliens of all descriptions, strange, and really strange; alien ships and UFOs sending beams into your head and the rest of your body, activating metallic boxes, devices, things that look like multi-pronged electrical outlets. Hundreds of wispy beings, whispering in your ear, offering to take your hand and guide you through the spiritual worlds, some falsely.

Thousands of little pieces of confetti, like rain falling through your astral body, each a pain picture, each a gesture of unexpiated outrage, rape, murder, damage, hurt, grievance, grief, insecurity, pain. And behind them throbbing dots of red, each an encapsulation of a past trauma, when you were beheaded, betrayed, left to rot, stabbed outright, burned, dismembered, when you went crazy, left your body, killed yourself, got crucified, got lost in the black arts, thrown off a cliff, or when you did all these things to other people.

Victim and victimizer, Roman and Christian. Hitler and Jew. They're all you, monster and saint, whore and virgin, nice guy, bad guy, rotten guy. And all the pictures and red throbbing dots like cheese on crackers for the beings at the great feast of your pain.

As I said, mercifully, we don't get this image at first. It would scare everybody away, and nobody would try to individuate and work through all this appalling crap. It's only later, when you've gained a little space, enjoy a little breathing room, know finally how to deal with the dark side and carve out your own space in this almost inconceivably vast astral space that is yourself, that you can entertain the dark image of yourself that, unbelievably, the angels must see all the time, and see through, and still, and always, love you to death.

Why go through all this? Why did *I* go through it? I got an answer to this one afternoon when Russell and me were at Lincoln Cathedral in Lincolnshire.

Russell and me had walked down the central axis of the cathedral doing a new Blaise image the boys had taught us. This was a dynamic one, involving a cycling torus donut, spurting lilac flames, a rain of golden stars, and hoops. Complicated, in other words. We had done it together like this a few weeks earlier at another cathedral and when we stood at the central axis, Blaise and the Archangel Michael had amplified it a hundred times, making it bigger than the church.

It must have had a good effect, because over the course of twenty minutes, three representatives of the cathedral — deacons, ushers, ministers, whatever — invited us to join in the communion service. I don't know exactly what they wanted, but they were all smiling and seemed to think we'd had something to do with their good mood. Russell and I were used to doing our Blaise work unobtrusively and without ever being acknowledged, so this was unusual.

At Lincoln Cathedral, however, when we reached the central axis, nothing happened. The Blaise image wobbled, like somebody had kicked it. It grew chaotic, enervated, and neither Blaise nor Michael seemed able to amplify it.

I noticed a point of disturbance a few feet beyond where we were standing. It was in a blocked off space, about ten feet wide, just before the choir. Under the stone floor I saw a flattened dark head, the vast weight of the cathedral squashing it, as if the church had been thrown at the being belonging to this head in an effort to hammer it into the ground and keep it there. I sensed its anger, down there, buried under many tons of stone. It looked like an octopus with a severely flattened head, but I sensed another being deeper down.

Russell and I took a lunch break to figure out what we would do and who was down there. I thought of King Solomon imprisoning the demons. I thought of Taranis, the malevolent Celtic thunder god, often summoned by black magicians. I thought of the Christian image of the Pit. Then the bigness of the event, the bigness of the being, got to us, because we both knew who it was.

It was Lucifer. It was exhilarating more than anything else to know this. Blaise had prepared us for this years ago. It was conceptual then; now it was real.

Before I go further into this Lucifer business, let me distract your attention for a moment with how the Greeks saw him. They called this being Prometheus. Prometheus, one of the Titans, stole the gods' fire and against the will of Zeus gave it to humanity. In other words, he helped humankind in defiance of the gods. As punishment, Zeus chained him to Mount Caucasus where an eagle ate his liver every day but eventually Herakles came and unbound him.

The Christians took the same occult fact and gave it a different spin. Lucifer, the Light-Bearer and Lord of Light, defied God and the gods and refused to serve humanity, and for this he was thrown into the Pit. He fell flaming, glorious, and unrepentant to the Earth. He was to languish forever in the Pit. Forget Herakles. Lucifer was toast. So which story was right? In certain respects, neither.

'Lucifer was the closest to the Lord of Absolute Infinite Love and Light, His Holiness Extreme in Excelsius,' Blaise told us. 'He wished to experience something which none of us had even thought possible. Lucifer achieved a part of the Plan, and is most blessed amongst angels for his part in the whole.'

The daring thing Lucifer wanted to achieve was to give humanity free will. He did through dropping the emerald, one of the jewels in his crown – the 'fire' that Prometheus 'stole' – into the human organism, Blaise explained. 'The emerald was dropped into Man's biophysical base at the time of the Fall, at that point when form was brought into matter by the Lord of Light.

'Lucifer, on a commission from the Arch Architect Most

Precious on High made his first step towards matter, described by some as the Fall. His mission is the shifting of consciousness from the point it is at to the Christed initiation in the Buddha Body.

'The emerald is a tiny electromagnetic doorway in the field of your heart chakra, in the heart of the heart. The emerald is purely in the etheric. It is the manifestation of the star in the emotional body or etheric body of recognition. It is the access point where that in you which is love is in love with that in others which is love. When two emeralds open synchronously, there is a spontaneous transmission of love from heart to heart. When a man or woman begins to awaken the Luciferian aspect of themselves, the emerald glows within them. It is a positive aspect of the Lord of Light awakening in the One.'

There's a good reason to get concerned about this emerald. The Grail's inside it. That's where the Grail Quest will unfailingly take you, to the edge of the emerald. You get six choices, six approaches, depending on your temperament. That's why the emerald has six sides, each representing an aspect of the truth of ourselves: understanding, knowledge, compassion, intuition, peace, bliss. Once you balance one of these aspects, you can penetrate the facet and enter. 'When penetrated,' Blaise said, 'each side removes the emerald's outer layer and reveals the light within, and the source of the light within.'

It's a light you don't want to approach lightly, if you'll pardon the irony. 'The light that the emerald contains is beyond any description, as is the experience. What you become after experiencing the light in the emerald is beyond what you commonly call the experiencer. Were you to be exposed to the source of love and light within the emerald, you would lose your sense of spacetime continuity.

'Therefore you must progress gently towards something that is not dependent upon the ordinary sense of 'going towards' something. You cannot get to the Grail and the scarlet drop of Christ without first passing through the emerald. The emerald is the temple for the Christed initiation in the Buddha Body.'

There is intensively but one emerald, Blaise continued. 'When all those who have emeralds awaken spontaneously at the same moment in time and space, then Lucifer will be united again with the Father. You see, any prejudice towards Lucifer is ludicrous. He is an intimate part of yourself and of your collective self. The Lord of Light has made many attempts in the past to reunite with this One. Always through Man's unknowing and unforgiving, he has remained tied to the material plane. Ever since the Elohim came to Earth he has been bound here.

'Now with your choice and by the means we have shown, we open the door for Lucifer to be forgiven, to find his rightful place at the right hand of the Absolute where he was shining brighter and more brilliantly than the most infinite source of light you can imagine – 10,000 times brighter than the brightest star.'

Following this debriefing – I should more properly call it a deprogramming of our innate but slumbering cultural prejudices about Lucifer – Blaise gave us a glimpse of an event in the remote planetary past.

'We will take you through time and space to a chamber within a dome. Within the dome is a group of people who await our presence. We are brought here to witness an event of some importance. There is above us all an angel of extra-ordinary proportions. He is bright. He is brighter than the brightest star. Within his chest is a green light that is so bright it casts a green glow for miles around. Each of you gathered here at this time may experience this green energy, this emerald light, within yourselves, if you wish.'

It was Lucifer, of course, at the beginning of the world. His robes were covered in jewels and he was exquisitely beautiful, truly 'the angel of my presence,' as Blake wrote. An emission like a green laser beam came out of his chest, or a green searchlight from a lighthouse, sweeping across the land. Illu-minating everything in its lovely light. Numerous beings, more or less human in appearance, were joyously receiving this green beam in their chests.

Blaise gave us a few moments to collect ourselves then returned to clarify matters, starting with when that was and who the people were.

'It was pre-first dome period, in a single dome in the southernmost tip of South America. The people were repre-sentatives from various galactic stations, such as Pleaidians, Sirians, and others. You were simultaneously present as yourselves and as part of our presence.'

'What was going on then? That was Lucifer, right?'

'Correct. Within each of the beings there he was activating the heart within the heart, known as the emerald. This first dome, before all the other domes came, was visited by Lord Lucifer in his full manifestation on his first visit to Gaia. Here he made a commitment to Earth as a being and thereby to the humanity that would reside on it. It was necessary for this to have happened before the implantation of the first domes over the surface of the Earth. This type of planetary initiation also occurred synchronously and coincidentally on other planets.'

Later Lucifer implanted the emeralds within incarnating humanity, and he projected his own emerald at a specific place on the planet. That place was the focus of a global event in August 1987 and is known as the El Tule tree, a gigantic, two thousand year old tree in the modest courtyard of El Templo del Santa Maria some six miles outside of Oaxaca in Southern Mexico. During the Harmonic Convergence, Lucifer — known in Mexican myth as Quetzalcoatl — returned to El Tule and his one emerald, plumed with Elohim.

The Zapotec myths predicted that Quetzalcoatl would return to the place where he buried his heart eons ago and like a pomegranate it would burst and spread its seed beneficently around the world. In practical terms, the Harmonic Convergence took place inside the emerald, yours, mine, Gaia's, Lucifer's.

Like the original 'Fall' of Lucifer, his return to El Tule in 1987 was part of a plan commissioned at the highest level, Blaise said. At that time, under the auspices of what Blaise refers to as 'His Most Highly Evolved Conscious Architect of the Cosmic Plane,' work began on opening receptive areas of the material plane to a new source of cosmic energy.

'This was focussed through Lucifer at Oaxaca. He illumined the astral sphere around Earth, feeding into those who had any degree of receptivity at an astral or higher mental level, illumination of a specific type. This coincided or converged with the opening of those doorways on a material plane that will activate the Earth grid in a new way, bringing eco-balance that was becoming sorely misplaced.' The humble El Tule tree, Blaise said, 'formed the link between the etheric, astral, and physical planes.'

'The one Emerald was Lucifer's gift to the Earth, and it was the birthing of the emerald in the consciousness of Man. The emerald was one. The emerald is an integral part of the Earth grid. In fact, the entire Earth is inside Lucifer's emerald, as are all humans, each person as a particle of the Earth, as the green of the grid within the emerald within their hearts. The emerald in the heart of the heart is the gift of the Lord of Light and therefore of the awakening of Gaia.

'Lucifer has an important role today that is initiatory. Lucifer brings the emeralds to a new state of refinement, as preparation for the immediate awakening of the next phase. Gaining familiarity with the emerald is also part of the preparation for the Christed initiation in the Buddha Body.'

So these thoughts and this background were with us both as we ate our lunch in a restaurant just off the Cathedral square. I tuned into Lucifer under the church. His energy color was a dark rich blue, and I matched my crown chakra to this to be able to see him better. I felt his grief, anger, disappointment, despair, isolation. 'Why have you forsaken me?' Lucifer cries out, the weight and scorn of an entire cathedral on his head. Crucified in the Earth and still on the cross.

Russell and I finished our lunch and headed back to the cathedral. We would work at opposite ends. He positioned himself by the front door, and maintained the Blaise image around the church, while I went way around the back, to sit on the furthest bit of lawn away from the top end of the church (beyond the crown chakra of it, architecturally) and practically in the street. You don't want to be right in the line of fire when you're doing this.

I called on Blaise, the Archangel Michael, and some of the Ray Masters for backup. When I say backup you may think I'm taking all the credit for myself. Believe me, I would have much preferred not to have to do this thing at the cathedral, but it's human karma that put Lucifer under the stone so it has to be humans who unbind him, with appropriate help from the spiritual worlds. We're stuck with it because we did it, so we have to undo it — we, you know, anybody willing to do it on the part of everybody when the moment is right.

I have to tell you one more thing before I tell you how we got the church off Lucifer's back. In the Grail stories, including Wagner's, Parsifal gets into the Grail Castle the first time by grace; he is basically a jackanapes, like I was. The second time he has to earn it, and that took him some years. He went off into the forest of incarnation, had some adventures, some misadventures, figured out some things, learned a few techniques, came back, walked in the front door, and healed the Fisher King like he was supposed to. He was a well-trained Grail Knight, a model for us all. I'll just say that I went off and learned how to deal with all these goddam entities, and now I'm back at Lincoln Cathedral doing this.

I had a look at Lucifer to see what the damage was. The octopus was sitting on top of him, like a jailor. When I say octopus, that being also looked like the aliens in *Independence Day*, giant flattened heads, really ugly, malevolent, snakelike. Something was holding it in place.

High above the cathedral there were twelve alien space-ships, each with a device, a machine, that sent down a beam that acted like an anchor bolt, holding the octopus in place. The ships were arrayed in three tiers, four per tier, and their beams created three overlapping squares, a perverse geometric mandala of astral rivets. This sounds like science fiction, but to tell you the truth, this is where science fiction comes from.

The work is to erase the beams and the machines, then the ships go away. I think technically you're easing a hologram and not the actual, quasi-physical device wherever and whatever it is. But once I erased the twelve devices and their beams, it was like unscrewing twelve long screws. The ships backed off and the alien octopus, now unanchored — unsupported — flew off as if sucked away by a reverse kind of gravity back into the astral realm where it came from. Then the heavy lid of a sarcophagus started to slide off.

As if on a slow-moving freight elevator, dozens of alien beings start to rise out of the sarcophagus, control-beings resembling gorillas, demons, bats, weird birds, all the baleful low life ejected in a kind of violent purgative heave. Things started to lighten up. All eighteen of the archangels now stood around the sarcophagus; they were as tall as the cathedral, their swords upraised. Behind, around, and above them were thousands of Blaises in their regal angelic form.

Then Lucifer arose from the Pit, attired in rich royal blue robes. He had at least one hundred wings, cramped for centuries against his magnificent body, now unfurling, stretching, extending, ready to enable him to soar again. He was an awesome sight. Blake and Blaise were not exaggerating when they said he was bright.

But then his valence shifted, and his color became bright

red, shockingly red. Innumerable demons fly out of the Pit making a halo around Lucifer. For a moment, Lucifer himself looks like Christianity's Satan, like Goethe's Mephistopheles, like every thoughtform of the chief of demons the Western mind has ever conjured up. Oh boy, I thought. What have I done? You can't put the genie back in the bottle, not this genie. I breathed a few times, then laughed.

Of course. That's the whole point, Grail Knight. The *two* aspects. With that insight, I now saw a celestial being with two faces, two sides, the magnificent Lucifer side, the demonic Mephistophelean side. Both were valid. Here's why. Lucifer's commission was to model what it would be like to hold free will consciousness in the context of being both good and evil.

He was – *he is* – the living demonstration, the embodiment of the Tree of the Knowledge of Good and Evil and what it's like to be conscious and able to choose *freely*. His job was to show us how to handle the polarity, to act out the consequences of either choice. He was the Old Adam in the Garden of Eden, not the serpent. He ate the golden apple freely, not out of coercion, and so gained the knowledge of the polarity between good and evil. Here's the key part: He has his knowledge in the context of an individuated *and* unitive consciousness. It's really what the Grail Quest is all about. It wasn't a Fall; it was an incarnation.

Christianity couldn't handle both aspects of Lucifer, so they took the light side and demonized the dark. One half of Lucifer got thrown in the Pit and they threw away the key. He became the dreadful bogeyman in the closet of the Western psyche, and the theologians went hysterical if anybody even looked in the direction of the closet. So we got deprived of the fullness of being, and started running scared of this unface-able Shadow, the wild man in the basement. We repudiated, invalidated, crucified, spat on, demonized, bound and chained him, even though he took on this polarized approach to matter on our behalf.

The trouble is what you won't look at, looks at you all the time. So when the Shadow is so demonic that no one will look at it, or even discuss it calmly, then we've lost our freedom and all the low lifes of the cosmos, the aliens, the bad Pleiadians, the idiot Euripideans, can manipulate us and control con-sciousness behind the scenes and keep us in fear and basically get the run of the place.

We're so much in denial we don't believe in demons and their ilk at all, so we can't see what they do in our space, and we never look at our Shadow, and so it runs us from the darkness. I see now why Blaise allowed the entities to harass me all those years; so I could come to terms with the bogey-man. It's really part of the Grail Knight training, I see now.

You see, we have to deal with this. We have to go through the Lucifer initiation, the appalling feast of the Shadow. Because we've got *his* emerald in our heart of hearts, and so has the planet. There's no way around this. If we want the Grail, that's where it is, in Lucifer's emerald. If we want peace on Earth, that's where it is, in Gaia's emerald.

A few days later Blaise debriefed us. We were a bit tired from the event at Lincoln and certain parts of our being were in a bit of shock, and still processing the experience.

'So, Blaise, I'm beginning to see how all those problems I had with entities over the years may have something to do with all this.'

'It was preparation for clearing larger things such as dimensional doorways. They are very congested. You have been getting familiar with the poisons.'

'Would you give us a perspective on Lucifer, based on what we did.'

'When Lucifer came to Earth, he was seduced by Satan, who bound him and his angel legion, through his will, into the material realm. Now, through effort and a turning round of will, Lucifer begins to associate again with the Christ towards the One. This process is being accelerated.

'The dark forces exert much effort at this time because they know they are losing their hold over Lucifer and his angels. Satan, or Mammon, is the lord of materiality, the lord of fame. These two are his main weapons. You have a responsibility to the Earth as you helped in its formation. Therefore you are an integral part of its redemption.'

'Was Lincoln Cathedral the only place where Lucifer was bound?'

'No. Hardly. You understand a little more now. Your prejudices and conditioning are less, so you can be informed a little more. It is part of the potential development for human consciousness to release that which is bound. Each place involves the other places – they are interconnected. At Lincoln, it is very possible that through releasing something there in terms of structure and form it will repercuss in many places.

'There are in fact 3,496 such places on the Earth. This is really an ongoing situation. You need to see it like time lapse photography. One event appears to be stationary, but each moment these things are taking place to a greater or a lesser extent. Lucifer is still being bound and unbound. This is part of the setup.'

I could see that, as Blaise relayed the number. The El Tule courtyard had been one such place. So had the dome in South America. Lucifer arriving in splendor. Lucifer being bound and thrown into the Pit. Lucifer being unbound. It was a continual gesture, or perhaps a cyclic one with three phases. Unbind Lucifer at one site you let a little of the projected darkness into the light and relieve the incessant pressure on the psyche of the unacknowledged Shadow. Bind him up here because the people can't cope or things are too volatile. And watch him arrive on Earth joyous as the appointed envoy from the Supreme Being.

10

Of course everything that happened up to this point, including the histrionics with the demons, was to get me ready for the main event. To see what's beyond that star.

Blaise was patient. They're good at waiting. Evidently they had planned all this in advance, and now were wiggling their wings a bit in anticipation of the *coup de grâce* – my sorry ass cooking in the Grail no doubt. They had importuned the Arch Architect Himself to let me participate in this astronomically mandated event. There was also the suggestion – maybe I misheard them or misunderstood, but it sounded good – that the Architect had pulled a few strings, shifted a few galactic timetables, to get things into auspicious alignment for my visit so as to maximize the impact. Whatever that meant.

It was about nine in the morning when I rolled into the parking lot at Avebury in Wiltshire. Brits will know this as the 28-acre stone circle a couple dozen miles north of Stonehenge, the one where you can touch the stones and won't trip over Druids at the solstices. These are *big* stones. The ones still standing – some 27 out of an estimated original count of almost 100 – are from 9 to 20 feet in height and weigh up to 40 tons each.

They are bizarre and wondrous to look at: they can't be stones. Nobody can quarry stones and have them end up looking like this, dressed or undressed. These stones look like they slowly congealed out of something liquid or perhaps molten. Look at them from the right angle and you can see faces in them, of people, animals, strange beings, images from an antique and foreign past.

The big stones encircle the village of Avebury which seems to have grown up in the midst of them. In fact there are two roads that pass through the place, dividing it into quadrants. Most people think it's either weird or slightly indecent to have carved up a stone circle with a village and its roads, but I think it would be great fun to live inside a stone circle as ancient as this one. Imagine the dreams you'd have.

My first impression of the stones, especially when I stood right next to one, my nose only an inch from its rough surface, was that these were stones the angels had touched, in fact, had probably made. I read somewhere that while archeologists propose the stone circle is perhaps 5,000 years old at most, the stones themselves may be 25 million years old. I let my imagination run with that one, that here before me is a stone created 25 million years ago out of thin air by one of the Elohim. Why not? They created most of the other megalithic features on the Earth. The scale of Avebury has their trademark, if you ask me.

On the outside of the big stones is a ditch that also encircles all of Avebury. Today the ditch is the grassy domain of grazing sheep, but you can walk through it if you like. You feel like you're a needle running the groove of an old phonograph record. From the base of the groove to the top of the ridge is about 18 feet, but archeologists think it was originally more like 50 feet and they guess that some 200,000 tons of earth and rock had to have been dug out of the ground here to excavate the ditch and make the ridge. I had a hunch who had done *that* spadework. Probably the work of a couple long afternoons for them.

As usual Blaise hadn't given me much in the way of directions. Just go to Avebury, they suggested. But I'd been around the block a few times with the boys and I was getting a sense of how they worked. I'd learned to use my star as a geiger counter or dowsing rod, watching it to see where it got brighter. So I sauntered around Avebury, through the ditch, along the embankment, about the stones, observing when my star got hot. Of course anywhere you stand at Avebury with your attention on your star, the star will be much brighter and bigger, but there was one spot where it got seriously enlarged.

It was an odd place to have a mystical experience. It's a little patch of greenery, a tiny traffic island set like a flat stone in the current of the busy road. It's diagonally in front of the public toilets and the Red Lion Inn and where the road from Marlborough (the A4361) enters Avebury, passes through, then leaves on its way to Swindon. Over the years millions of drivers must have passed right by this island and never given it any notice. Why should they? But it was certainly giving my star notice.

I stood there, trying to be inconspicuous, as my star started to engulf me. It was going supernova with special effects courtesy of George Lucas' finest. I didn't have to do anything, breathe, focus, smile – nothing. That star had a mind of its own. Usually when the star goes supernova, it pops and dumps me into the pale blue sphere. This time it kept growing, getting still brighter. Somehow I was able to see myself as if from above or afar. I had become a burning white stone. It was a big stone, like one of Avebury's biggest, like a sculptor's slab

— a rectangular block perhaps fifteen feet long and ten feet high. White and burning.

Then my field of vision suddenly expanded and I was looking at all of Avebury, again as if from a short distance above. That big burning white stone I had seen myself turn into was now the size of the entire 28-acre stone circle.

I felt something like a corkscrew passing through me and into the ground. It didn't hurt or tickle, but it was like being in the middle of a living double helix. I looked up and saw two brilliant cords, one gold, the other silver, interweaving, almost dancingly, as they descended from high above Avebury to the big white burning stone and into the ground, and me.

Somehow that stone anchored this incoming helix of gold and silver. The two lines then headed out across the countryside, and what was surprising was that they followed the orientation of the two roads that cut Avebury into quadrants. The gold line went in opposite directions at once, and so did the silver, making an equal-armed cross of light at Avebury. I was standing at the junction of both lines where they left Avebury in opposite directions. I realized, or maybe I saw it, that these two lines went completely around the Earth and came back to where they started, like the oroboros eating its tail.

I sensed my white stone block being continually enlivened by the gold and silver cords as they grounded themselves through it then set off in their own directions to encircle the planet. I couldn't see where the lines came from, but I guessed it was somewhere in the galaxy, and probably someplace important.

As if out of the corner of my eye, I saw something else.

Remember that stone I mentioned that's now at Glastonbury Abbey but should be at Beckery? I saw a dozen of these around the planet, symmetrically distributed, and each one was receiving and grounding a colored line of light, then sending this line in opposite directions around the planet, just like Avebury's gold and silver lines.

All the lines together created an elegant and beautiful webwork of light around the Earth. The planet was like a lovely blue-white beachball in an open-mesh designer beach bag whose fabric somehow glowed with its own light. And the star, in me and at Avebury — I couldn't tell them apart any more — was the key to the entire system, the lock that opened the door and started the motor.

That was enough for one day. I packed up my Grail equipment and drove back to Wick. Over the next few weeks, between conversations with Blaise and meditations on my experiences there, I put a kind of picture together.

The reason my star got so big and went supernova so fast is that it's supposed to at Avebury. That's one of the reasons Avebury was built. That's why we should go there. It's where the angelic realm put the Blazing Star for Earth. Humans have a star, and so does the Earth. Go to Earth's star and your star will swell in recognition. So my star met Earth's star and had a party in the form of that big burning white stone. Avebury is our home away from home.

Avebury is also Blaise central. It would be silly to say it's their home away from home, for when is an angel not at home, which is to say, not with God? But the Earth's star at Avebury is Blaise, the Ofanim, the Wheels parked on our planet.

It's even better than that. Avebury is where the Earth plugs into the galaxy, its umbilicus to the larger world. The gold and silver lines I saw coming down in a double helix into the vicinity of the traffic island are the two strands of Earth's umbilicus. They plug in at the other end to Sirius and Canopus, the two brightest stars in our galaxy. The gold line goes to Sirius, the silver to Canopus. So when you stand there like a fool on the traffic island in the midst of traffic urgent to get elsewhere, you are in the center of this shower of energies from Sirius and Canopus.

In a sense, you're the Hanged Man of Tarot, hanging upside down from the Tree of Life, dangling over the ground, but in this case one leg stands on Sirius, the other on Canopus, and your head is a big burning stone of white fire.

Not only is Avebury the planet's plug-in point for the galaxy, but it's also the central plug-in point for all the Earth's domes. They all have gold and silver cords coming into them the way these cords come into Avebury; the difference is that all the gold and silver cords from the hundreds of domes get gathered up into one gold and silver cord at Avebury. All the cords come back to here.

In other words, all the planet's domes are wired into Avebury, and through Avebury, into Sirius and Canopus. Which means if you're at a dome somewhere on the Earth you can get a similar kind of expansive effect with your star as you would get at Avebury — a kind of twice-removed visit to the two brightest stars. At Avebury you're only once removed, and perhaps not at all. Maybe, if you can imagine it or experience it, you're at the heart of the galaxy.

The other colored lines I saw around the Earth all come from the Great Bear. They have to do with the Ray Masters and the energies they work with on Earth. Each of those twelve lines is grounded at a specific point on the Earth through one of those rounded stones. Delphi on Mount Parnassus in Greece had one and called it the omphalos; there's another one inside the Ka'aba at Mecca in Saudi Arabia.

These oroboros lines, or great circle lines, or planetary ley lines, if you like, comprise a fair part of the Earth's energy body. They're like an armature around which the physical Earth was woven. Blaise said there are fifteen of these lines in all: twelve from the Great Bear, one from Sirius, one from Canopus, with a fifteenth from Polaris entering the Earth in the South Pacific at Mount Meru.

That night I sat on my bed upstairs at Wick and reviewed the events and images of the day. I loved that magic wand effect on my star that Avebury had. Even to think of Avebury apparently had potency, because my star started to expand again as if I was still there. Maybe energetically I'd never left; in fact, maybe once you go to Avebury and have your star ignited, you're always there.

My star went supernova and popped me into the pale blue sphere. I laid back into this image and allowed the blue dish to form and laid back in that as if it were a float on a salt sea, buoyant, tranquil, and ever so sky blue. Then the emerald formed above me, like a bright green skyscraper with six sides all terminating in a point directly in front of me.

Effortlessly, I walked through one of the sides and entered the 'building' of the emerald. I made straight for the Round Table where I took my seat and waited for the Sun to appear. In a moment it did, and an intensely gold light throbbed at the center of the Table, like a sun were being born out of the Table.

Soon the Sun filled my field of vision and either it rushed towards me or I walked into it, but all there was around me was gold. There was no place that was not gold. Where my body had been was gold. Where my mind had been was gold. But now the gold started to congeal into a shape. Circular, like a bowl, with a big hollow interior: the Grail chalice.

I was nowhere in particular, but everywhere. I was the sides and rim and handles and empty interior of the bowl. Where my body should have been that was the empty insides of the chalice; where the space around my body should have been, that's where I was, occupying all 360 degrees of the round bowl. It felt like I was zipping around the sides of the bowl at nearly the speed of light, occupying every atomic crevice at the same moment, yet it also felt as if I were motionless yet distributed everywhere *as* the Grail. I'll tell you, you could spend a lot of time trying to figure this one out; it's easier just to experience it.

Then it started to rain. Just one drop, but it was so wet, it felt like all the rain in the world falling on me at once. It was a scarlet drop, such a vivid red. It stained the Grail bowl as if the chalice were blotting paper and the drop were ink. The golden chalice flushed scarlet, everything was scarlet, then it popped.

No scarlet. No Grail. Just the sense of a geometric space, like a glass house with maybe eight equal sides. It was the kind of glass house you felt could travel on its own, could go places, pass through things yet be impenetrable. Then it started to rotate slowly as if turned by an invisible axle. I sat with this sensation, as if, somehow, I was in a glass house at the top of the world, spinning slowly, surveying everything, *seeing* everything even though I didn't know what I was seeing and if you'd asked me what I saw, I would have drawn a blank.

Here was the whole Blaise toolkit – star, blue dish, emerald, round table, golden sun, Grail, scarlet drop, glass house, axle. And the stone, sword, and Christ child too, though I'm not sure where they fit in the sequence. I saw how you put it all together, like an angel's erector set with easy-to-follow instructions. But what had I built? What had I been building all these months with these parts?

'Those are the stages of the Christed initiation in the Buddha Body,' Blaise explained on their next visit. 'The Christed initiation in the Buddha Body is the central theme of what you've been doing with us. We are instruments of the Archangel Michael in this activity. He brings the Christ spirit from the final event at Golgotha. He prepares the Christed initiation now for the coming Maitreya, the event of your future. It is about the event at Golgotha when matter became spirit. It is the inner and outer Heart, and the planetary grid system of Earth.'

'What's that new element, the glass house and axle?'

'This was a direct experience of the activation of the Buddha Body, the dynamic form of the Buddha Body. The spinning octahedron is the three dimensional aspect of the turning Wheel. It is the Buddha Body. Now the Wheel becomes 3D as the Dharma becomes living in the light of Christ Consciousness.'

'You talked about an initiation, Blaise, but it seems I've been getting initiated all over the place. Not just one place where some archangel touches my shoulder with a sword or any-thing straightforward like that.'

'Hardly. You are experiencing a single initiation, in stages, spread out across many landscape nodes. This is part of the dedication of the Grail. These stages are also elements of the Christed initiation in the Buddha Body.'

'What did you mean a moment ago when you said this Christed initiation also involved the Earth's grid system?'

'We'll try to show you.'

I won't relate everything Blaise showed us, because it was a lot and some of it I'm still decoding, or in computer terms, unpacking, uncompressing. But here is the essential idea: The new kind of initiation is happening through the Earth and over time. The Earth's sacred sites are the initiation temples. The theme of the initiation is the Christ and the Buddha, with the quality of awareness being exemplified.

It may take you years to go through the stages of the initiation, to assemble the kit of stone, star, dish, emerald, Grail, and the rest, to build it inside you while meditating out in the landscape. That's the key part: whatever you do for yourself while in the landscape, you do equally for the planet. It's reciprocal. Your initiation enables the Earth to get initi-ated, and She provides you with the venues. The angelic realm supervises and the elemental kingdom helps out.

The Earth is a Grail Knight too in an odd kind of way. Albion is her name. Albion is the essence of the essence within Gaia, Blaise said. Albion is the Light Bearer, the Lord of Light, Lucifer, brought to Earth as Gaia's Grail Knight. You could think of Albion as a hologram of Lucifer in his original resplendent state. The Christed initiation in the Buddha Body is the same thing as Walking in Albion. I know it sounds like a secret code, but it's the most direct way to say it.

You walk through the Earth's sacred sites while in your star – you're actually walking through the giant geomythic body of Albion who's as big as a planet. You have a mystical experience at one of the sites, and it has a positive impact on Albion. It's a little pinprick of consciousness and he stirs in his slumber. You start waking up Albion and it's a step towards redeeming Lucifer.

Lucifer fell, Albion sleeps. Wake Albion, Lucifer arises. Lucifer's redemption is the same thing as achieving the Christ in the Buddha Body, Blaise said. And it's up to us, Grail Knights around the world, co-creators and angels manqué, to help create this 'positive possibility,' as Blaise calls it.

'Walking in Albion means walking consciously, step-by-step, contacting the essence, making an imprint in the energy matrix of the Earth, producing a tangible effect in the consciousness of Gaia that the initiation of Christ in the Buddha Body may come to be a positive practicality and a recurrent possibility.'

All the subtle architecture of the Earth, the domes, zodiacs, eggs, celestial cities, Grail castles, the whole galaxy on Earth, the galaxy turned inside out for us, all the structures of Heaven imprinted on our planet – it's all for us. To make it easier to do. To make it *possible* to do. To walk in Albion in bodies on Earth.

It was all planned out, long ago, far longer ago, in fact, than the mind can comfortably conceive. But not such a long stretch of time for the Arch Architect. For that old boy, it's just a day in the life. Even so, the strategy is awesome.

Implant the Christ in the heart chakra of the planet's consciousness, Glastonbury. Let it germinate. Bury the Star at Avebury. Let it go supernova. Connect the Christ and the Buddha in one focus, a single magnificent, protracted initiation. Wait for some Grail Knights game enough to try it, to get wet, and like it. Then take the show on the road. Make the Grail Knight game irresistible. Give them a handicap, a few clues, a few timely boosts up, and hope for the best. Hope they can find what's beyond the star.

That's the joke, you know, what's beyond that star. One day I realized that the answer depends on who's asking the question. The Grail Knight asks it, climbs the Grail scaffolding, the Christed initiation ladder, and penetrates through the layers of planetary and cosmic mystery to the one star, Blaise's realm, to the pinprick of absolute light at the heart of existence.

But maybe the question is being asked from Blaise's side of things: what's beyond that star? What's beyond *us*? What if you are that pinprick of absolute brilliance, brighter by far, at the core of it all. What's beyond this, beyond that star?

Outside of the seemingly insular enlightenment of being *this* close and almost forever so to the sublime Arch Architect, you wonder what the rest of the world is like, that multiplicity of universes, innumerable galaxies, and inhabited planets, the whole fantastic circus of existence your almost eternal life is dedicated to serving. What's it like from inside the inside, there at the extreme other end of pure spirit, deep in the trenches of unyielding matter.

Sure, you can *see* it all, understand why it is the way it is, know where it's likely to go and when, but what does it *feel* like to be in the thick of it, perspiring, tying up your sneaker laces, trying to stay conscious of the Grail as you thread your way through traffic, intermittently remembering you are the star even though here you are seemingly just a human body on the Earth. Or *also* a human body. Or both, angel and man, star and flesh.

I remembered some of the ways Blaise defined themselves when we asked them to help us understand who they are. They'd give us a few sentences now and then. One day I put a lot of them together to see if they could precipitate me into a new understanding. For most of the time it was a palimpsest of riddles, whose meaning was just beyond my reach. Now it felt closer, more to the point.

'We are pointless. From the tiniest point you can imagine, we are in the middle of that point. We express ourselves as the point within the point of pointlessness. We are an exploding star. We are the big bang at the beginning of the universe. We are the dark hole in space that contains all space. We are infinite life beyond light and darkness. We are a point of light within the depths of being. We are the little point of light that fills infinite space.

'We are that which is a part of the Christ within. We are the point, the Nimitta, within the Buddha Body. We are that Blazing Star, that pinpoint of light, so bright that it goes beyond imagination into comprehension, into the lucid clarity of being. We are the point of absolute light. We are like thousands and thousands of pinpoints of light at the tip of the needle. We are the Star you are. We are *your* Blazing Star.'

Thinking about all this, you begin to wonder if you're talking to yourself.

You also sense that what's beyond that star is the star, a full circle return.

It was time to have another visit to Avebury. This time I stayed a week. A lot happened, though I became aware of it only in fragments, as if I were getting snapshots of a complex event. After a while I put it all together in a living picture.

I felt like I was sitting in the bleachers, a bit removed from Avebury but with an excellent close-up view of the events in the stone-circled amphitheater. A massive, majestic, celestial being stands in the Avebury circle, towering many hundreds of feet above the green. He has a crystalline crown on his head, rising from his forehead and made of six layers of diamonds, his face and neck are blue, and he is slowly turning, making a slow-motion pirouette, one leg raised, the other pivoting his body.

He has a consort in this slow dance, a female of equal stature. The two dancers occupy all of Avebury; in fact, its 28 acres cannot contain them, and their forms spill out into the Wiltshire countryside, making me think perhaps their dance floor is the size of the Avebury dome which is fourteen miles wide and maybe the stone circle has room enough only for their big toes. Their turning reminded me of a corkscrew; they were the two halves of a single downward spiraling motion, a double helix in god form.

At their feet is an elephant, but it's more like an elephant god, a celestial being with an elephant's head. Of course: Ganesh, the elephant-headed god. But there's a deeper 'of course' to this because Ganesh is one of Blaise's favorite forms. Over the years Russell, Berenice, myself, and a few others have tended to see Blaise as a group of dancing, cavorting elephants. Blaise once joked that they liked the long trunks. They also said they've taken many forms, every cultural form you could think of, actually, but the elephant god, Ganesh, the benign remover of obstacles, was one of their favorites.

It was amusing to see Blaise in their Ganesh form – there were in fact many dozens of Ganeshes about the feet of the two dancing celestial figures. It also gave me a clue as to who these two vast beings were. Ganesh's parents in Hindu myth are Shiva and Parvati, and Shiva has a blue throat, and he is associated with Sirius in Hindu myths about the stars. Parvati must be Canopus.

The Ganesh elephants were arrayed about the edge of the Avebury circle, interspersed amidst the big stones, creating a kind of nimbus about the feet of Shiva and Parvati. In the center of this nimbus was a giant seed of light, and it was jam-packed with things.

Imagine everything that's part of the Earth's energy body stuffed inside this seed of light – the domes, celestial cities, eggs, Grail castles, blue dishes, emeralds, zodiacs, dragons, the entire DNA array of possible light forms and geomantic structures all inside this seed. But not jumbled together, like they'd been tossed into a big closet, but set up, organized, the Earth's light body in miniature. The Earth's geomythic body without the planet. The prototype of the whole thing, the original hologram, the engineer's original scale model of how it would be.

It was a tableau in multiple dimensions of the whole idea of Earth's geomancy, a fantastic celestial city. 'It is Varuna's House of Light,' Blaise said.

More myth, but you know, it's often the only way to make sense of geomantic visions. It's one of the few languages of light we have to decode celestial data and to speak of remarkable things we see in the galaxy on Earth. So Varuna: He's the Hindu equivalent of the Greek Ouranos, Kronos's father, and Zeus' grandfather, and Varuna's 'father' is infinity itself.

Varuna is the king of the universe and the starry sky; he fixed the stars and the planets in their positions, he knows all the secrets of creation, he owns the magic power of maya by which forms are created. Varuna's a magician, the justice giver; his laws are unassailable; he binds and sustains the worlds, he surrounds, envelops and covers everything with his thousand eyes. He's known as the Abode of Life, the Vast, the Immense, the Nourisher. His golden city is the most beautiful city in the world, known as Starry Night, Earthly City, and Joyful.

So Avebury is Varuna's House of Light, his celestial play-house on Earth, and it's Shiva's dance hall. Shiva of course is the Lord of Dancers, and the cosmos is his theater as he dances with the primal rhythmic energy of creation revealing the supreme reality. His dance is the activity of God, the Hindu mystics tell us, and all the gods witness this sublime dance in the golden hall of Chitamparam, the center of the universe.

Some of the gods accompany Shiva's dance with musical instruments, notably the Gandharvas. I had seen these celestial musicians in Glastonbury when I visited Avalon, and today at Avebury they were all over the place. The big stones on the edge of the Avebury circle are portals for the Gandharvas, yellow-enflamed archways leading back to their celestial city of Gandhavati, which looks like a marble citadel on a mountaintop. Gandharvas, clothed in yellow robes and playing flutes, troop into Avebury out of the stones by the thousands, in seemingly endless ranks of six abreast. They walk from their realm through the stones into Avebury, as effortlessly as through an open door.

Shiva and Parvati together are like the musical cleft in a piece of music, and the Gandharvas are the notes. Flowing into Avebury, they array themselves around the dancing figures in innumerable concentric circles. Their music is alive; it takes forms; it flows like a river of nymphs; it circulates through the ditch like a current of ideas, light forms, beings, delight, things my mind cannot interpret.

The ditch around Avebury contains and amplifies the music, raising it up into curtains of sounds that are also lights surrounding, informing the spectacle. It is a kind of informing, or form-making, because the Ghandarva music is generating the soundscape of Varuna's maya, taking that abundance of light and shaping it, structuring the elementary vibratory field that underlies our spacetime reality, making our reality what it is, but from behind the scenes.

I felt like I was in the Emerald City of Oz, and had just pulled back the curtains to see the Wizard, except this time he wasn't a fake, but the real thing, a world creator, and he was allowing me to watch some of the hand movements on the levers and wheels. I felt as if I were seeing our reality being created, from the dance to the sound to the forms in light. Avebury as Shiva's maya machine.

My attention shifted to the two bright energy lines that cut the Avebury circle into quadrants. Each of these quarters was filled with a vast face. In one I saw a lion, but it was made of millions of small angels, like a pointillist painting. In another quadrant was the face of a bull, similarly made of tiny angels packed together; next to this quadrant was the image of an eagle, and next to it, a man.

For a while I was dumbfounded. I didn't understand what I was seeing. Then Blaise gave me a clue. 'These are the Four Beasts of the Apocalypse, also known as the Cherubim or Living Creatures. This is really about the mystery of the Face of the Ancient of Days.' Right: Ezekiel's vision of the Chariot of God, with the faces of the four 'Beasts' depicted around the Wheels. The Four Beasts, made of millions of Cherubim, the living reality of earth, air, fire, and water, giving new born reality its elemental stamp, its tattoo, at the core of matter.

So this is where our reality is made every day. This is where the energy web of the Earth's geomythic body is spun. This is where it's all sustained. In the star. My star, your star, Blaise's star, the Arch Architect's star. The Blazing Star.

Everything shifted then or perhaps Avebury's second act got rolled onto the stage. Now I am aware of all of it being inside my star. I had deliberately put Avebury inside my star and let the star get big and then go supernova. Now Avebury is in the blue dish which is as wide as the dome overhead.

But since my star is also the star at the center of Avebury, things jump a level, and the blue-white planet is inside my star. I am Love from Above to the Earth and the planet sits in my starry womb. My head is gold with Sirius, my heart is silver with Canopus, and both energies braid together to create the placenta around the Earth. The fourteen rays from the Great

Bear form rainbow ribbons around the planet. All of this is inside the star.

In the center of the blue dish at Avebury there is a baptismal fount. I immerse myself in it and emerge refreshed and purified. Some dozen feet above it is a white rotunda — the familiar Blaise meeting place. It's hard to tell how big it is; for a moment it seems as large as the Avebury dome. In the center of the rotunda is the Grail, and I stand in it. I feel naked, but it's not a clothes thing. I'm naked in the sense that I don't have a human physical body at all, but one of light. I feel human, but I have no gender.

I hear the phrase 'I am the Light and the Life of the World' repeated continuously like a chant. The scarlet Christ light starts to burn in me as I stand naked in the Grail. Every cell and photon of my body burns with the Christ light. Even though I don't have any palpable body, I am burning up. Yet at the same time I am still that larger being who holds the Earth in its star womb enveloping it with the gold and silver placenta and the rainbow ribbons around that.

The Christ flames fill me up, inflating me with *life* like a flat bicycle tire getting air. Angels surround me. The red-flaming Seraphim, the accompanists of the Christ in his Ascension, stand round the Grail. Behind them, the Elohim stand like translucent columns at the big stones on the edge of the ditch, and thousands of Blaises in their angelic forms make a stacked halo about the rotunda. Standing in the midst of everything, as if rising up from within everything, are the eighteen archangels.

Now someone joins me in the Grail crucible, a female. It's Gaia. I know it. How do you picture a goddess the size of a planet? Whose face do you give her? The Welsh myth-makers tackled this problem long ago and came up with *Blodeuwedd*, the Flower Maiden. One of the characters in the *Mabinogion* says by our magic we will conjure up a wife for him made of flowers, and we will call forth the 'very fairest and best endowed maiden that mortal ever saw.'

It dawns on me that this is a marriage ceremony I'm in the middle of. In fact, at one level of my participation, I'm taking the role of parent. Even to say I'm taking a role is inaccurate. My awareness has been invited into a mythic tableau in which I am allowed to move around inside the characters and see the event from their differing perspectives. So now 'I' am a Pleiadian guardian, one of Gaia's many cosmic fathers who will formally give her away at the wedding. But 'I' am also Sirius her father and Canopus her mother, and this is a day long awaited.

I escort Gaia, my daughter, down the steps from the rotunda to the baptismal fount. She anoints herself in the living waters. We walk back up to the Grail and stand in the Christ flames, utterly burning up yet still there as if untouched. She seems sad, frightened, upset, tearful, anxious as she prepares to meet her husband, Albion. In the vast age of the planet, this is her first marriage. 'Stay with me,' she says, meaning don't let her lapse from my attention today.

But where is Albion? None of the Earth's Albions is awake yet though a few are close. Then I understand. Albion after all is a hologram. Here comes the original. Descending slowly from above in almost incomprehensible splendor was the Lord of Light, Lucifer, the original of Albion's virtual reality. Lucifer arrives and irradiates the entire vast tableau of angels, humans, and Gaia with the green light of his emerald. He stands in Avebury like a giant, his head high above the top of the dome, his emerald throbbing. Avebury is his Earth circle, its 28 acres cut to his celestial body measurements in the context of this planet.

All of this – marriage, angels, Avebury, planet, its energy body – all of it, in truth, is inside Lucifer's emerald as he stands before us at Avebury.

Lucifer, with his crown and emerald, and next to him the Archangel Michael, with his sword and shield, as familiar and cordial as brothers.

And Lucifer, fingertips touching Gaia's, summons Albion from out of himself, from out of the skin of the Earth, from out of every man and woman who ever lived on the Earth, from out of the myriads of stars in the galaxy. Albion: pristine, newborn, freshly awakened, adamantly betrothed, ready.

The Christ light inflames Avebury and everything and everybody in it. The stones, roads, ditch, sheep, grass, tourists, buildings, baptismal fount, rotunda, Grail, the Seraphim, Cherubim, Elohim, archangels, Blaises, Gaia, Albion, Lucifer – all aflame. The Christ light burns reality from within, but it's a purifying not destructive inferno, and marries Heaven and Earth from within.

As the final act of this midday marriage of Gaia and the Lord of Light we make a grand procession around the ridge encircling Avebury. A griffin leads. It was in fact that same griffin I had months earlier encountered at a location I then did not recognize but now do. Avebury. The griffin is easily a hundred feet tall.

He's followed by Lucifer and Michael, then Gaia and Albion,

the angels, gnomes and the other elementals, and us, the Grail Knights, and the many who have come here during the long life of the planet to attune themselves with their purpose; to remember their home in the cosmos, and to send their best wishes to the planet. We parade merrily along the ridge and I see that all of Avebury is festooned for the wedding reception, for the imminent lost weekend of light. . . .

It was late in the afternoon. I was getting ready to leave Avebury for the day when Blaise gave me a coda, a little angel food. Look up, they whispered. There above Avebury were hundreds, no, thousands, probably millions, of winged elephants floating luxuriously down the sky to Avebury. They had parachutes. They wore bowlers. They sported canes. They were trumpeting. If elephants can wag their tails, they were wagging them. If elephants can wink, they were winking. And if they could sing, they were singing.

Forty million, forty million of us. Count us up – we're all here. There's so many of us we always travel by bus. That's because there's forty million, forty million, forty million of us!

www.clairviewbooks.com

AND THE WOLVES HOWLED
Fragments of two lifetimes
Barbro Karlén
ISBN 1 902636 18 X

LIGHT BEYOND THE DARKNESS
How I healed my suicide son after his death
Doré Deverell
ISBN 1 902636 19 8

LIVING WITH INVISIBLE PEOPLE
A Karmic autobiography
Jostein Saether
ISBN 1 902636 26 0

A MESSAGE FOR HUMANITY
The call of God's angels at a time of global crisis
K. Martin-Kuri
ISBN 1 902636 27 9

MY DESCENT INTO DEATH
and the message of love which brought me back
Howard Storm
ISBN 1 902636 16 3

PSYCHIC QUEST
Episodes from the life of a ghost hunter
Natalie Osborne-Thomason
ISBN 1 902636 34 1

PSYCHIC WARRIOR
The true story of the CIA's paranormal espionage programme
David Morehouse
ISBN 1 902636 20 1

SEVEN STEPS TO ETERNITY
The true story of one man's journey into the afterlife
as told to 'psychic surgeon' Stephen Turoff
ISBN 1 902636 17 1

WHEN THE STORM COMES
and A MOMENT IN THE BLOSSOM KINGDOM
Barbro Karlén
ISBN 1 902636 23 6

www.clairviewbooks.com